Quantitative Methods in Linguistics

For Erin

Quantitative Methods in Linguistics

Keith Johnson

BLACKWELL PUBLISHING
350 Main Street, Malden, MA 02148-5020, USA
9600 Garsington Road, Oxford OX4 2DQ, UK
550 Swanston Street, Carlton, Victoria 3053, Australia

First published 2008 by Blackwell Publishing Ltd

3 2009

Library of Congress Cataloging-in-Publication Data

Johnson, Keith, 1958–
Quantitative methods in linguistics / Keith Johnson.
p. cm.
Includes bibliographical references and index.
ISBN 978-1-4051-4424-7 (hardcover : alk. paper) — ISBN 978-1-4051-4425-4 (pbk. : alk. paper) 1. Linguistics—Statistical methods. I. Title.

P138.5.J64 2008
401.2′1—dc22

2007045515

A catalogue record for this title is available from the British Library.

Set in Palatino 10/12.5
by Graphicraft Limited Hong Kong
Printed and bound in Singapore
by Utopia Press Pte Ltd

The publisher's policy is to use permanent paper from mills that operate a sustainable forestry policy, and which has been manufactured from pulp processed using acid-free and elementary chlorine-free practices. Furthermore, the publisher ensures that the text paper and cover board used have met acceptable environmental accreditation standards.

For further information on
Blackwell Publishing, visit our website at
www.blackwellpublishing.com

Contents

Acknowledgments

This book began at Ohio State University and Mary Beckman is largely responsible for the fact that I wrote it. She established a course in "Quantitative Methods in Linguistics" which I also got to teach a few times. Her influence on my approach to quantitative methods can be found throughout this book and in my own research studies, and of course I am very grateful to her for all of the many ways that she has encouraged me and taught me over the years.

I am also very grateful to a number of colleagues from a variety of institutions who have given me feedback on this volume, including: Susanne Gahl, Chris Manning, Christine Mooshammer, Geoff Nicholls, Gerald Penn, Bonny Sands, and a UC San Diego student reading group led by Klinton Bicknell. Students at Ohio State also helped sharpen the text and exercises – particularly Kathleen Currie-Hall, Matt Makashay, Grant McGuire, and Steve Winters. I appreciate their feedback on earlier handouts and drafts of chapters. Grant has also taught me some R graphing strategies. I am very grateful to UC Berkeley students Molly Babel, Russell Lee-Goldman, and Reiko Kataoka for their feedback on several of the exercises and chapters. Shira Katseff deserves special mention for reading the entire manuscript during fall 2006, offering copy-editing and substantive feedback. This was extremely valuable detailed attention – thanks! I am especially grateful to OSU students Amanda Boomershine, Hope Dawson, Robin Dodsworth, and David Durian who not only offered comments on chapters but also donated data sets from their own very interesting research projects. Additionally, I am very grateful to Joan Bresnan, Beth Hume, Barbara Luka, and Mark Pitt for sharing data sets for this book. The generosity and openness of all of these "data donors" is a high standard of research integrity. Of course, they are not responsible for any mistakes that I may have made with their data. I wish that I could have followed the recommendation of Johanna Nichols and Balthasar Bickel to add a chapter on typology. They were great, donating a data set and a number of observations and suggestions, but in the end I ran out of time. I hope that there will be a second edition of this book so I can include typology – and perhaps by then some other areas of linguistic research as well.

Finally, I would like to thank Nancy Dick-Atkinson for sharing her cabin in Maine with us in the summer of 2006, and Michael for the whiffle-ball breaks. What a nice place to work!

Design of the Book

One thing that I learned in writing this book is that I had been wrongly assuming that we phoneticians were the main users of quantitative methods in linguistics. I discovered that some of the most sophisticated and interesting quantitative techniques for doing linguistics are being developed by sociolinguists, historical linguists, and syntacticians. So, I have tried with this book to present a relatively representative and usable introduction to current quantitative research across many different subdisciplines within linguistics.[1]

The first chapter "Fundamentals of quantitative analysis" is an overview of, well, fundamental concepts that come up in the remainder of the book. Much of this will be review for students who have taken a general statistics course. The discussion of probability distributions in this chapter is key. Least-square statistics – the mean and standard deviation, are also introduced.

The remainder of the chapters introduce a variety of statistical methods in two thematic organizations. First, the chapters (after the second general chapter on "Patterns and tests") are organized by linguistic subdiscipline – phonetics, psycholinguistics, sociolinguistics, historical linguistics, and syntax.

[1] I hasten to add that, even though there is very much to be gained by studying techniques in natual language processing (NLP), this book is not a language engineering book. For a very authoritative introduction to NLP I would recommend Manning and Schütze's *Foundations of Statistical Natural Language Processing* (1999).

This organization provides some familiar landmarks for students and a convenient backdrop for the other organization of the book which centers around an escalating degree of modeling complexity culminating in the analysis of syntactic data. To be sure, the chapters do explore some of the specialized methods that are used in particular disciplines – such as principal components analysis in phonetics and cladistics in historical linguistics – but I have also attempted to develop a coherent progression of model complexity in the book.

Thus, students who are especially interested in phonetics are well advised to study the syntax chapter because the methods introduced there are more sophisticated and potentially more useful in phonetic research than the methods discussed in the phonetics chapter! Similarly, the syntactician will find the phonetics chapter to be a useful precursor to the methods introduced finally in the syntax chapter.

The usual statistics textbook introduction suggests what parts of the book can be skipped without a significant loss of comprehension. However, rather than suggest that you ignore parts of what I have written here (naturally, I think that it was all worth writing, and I hope it will be worth your reading) I refer you to Table 0.1 that shows the continuity that I see among the chapters.

The book examines several different methods for testing research hypotheses. These focus on building statistical models and evaluating them against one or more sets of data. The models discussed in the book include the simple *t*-test which is introduced in Chapter 2 and elaborated in Chapter 3, analysis of variance (Chapter 4), logistic regression (Chapter 5), linear mixed effects models and logistic linear mixed effects models discussed in Chapter 7. The progression here is from simple to complex. Several methods for discovering patterns in data are also discussed in the book (in Chapters 2, 3, and 6) in progression from simpler to more complex. One theme of the book is that despite our different research questions and methodologies, the statistical methods that are employed in modeling linguistic data are quite coherent across subdisciplines and indeed are the same methods that are used in scientific inquiry more generally. I think that one measure of the success of this book will be if the student can move from this introduction – oriented explicitly around linguistic data – to more general statistics reference books. If you are able to make this transition I think I will have succeeded in helping you connect your work to the larger context of general scientific inquiry.

Table 0.1 The design of the book as a function of statistical approach (hypothesis testing vs. pattern discovery), type of data, and type of predictor variables.

Hypothesis testing		*Predictor variables*		
		Factorial (nominal)	**Continuous**	**Mixed random and fixed factors**
Type of data	Ratio (continuous)	t-test (Chs 2 & 3)	Linear regression (Chs 2 & 3)	Repeated measures ANOVA (Ch. 4)
		ANOVA (Ch. 4)		Linear mixed effects (Ch. 7)
	Nominal (counting)	χ^2 test (Ch. 5) Logistic regression (Ch. 5)	Logistic regression (Ch. 5)	Logistic linear mixed effects (Ch. 7)

Pattern discovery		*Type of pattern*	
		Categories	**Continuous**
Type of data	Many continuous dimensions	Principal components (Ch. 3)	Linear regression (Ch. 3) Principal components (Ch. 3)
	Distance matrix	Clustering (Ch. 6) MD Scaling (Ch. 6)	
	Shared traits	Cladistics (Ch. 6)	

A Note about Software

One thing that you should be concerned with in using a book that devotes space to learning how to use a particular software package is that some software programs change at a relatively rapid pace.

In this book, I chose to focus on a software package (called "R") that is developed under the GNU license agreement. This means that the software is maintained and developed by a user community and is distributed not for profit (students can get it on their home computers at no charge). It is serious software. Originally developed at AT&T Bell Labs, it is used extensively in medical research, engineering, and science. This is significant because GNU software (like Unix, Java, C, Perl, etc.) is more stable than commercially available software – revisions of the software come out because the user community needs changes, not because the company needs cash. There are also a number of electronic discussion lists and manuals covering various specific techniques using R. You'll find these resources at the R project web page (http://www.r-project.org).

At various points in the text you will find short tangential sections called "R notes." I use the R notes to give you, in detail, the command language that was used to produce the graphs or calculate the statistics that are being discussed in the main text. These commands have been student tested using the data and scripts that are available at the book web page, and it should be possible to copy the commands verbatim into an open session of R and reproduce for yourself the results that you find in the text. The aim of course is to reduce the R learning curve a bit so you can apply the concepts of the book as quickly as possible to your own data analysis and visualization problems.

Contents of the Book Web Site

The data sets and scripts that are used as examples in this book are available for free download at the publisher's web site – www.blackwellpublishing.com. The full listing of the available electronic resources is reproduced here so you will know what you can get from the publisher.

Chapter 2 Patterns and Tests

Script: Figure 2.1.
Script: The central limit function from a uniform distribution (central.limit.unif).
Script: The central limit function from a skewed distribution (central.limit).
Script: The central limit function from a normal distribution.
Script: Figure 2.5.
Script: Figure 2.6 (shade.tails)
Data: Male and female F1 frequency data (F1_data.txt).
Script: Explore the chi-square distribution (chisq).

Chapter 3 Phonetics

Data: Cherokee voice onset times (cherokeeVOT.txt).
Data: The tongue shape data (chaindata.txt).
Script: Commands to calculate and plot the first principal component of tongue shape.
Script: Explore the F distribution (shade.tails.df).
Data: Made-up regression example (regression.txt).

Chapter 4 Psycholinguistics

Data: One observation of phonological priming per listener from Pitt and Shoaf's (2002).
Data: One observation per listener from two groups (overlap versus no overlap) from Pitt and Shoaf's study.
Data: Hypothetical data to illustrate repeated measures of analysis.
Data: The full Pitt and Shoaf data set.
Data: Reaction time data on perception of flap, /d/, and eth by Spanish-speaking and English-speaking listeners.
Data: Luka and Barsalou (2005) "by subjects" data.
Data: Luka and Barsalou (2005) "by items" data.
Data: Boomershine's dialect identification data for exercise 5.

Chapter 5 Sociolinguistics

Data: Robin Dodsworth's preliminary data on /l/ vocalization in Worthington, Ohio.
Data: Data from David Durian's rapid anonymous survey on /str/ in Columbus, Ohio.
Data: Hope Dawson's Sanskrit data.

Chapter 6 Historical Linguistics

Script: A script that draws Figure 6.1.
Data: Dyen, Kruskal, and Black's (1984) distance matrix for 84 Indo-European languages based on the percentage of cognate words between languages.
Data: A subset of the Dyen et al. (1984) data coded as input to the Phylip program "pars."

Data: IE-lists.txt: A version of the Dyen et al. word lists that is readable in the scripts below.
Script: make_dist: This Perl script tabulates all of the letters used in the Dyen et al. word lists.
Script: get_IE_distance: This Perl script implements the "spelling distance" metric that was used to calculate distances between words in the Dyen et al. list.
Script: make_matrix: Another Perl script. This one takes the output of get_IE_distance and writes it back out as a matrix that R can easily read.
Data: A distance matrix produced from the spellings of words in the Dyen et al. (1984) data set.
Data: Distance matrix for eight Bantu languages from the Tanzanian Language Survey.
Data: A phonetic distance matrix of Bantu languages from Ladefoged, Glick, and Criper (1971).
Data: The TLS Bantu data arranged as input for phylogenetic parsimony analysis using the Phylip program pars.

Chapter 7 Syntax

Data: Results from a magnitude estimation study.
Data: Verb argument data from CoNLL-2005.
Script: Cross-validation of linear mixed effects models.
Data: Bresnan et al.'s (2007) dative alternation data.

1 Fundamentals of Quantitative Analysis

In this chapter, I follow the outline of topics used in the first chapter of Kachigan, *Multivariate Statistical Analysis*, because I think that that is a very effective presentation of these core ideas.

Increasingly, linguists handle quantitative data in their research. Phoneticians, sociolinguists, psycholinguists, and computational linguists deal in numbers and have for decades. Now also, phonologists, syntacticians, and historical linguists are finding linguistic research to involve quantitative methods. For example, Keller (2003) measured sentence acceptibility using a psychophysical technique called magnitude estimation. Also, Boersma and Hayes (2001) employed probablistic reasoning in a constraint reranking algorithm for optimality theory.

Consequently, mastery of quantitative methods is increasingly becoming a vital component of linguistic training. Yet, when I am asked to teach a course on quantitative methods I am not happy with the available textbooks. I hope that this book will deal adequately with the fundamental concepts that underlie common quantitative methods, and more than that will help students make the transition from the basics to real research problems with explicit examples of various common analysis techniques.

Of course, the strategies and methods of quantitative analysis are of primary importance, but in these chapters practical aspects of handling quantitative linguistic data will also be an important focus. We will be concerned with how to use a particular statistical package (R) to discover patterns in quantitative data and to test linguistic hypotheses. This theme is very practical and assumes that it is appropriate and useful to look at quantitative measures of language structure and usage.

We will question this assumption. Salsburg (2001) talks about a "statistical revolution" in science in which the distributions of measurements are the objects of study. We will, to some small extent, consider linguistics from this point of view. Has linguistics participated in the statistical revolution? What would a quantitative linguistics be like? Where is this approach taking the discipline?

Table 1.1 shows a set of phonetic measurements. These VOT (voice onset time) measurements show the duration of aspiration in voiceless stops in Cherokee. I made these measurements from recordings of one

Table 1.1 Voice onset time measurements of a single Cherokee speaker with a 30-year gap between recordings.

	1971		**2001**
k	67	k	84
k	127	k	82
k	79	k	72
k	150	k	193
k	53	k	129
k	65	k	77
k	75	k	72
k	109	k	81
t	109	k	45
t	126	k	74
t	129	k	102
t	119	k	77
t	104	k	187
t	153	t	79
t	124	t	86
t	107	t	59
t	181	t	74
t	166	t	63
		t	75
		t	70
		t	106
		t	54
		t	49
		t	56
		t	58
		t	97
Average	113.5		84.7
Standard Deviation	35.9		36.09

speaker, the Cherokee linguist Durbin Feeling, that were made in 1971 and 2001. The average VOT for voiceless stops /k/ and /t/ is shorter in the 2001 dataset. But is the difference "significant"? Or is the difference between VOT in 1971 and 2001 just an instance of random variation – a consequence of randomly selecting possible utterances in the two years that, though not identical, come from the same underlying distribution of possible VOT values for this speaker? I think that one of the main points to keep in mind about drawing conclusions from data is that it is all guessing. Really. But what we are trying to do with statistical summaries and hypothesis testing is to quantify just how reliable our guesses are.

1.1 What We Accomplish in Quantitative Analysis

Quantitative analysis takes some time and effort, so it is important to be clear about what you are trying to accomplish with it. Note that "everybody seems to be doing it" is not on the list. The four main goals of quantitative analysis are:

1 data reduction: summarize trends, capture the common aspects of a set of observations such as the average, standard deviation, and correlations among variables;
2 inference: generalize from a representative set of observations to a larger universe of possible observations using hypothesis tests such as the *t*-test or analysis of variance;
3 discovery of relationships: find descriptive or causal patterns in data which may be described in multiple regression models or in factor analysis;
4 exploration of processes that may have a basis in probability: theoretical modeling, say in information theory, or in practical contexts such as probabilistic sentence parsing.

1.2 How to Describe an Observation

An observation can be obtained in some elaborate way, like visiting a monastery in Egypt to look at an ancient manuscript that hasn't been read in a thousand years, or renting an MRI machine for an hour of brain imaging. Or an observation can be obtained on the cheap –

asking someone where the shoes are in the department store and noting whether the talker says the /r/'s in "fourth floor."

Some observations can't be quantified in any meaningful sense. For example if that ancient text has an instance of a particular form and your main question is "how old is the form?" then your result is that the form is at least as old as the manuscript. However, if you were to observe that the form was used 15 times in this manuscript, but only twice in a slightly older manuscript, then these frequency counts begin to take the shape of quantified linguistic observations that can be analyzed with the same quantitative methods used in science and engineering. I take that to be a good thing – linguistics as a member of the scientific community.

Each observation will have several descriptive properties – some will be qualitative and some will be quantitative – and descriptive properties (variables) come in one of four types:

Nominal: Named properties – they have no meaningful order on a scale of any type.

> Examples: What language is being observed? What dialect? Which word? What is the gender of the person being observed? Which variant was used: *going* or *goin'*?

Ordinal: Orderable properties – they aren't observed on a measurable scale, but this kind of property is transitive so that if *a* is less than *b* and *b* is less than *c* then *a* is also less than *c*.

> Examples: Zipf's rank frequency of words, rating scales (e.g. excellent, good, fair, poor)?

Interval: This is a property that is measured on a scale that does not have a true zero value. In an interval scale, the magnitude of differences of adjacent observations can be determined (unlike the adjacent items on an ordinal scale), but because the zero value on the scale is arbitrary the scale cannot be interpreted in any absolute sense.

> Examples: temperature (Fahrenheit or Centigrade scales), rating scales?, magnitude estimation judgments.

Ratio: This is a property that we measure on a scale that does have an absolute zero value. This is called a ratio scale because ratios of these measurements are meaningful. For instance, a vowel that is 100 ms long is twice as long as a 50 ms vowel, and 200 ms is twice 100 ms. Contrast this with temperature – 80 degrees Fahrenheit is not twice as hot as 40 degrees.

Examples: Acoustic measures – frequency, duration, frequency counts, reaction time.

1.3 Frequency Distributions: A Fundamental Building Block of Quantitative Analysis

You must get this next bit, so pay attention. Suppose we want to know how grammatical a sentence is. We ask 36 people to score the sentence on a grammaticality scale so that a score of 1 means that it sounds pretty ungrammatical and 10 sounds perfectly OK. Suppose that the ratings in Table 1.2 result from this exercise.

Interesting, but what are we supposed to learn from this? Well, we're going to use this set of 36 numbers to construct a frequency

Table 1.2 Hypothetical data of grammaticality ratings for a group of 36 raters.

Person #	Rating	Person #	Rating
1	5	19	3
2	4	20	9
3	6	21	5
4	5	22	6
5	5	23	5
6	4	24	1
7	6	25	5
8	1	26	7
9	4	27	4
10	3	28	5
11	6	29	2
12	3	30	4
13	4	31	5
14	5	32	3
15	4	33	3
16	5	34	6
17	5	35	3
18	4	36	5

distribution and define some of the terms used in discussing frequency distributions.

R note. I guess I should confess that I made up the "ratings" in Table 1.2. I used a function in the R statistics package to draw 36 random integer observations from a normal distribution that had a mean value of 4.5 and a standard deviation of 2. Here's the command that I used to produce the made up data:

```
> round(rnorm(36,4.5,2))
```

If you issue this command in R you will almost certainly get a different set of ratings (that's the nature of random selection), but the distribution of your scores should match the one in the example.

Look again at Table 1.2. How many people gave the sentence a rating of "1"? How many rated it a "2"? When we answer these questions for all of the possible ratings we have the values that make up the frequency distribution of our sentence grammaticality ratings. These data and some useful recodings of them are shown in Table 1.3.

You'll notice in Table 1.3 that we counted two instances of rating "1", one instance of rating "2", six instances of rating "3", and so on. Since there were 36 raters, each giving one score to the sentence, we have a total of 36 observations, so we can express the frequency counts in relative terms – as a percentage of the total number of observations. Note that percentages (as the etymology of the word would suggest) are commonly expressed on a scale from 0 to 100, but you could express the same information as proportions ranging from 0 to 1.

The frequency distribution in Table 1.3 shows that most of the grammaticality scores are either "4" or "5," and that though the scores span a wide range (from 1 to 9) the scores are generally clustered in the middle of the range. This is as it should be because I selected the set of scores from a normal (bell-shaped) frequency distribution that centered on the average value of 4.5 – more about this later.

The set of numbers in Table 1.3 is more informative than the set in Table 1.2, but nothing beats a picture. Figure 1.1 shows the frequencies from Table 1.3. This figure highlights, for the visually inclined, the same points that we made regarding the numeric data in Table 1.3.

Table 1.3 Frequency distributions of the grammaticality rating data in Table 1.2.

Rating	Frequencies	Relative frequencies	Cumulative frequencies	Relative cumulative frequencies
1	2	5.6	2	5.6
2	1	2.8	3	8.3
3	6	16.7	9	25.0
4	8	22.2	17	47.2
5	12	33.3	29	80.6
6	5	13.9	34	94.4
7	1	2.8	35	97.2
8	0	0.0	35	97.2
9	1	2.8	36	100.0
Total	36	100.0	36	100.0

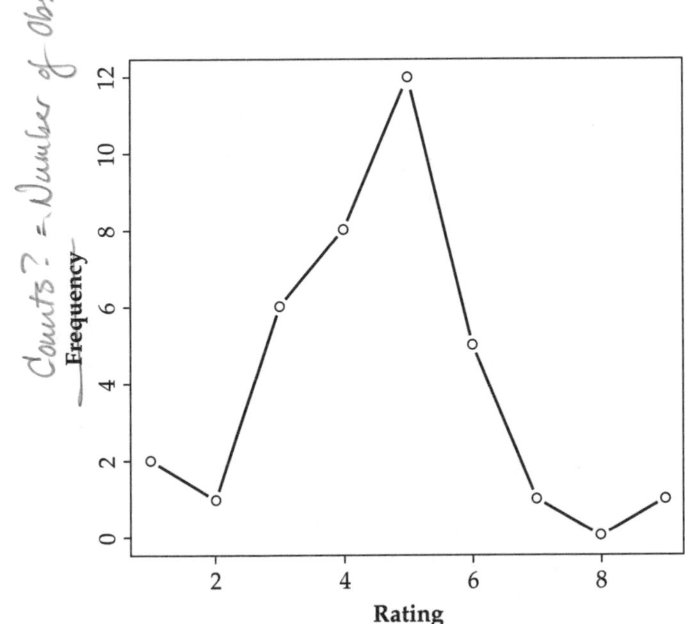

Figure 1.1 The frequency distribution of the grammaticality rating data that was presented in Table 1.2.

R note. I produced Figure 1.1 using the `plot()` command in R. I first typed in the frequency count data and the scores that correspond to these frequency counts, so that the vector `data` contains the counts and the vector `rating` has the rating values. Then I told `plot()` that we want a line plot with both (`type = "b"`) lines and points.

```
data = c(2,1,6,8,12,5,1,0,1)
rating = c(1,2,3,4,5,6,7,8,9)
plot(rating,data,type = "b", main = "Sentence rating frequency
      distribution", xlab = "Rating", ylab = "Frequency")
```

The property that we are seeking to study with the "grammaticality score" measure is probably a good deal more gradient than we permit by restricting our rater to a scale of integer numbers. It may be that not all sentences that he/she would rate as a "5" are exactly equivalent to each other in the internal feeling of grammaticality that they evoke. Who knows? But suppose that it is true that the internal grammaticality response that we measure with our rating scale is actually a continuous, gradient property. We could get at this aspect by providing a more and more continuous type of rating scale – we'll see more of this when we look at magnitude estimation later – but whatever scale we use, it will have some degree of granularity or quantization to it. This is true of all of the measurement scales that we could imagine using in any science.

So, with a very fine-grained scale (say a grammaticality rating on a scale with many decimal points) it doesn't make any sense to count the number of times that a particular measurement value appears in the data set because it is highly likely that no two ratings will be exactly the same. In this case, then, to describe the frequency distribution of our data we need to group the data into contiguous ranges of scores (bins) of similar values and then count the number of observations in each bin. For example, if we permitted ratings on the 1 to 10 grammaticality scale to have many decimal places, the frequency distribution would look like the histogram in Figure 1.2, where we have a count of 1 for each rating value in the data set.

Figure 1.3 shows how we can group these same data into ranges (here ratings between 0 and 1, 1 and 2, and so on) and then count the number of rating values in each range, just as we counted before, the

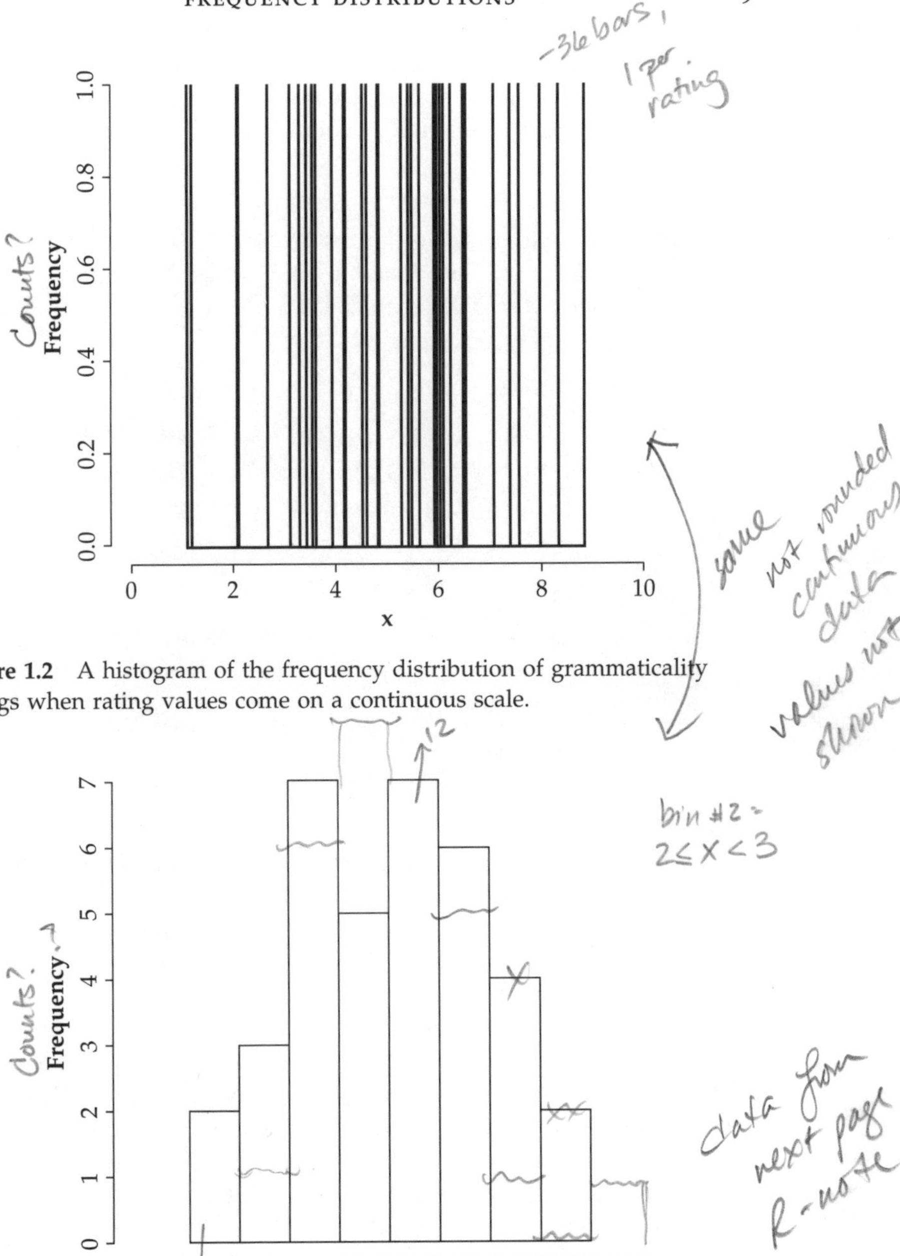

Figure 1.2 A histogram of the frequency distribution of grammaticality ratings when rating values come on a continuous scale.

Figure 1.3 The same continuous rating data that was shown in Figure 1.2, but now the frequency distribution is plotted in bins.

number of ratings of a particular value. So, instead of counting the number of times the rating "6" was given, now we are counting the number of ratings that are greater than or equal to 5 and less than 6.

R note. The histograms in figures 1.2 and 1.3 are really easy to produce in R. First, I produced a small set of 36 "observations" from a normal distribution that has a mean rating of 4.5 and a standard deviation of ratings of 2.

```
x = rnorm(36, 4.5, 2)
```

Then to produce Figure 1.2, I used the `hist()` command and told it that I wanted lots and lots of vertical bars. This large number gave me a separate bar for each of the 36 observations in the "x" data set.

```
hist(x, breaks = 30000,xlim = c(0,10))
```

Then to produce Figure 1.3, I used the same command, this time permitting the command to choose a good bar width for my data. Nice that the simpler command gives you the more sensible output.

```
hist(x,xlim = c(0,10))
```

OK. This process of grouping measurements on a continuous scale is a useful, practical thing to do, but it helps us now make a serious point about theoretical frequency distributions. This point is the *foundation* of all of the hypothesis testing statistics that we will be looking at later. So, pay attention!

Let's suppose that we could draw an infinite data set. The larger our data set becomes the more detailed a representation of the frequency distribution we can get. For example, suppose I keep collecting sentence grammaticality data for the same sentence, so that instead of ratings from 36 people I had ratings from 10,000 people. Now even with a histogram that has 1,000 bars in it (Figure 1.4), we can see that ratings near 4.5 are more common than those at the edges of the rating scale. Now if we keep adding observations up to infinity (just play along with me here) and keep reducing the size of the bars in the histogram of the frequency distribution we come to a point at which the intervals between bars is vanishingly small – i.e. we end up with a continuous curve (see Figure 1.5). "Vanishingly small" should be a tip-off

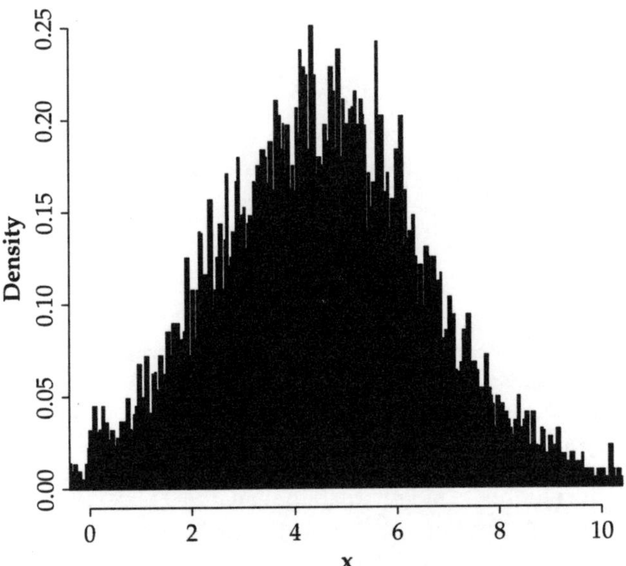

Figure 1.4 A frequency histogram with 1,000 bars plotting frequency in 10,000 observations.

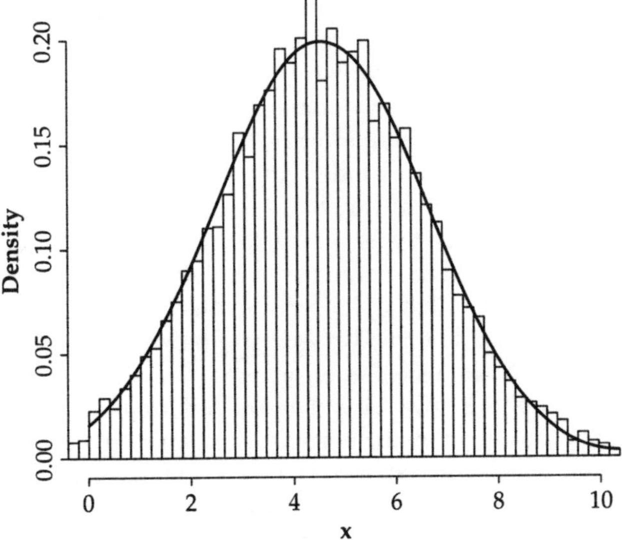

Figure 1.5 The probability density distribution of 10,000 observations and the theoretical probability density distribution of a normal distribution with a mean of 4.5 and a standard deviation of 2.

that we have entered the realm of calculus. Not to worry though, we're not going too far.

R note. The cool thing about Figure 1.5 is that we combine a histogram of the observed frequency distribution of a set of data with a theoretical normal distribution curve (see Chapter 2 regarding probability density). It is useful to be able to do this. Here are the commands I used:

```
x = rnorm(10000, 4.5, 2) # generate 10,000 data points
hist(x,breaks=100,freq=FALSE,xlim = c(0,10)) # plot them
in a histogram
  # now plot the normal curve
plot(function(x)dnorm(x, mean=4.5, sd=2), 0,10, add=TRUE)
```

Of course, the excellent fit between the "observed" and the theoretical distributions is helped by the fact that the data being plotted here were generated by random selection (`rnorm()`) of observations from the theoretical normal distribution (`dnorm()`).

The "normal distribution" is an especially useful theoretical function. It seems intuitively reasonable to assume that in most cases there is some underlying property that we are trying to measure – like grammaticality, or typical duration, or amount of processing time – and that there is some source of random error that keeps us from getting an exact measurement of the underlying property. If this is a good description of the source of variability in our measurements, then we can model this situation by assuming that the underlying property – the uncontaminated "true" value that we seek – is at the center of the frequency distribution that we observe in our measurements and that the spread of the distribution is caused by error, with bigger errors being less likely to occur than smaller errors.

These assumptions give us a bell-shaped frequency distribution which can be described by the normal curve, an extremely useful bell-shaped curve, which is an exponential function of the mean value (Greek letter μ "mew") and the variance (Greek letter σ "sigma").

$$f_x = \frac{1}{\sigma\sqrt{2\pi}} e^{-(x-\mu)^2/2\sigma^2} \quad \text{the normal distribution}$$

One useful aspect of this definition of a theoretical distribution of data (besides that it derives from just two numbers, the mean value and a measure of how variable the data are) is that sum of the area under the curve f_x is 1. So, instead of thinking in terms of a "frequency" distribution, the normal curve gives us a way to calculate the probability of any set of observations by finding the area under any portion of the curve. We'll come back to this.

1.4 Types of Distributions

Data come in a variety of shapes of frequency distributions (Figure 1.6).

For example, if every outcome is equally likely then the distribution is *uniform*. This happens for example with the six sides of a dice – each one is (supposed to be) equally likely, so if you count up the number of rolls that come up "1" it should be on average 1 out of every 6 rolls.

In the *normal* – bell-shaped – distribution, measurements tend to congregate around a typical value and values become less and less likely as they deviate further from this central value. As we saw in the section above, the normal curve is defined by two parameters – what the central tendency is (μ) and how quickly probability goes down as you move away from the center of the distribution (σ).

If measurements are taken on a scale (like the 1–9 grammaticality rating scale discussed above), as we approach one end of the scale the frequency distribution is bound to be *skewed* because there is a limit beyond which the data values cannot go. We most often run into skewed frequency distributions when dealing with percentage data and reaction time data (where negative reaction times are not meaningful).

The *J-shaped* distribution is a kind of skewed distribution with most observations coming from the very end of the measurement scale. For example, if you count speech errors per utterance you might find that most utterances have a speech error count of 0. So in a histogram, the number of utterances with a low error count will be very high and will decrease dramatically as the number of errors per utterance increases.

A *bimodal* distribution is like a combination of two normal distributions – there are two peaks. If you find that your data fall in a bimodal distribution you might consider whether the data actually represent two separate populations of measurements. For example, voice fundamental frequency (the acoustic property most closely related to the pitch of a person's voice) falls into a bimodal distribution when you

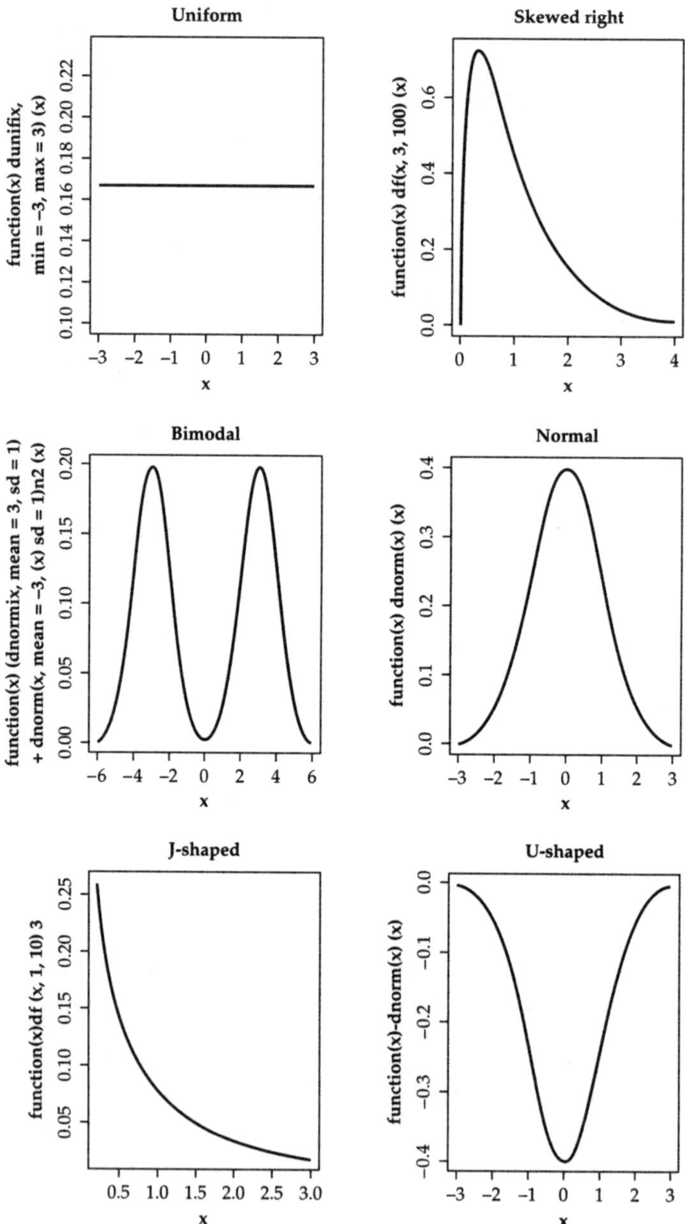

Figure 1.6 Types of probability distributions.

pool measurements from men and women because men tend to have lower pitch than women.

If you ask a number of people how strongly they supported the US invasion of Iraq you would get a very polarized distribution of results. In this *U-shaped* distribution most people would be either strongly in favor or strongly opposed with not too many in the middle.

R note. Figure 1.6 not only illustrates different types of probability distributions, it also shows how to combine several graphs into one figure in R. The command `par()` lets you set many different graphics parameters. I set the graph window to expect two rows that each have three graphs by entering this command:

```
> par(mfcol=c(2,3))
```

Then I entered the six plot commands in the following order:

```
> plot(function(x)dunif(x,min=-3,max=3),-3,3,
main="Uniform")
> plot(function(x)dnorm(x),-3,3, main="Normal")
> plot(function(x)df(x,3,100),0,4,main="Skewed right")
> plot(function(x)df(x,1,10)/3,0.2,3, main="J-shaped")
> plot(function(x)(dnorm(x, mean=3, sd=1)+dnorm(x,mean=-3,
sd=1))/2,-6,6, main="Bimodal")
> plot(function(x)-dnorm(x),-3,3,main="U-shaped")
```

And, voilá. The figure is done. When you know that you will want to repeat the same, or a very similar, sequence of commands for a new data set, you can save a list of commands like this as a custom command, and then just enter your own "plot my data my way" command.

1.5 Is Normal Data, Well, Normal?

The normal distribution is a useful way to describe data. It embodies some reasonable assumptions about how we end up with variability in our data sets and gives us some mathematical tools to use in two important goals of statistical analysis. In data reduction, we can describe the whole frequency distribution with just two numbers – the mean and the standard deviation (formal definitions of these are just ahead.) Also, the normal distribution provides a basis for drawing inferences about the accuracy of our statistical estimates.

So, it is a good idea to know whether or not the frequency distribution of your data is shaped like the normal distribution. I suggested earlier that the data we deal with often falls in an approximately normal distribution, but as discussed in section 1.4, there are some common types of data (like percentages and rating values) that are not normally distributed.

We're going to do two things here. First, we'll explore a couple of ways to determine whether your data are normally distributed, and second we'll look at a couple of transformations that you can use to *make* data more normal (this may sound fishy, but transformations are legal!).

Consider again the Cherokee data that we used to start this chapter. We have two sets of data, thus, two distributions. So, when we plot the frequency distribution as a histogram and then compare that observed distribution with the best-fitting normal curve we can see that both the 2001 and the 1971 data sets are fairly similar to the normal curve. The 2001 set (Figure 1.7) has a pretty normal looking shape, but there are a couple of measurements at nearly 200 ms that hurt the fit. When we remove these two, the fit between the theoretical normal curve and the frequency distribtion of our data is quite good. The 1971 set

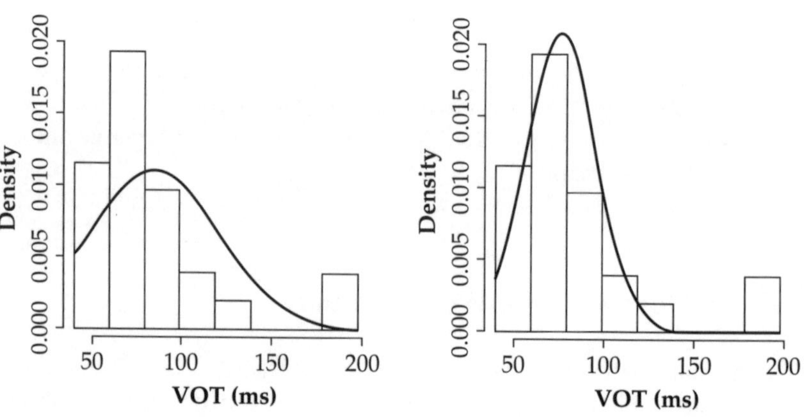

Figure 1.7 The probability density distribution of the Cherokee 2001 voice onset time data. The left panel shows the best-fitting normal curve for all of the data points. The right panel shows the best-fitting normal curve when the two largest VOT values are removed from the data set.

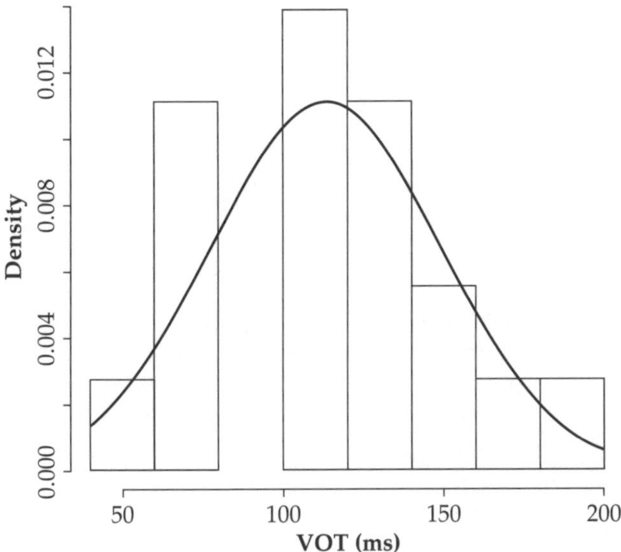

Figure 1.8 The probability density distribution of the Cherokee 1971 voice onset time data. The best-fitting normal curve is also shown.

(Figure 1.8) also looks roughly like a normally distributed data set, though notice that there were no observations between 80 and 100 ms in this (quite small) data set. Though if these data came from a normal curve we would have expected several observations in this range.

R note. In producing Figures 1.7 and 1.8, I used the `c()` function to type in the two vectors `vot01` for the 2001 data and `vot71` for the 1971 data. Just ahead I'll introduce methods for reading data from computer files into R – you don't usually have to type in your data. Then I used the `mean()` and `sd()` functions to calculate the means and standard deviations for these data sets. Finally, I used the `hist()` and `plot()` commands to draw the actual and theoretical frequency distributions in the figures.

```
> vot01 = c(84, 82, 72,193, 129, 77, 72, 81, 45, 74, 102, 77,
187, 79, 86, 59, 74, 63, 75, 70, 106, 54, 49, 56, 58, 97)
> vot71 =c(67, 127, 79, 150, 53, 65, 75, 109, 109, 126, 129,
119, 104, 153, 124, 107, 181, 166)
```

```
> mean(vot01)
  [1] 84.65385
> sd(vot01)
  [1] 36.08761
> hist(vot01,freq=FALSE)
> plot(function(x)dnorm(x, mean=84.654, sd=36.088), 40,
200, add=TRUE)
```

You might also be interested to see how to take the mean and standard deviation with outliers removed. I decided that the two VOT measurements in `vot01` that are greater than 180 ms are outliers and so calcuated the mean and standard deviation for only those numbers in the vector that are less than 180 using the following statements.

```
> mean(vot01[vot01<180])
[1] 75.875
> sd(vot01[vot01<180])
[1] 19.218
```

Read `vot01[vot01<180]` as "the numbers in `vot01` that are less than 180." When we have data sets that are composed of several linked vectors we can extract subsets of data using similar syntax.

Note though that I have just told you how to "remove outliers" as if it is perfectly fine to remove weird data. It is not! You should use *all* of the data you collect unless you have good independent reasons for not doing so. For example, data values can be removed if you know that there has been some measurement error that results in the weird value, or if you know that the person providing the data was different from the other participants in the study in some way that bears on the aims of the study (e.g. by virtue of having fallen asleep during a perception experiment, or by not being a native speaker of the language under study), or the token is different in some crucial way (e.g. by virtue of being spoken in error or with a disfluency). Because such variation on the part of the people we study is bound to happen, it is acceptable to trim the 5% most extreme data values from a large and noisy database where manual inspection of the entire database is not practical.

These frequency distribution graphs give an indication of whether our data is distributed on a normal curve, but we are essentially waving our hands at the graphs and saying "looks pretty normal to me." I guess you shouldn't underestimate how important it is to look at the data, but it would be good to be able to measure just how "normally distributed" these data are.

To do this we measure the degree of fit between the data and the normal curve with a quantile/quantile plot and a correlation between the actual quantile scores and the quantile scores that are predicted by the normal curve. The NIST *Handbook of Statistical Methods* (2004) has this to say about Q-Q plots.

> The quantile-quantile (q-q) plot is a graphical technique for determining if two data sets come from populations with a common distribution.
>
> A q-q plot is a plot of the quantiles of the first data set against the quantiles of the second data set. By a quantile, we mean the fraction (or percent) of points below the given value. That is, the 0.3 (or 30%) quantile is the point at which 30% percent of the data fall below and 70% fall above that value.
>
> A 45-degree reference line is also plotted. If the two sets come from a population with the same distribution, the points should fall approximately along this reference line. The greater the departure from this reference line, the greater the evidence for the conclusion that the two data sets have come from populations with different distributions.
>
> The advantages of the q-q plot are:
>
> 1 The sample sizes do not need to be equal.
> 2 Many distributional aspects can be simultaneously tested. For example, shifts in location, shifts in scale, changes in symmetry, and the presence of outliers can all be detected from this plot. For example, if the two data sets come from populations whose distributions differ only by a shift in location, the points should lie along a straight line that is displaced either up or down from the 45-degree reference line.
>
> The q-q plot is similar to a probability plot. For a probability plot, the quantiles for one of the data samples are replaced with the quantiles of a theoretical distribution.

Further regarding the "probability plot" the *Handbook* has this to say:

> The probability plot (Chambers et al. 1983) is a graphical technique for assessing whether or not a data set follows a given distribution such as the normal or Weibull.

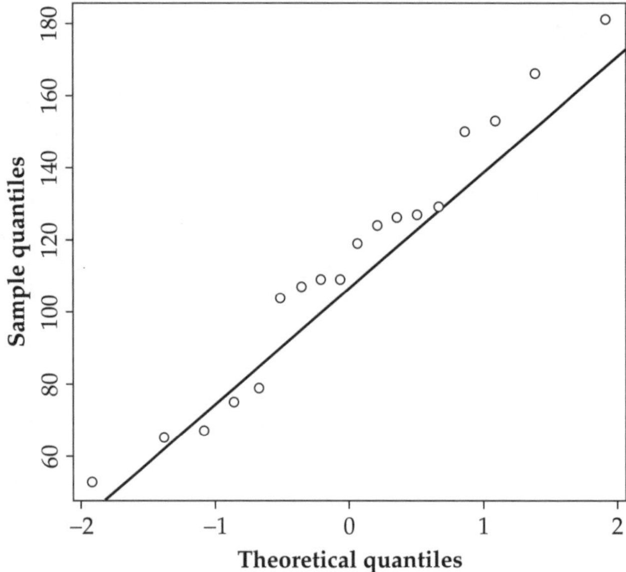

Figure 1.9 The quantiles-quantiles probability plot comparing the Cherokee 1971 data with the normal distribution.

> The data are plotted against a theoretical distribution in such a way that the points should form approximately a straight line. Departures from this straight line indicate departures from the specified distribution.

As you can see in Figure 1.9 the Cherokee 1971 data are just as you would expect them to be if they came from a normal distribution. In fact, the data points are almost all on the line showing perfect identity between the expected "Theoretical quantiles" and the actual "Sample quantiles." This good fit between expected and actual quantiles is reflected in a correlation coefficient of 0.987 – almost a perfect 1 (you'll find more about correlation in the phonetics chapter, Chapter 3).

Contrast this excellent fit with the one between the normal distribution and the 2001 data (Figure 1.10). Here we see that most of the data points in the 2001 data set are just where we would expect them to be in a normal distribution. However the two (possibly three) largest VOT values are much larger than expected. Consequently, the correlation between expected and observed quantiles for this data set (r = 0.87) is lower than what we found for the 1971 data. It may be that this distribution would look more normal if we collected more data

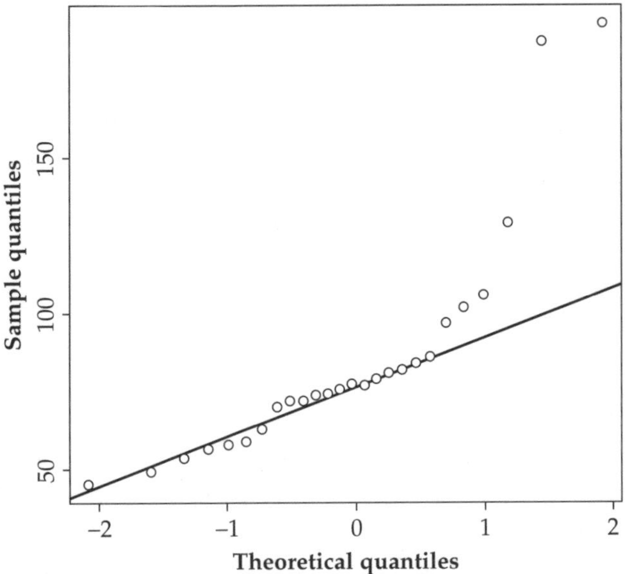

Figure 1.10 The quantiles-quantiles probability plot comparing the Cherokee 2001 data with the normal distribution.

points, or we might find that we have a bimodal distribution such that most data comes from a peak around 70 ms, but there are some VOTs (perhaps in a different speaking style?) that center around a much longer (190 ms) VOT value. We will eventually be testing the hypothesis that this speaker's VOT was shorter in 2001 than it was in 1971 and the outlying data values work against this hypothesis. But, even though these two very long VOT values are inconvenient, there is no valid reason to remove them from the data set (they are not errors of measurement, or speech dysfluencies), so we will keep them.

R note. Making a quantile-quantile plot in R is easy using the `qqnorm()` and `qqline()` functions. The function `qqnorm()` takes a vector of values (the data set) as input and draws a Q-Q plot of the data. I also captured the values used to plot the *x*-axis of the graph into the vector `vot71.qq` for later use in the correlation function `cor()`. `qqline()` adds the 45-degree reference line to the plot, and cor() measures how well the points fit on the line (0 for no fit at all and 1 for a perfect fit).

```
vot71.qq = qqnorm(vot71)$x # make the quantile/quantile plot
vot01.qq = qqnorm(vot01)$x # and keep the x axis of the plot

qqline(vot71) # put the line on the plot
cor(vot71,vot71.qq) # compute the correlation
[1] 0.9868212
> cor(vot01,vot01.qq)
[1] 0.8700187
```

Now, let's look at a non-normal distribution. We have some rating data that are measured as proportions on a scale from 0 to 1, and in one particular condition several of the participants gave ratings that were very close to the bottom of the scale – near zero. So, when we plot these data in a quantile-quantile probability plot (Figure 1.11), you

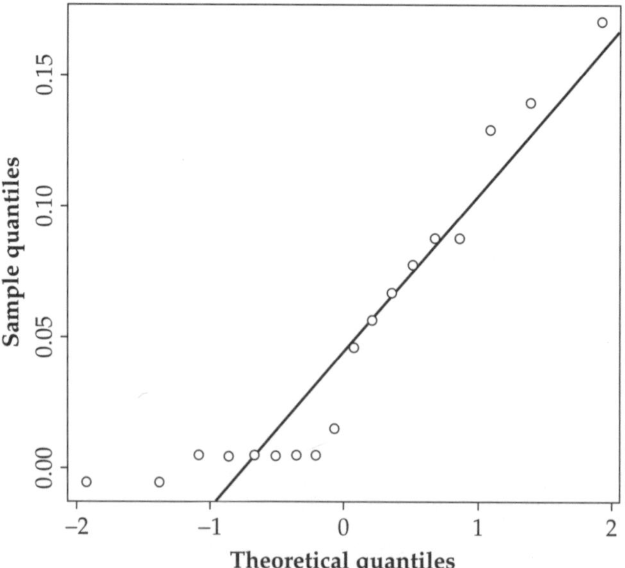

Figure 1.11 The Normal quantile-quantile plot for a set of data that is not normal because the score values (which are probabilities) cannot be less than zero.

can see that, as the sample quantile values approach zero, the data points fall on a horizontal line. Even with this non-normal distribution, though, the correlation between the expected normal distribution and the observed data points is pretty high (r = 0.92).

One standard method that is used to make a data set fall on a more normal distribution is to transform the data from the original measurement scale and put it on a scale that is stretched or compressed in helpful ways. For example, when the data are proportions it is usually recommended that they be transformed with the arcsine transform. This takes the original data x and converts it to the transformed data y using the following formula:

$$y = \frac{2}{\pi}\arcsin(\sqrt{x}) \quad \text{arcsine transformation}$$

This produces the transformation shown in Figure 1.12, in which values that are near 0 or 1 on the x-axis are spread out on the y-axis.

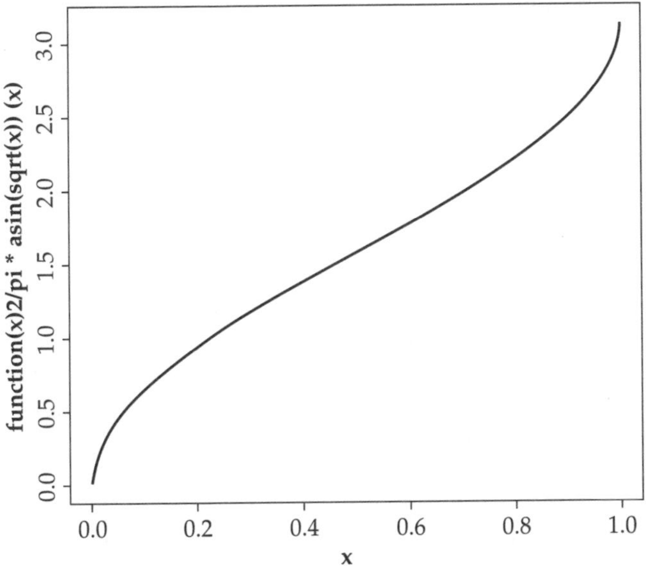

Figure 1.12 The arcsine transformation. Values of x that are near 0 or 1 are stretched out on the arcsine axis. Note that the transformed variable spans a range from 0 to π.

R note. The command for plotting the arcsine transformation in Figure 1.12 uses the plot function method.

```
> plot(function(x)2/pi*asin(sqrt(x)),0,1)
```

And as in this plot command, the command to transform the original data set (the vector "data") also uses the functions `asin()` and `sqrt()` to implement the arcsine and square root operations to create the new vector of values "x.arcsin." Read this as "x.arcsin is produced by taking the arcsine of the square root of data and multiplying it by 2 divided by π."

```
> x.arcsin = 2/pi*asin(sqrt(x))
```

The correlation between the expected values from a normal frequency distribution and the actual data values on the arcsine transformed measurement scale ($r = 0.96$) is higher than it was for the untransformed data. The better fit of the normal distribution to the observed data values is also apparent in the normal Q-Q plot of the transformed data (Figure 1.13). This indicates that the arcsine transform did what we needed it to do – it made our data more normally distributed so that we can use statistics that assume that the data fall in a normal distribution.

1.6 Measures of Central Tendency

Figure 1.14 shows three measures of the the central tendency, or mid-point, of a skewed distribution of data.

The *mode* of the distribution is the most frequently occurring value in the distribution – the tip of the frequency distribution. For the skewed distribution in Figure 1.14, the mode is at about 0.6.

Imagine ordering a data set from the smallest value to the largest. The *median* of the distribution is the value in the middle of the ordered list. There are as many data points greater than the median value then are less than the median. This is sometimes also called the "center of gravity".

The *mean* value, or the arithmetic average, is the least squares estimate of central tendency. First, how to calculate the mean – sum the data values and then divide by the number of values in the data set.

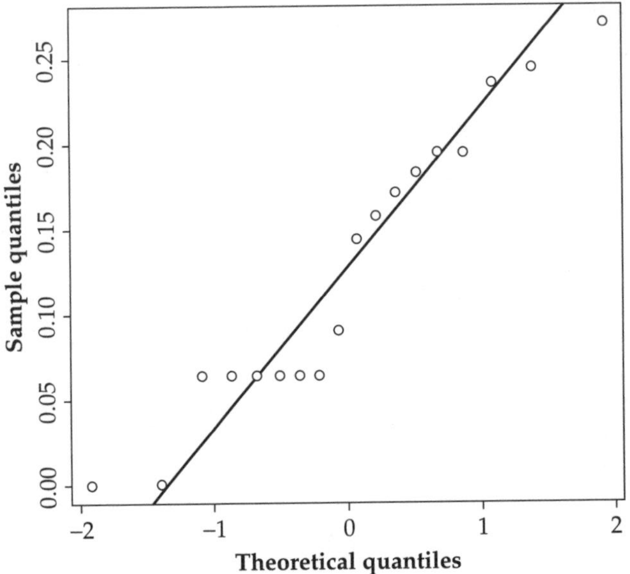

Figure 1.13 The normal quantile-quantile plot for the arcsine transform of the data shown in Figure 1.11.

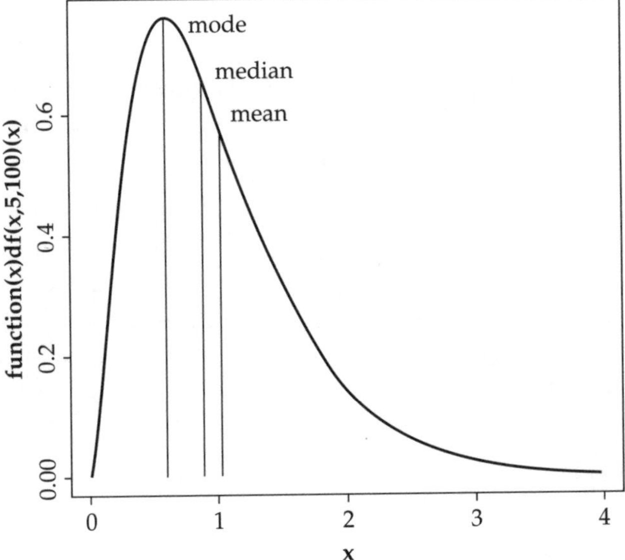

Figure 1.14 The mode, median, and mean of a skewed distribution.

$$\bar{x} = \frac{\sum_{i=0}^{n} x_i}{n} \quad \text{mean}$$

Second, what does it mean to be the least squares estimate of central tendency? This means that if we take the difference between the mean and each value in our data set, square these differences and add them up, we will have a smaller value than if we were to do the same thing with the median or any other estimate of the "mid-point" of the data set.

$$d^2 = \sum_{i=0}^{n} (x_i - \bar{x})^2 \quad \text{sum of the squared deviations (also called SS)}$$

So, in the data set illustrated in Figure 1.14, the value of d^2, the sum of the squared deviations from the mean, is 4,570, but if we calculate the sum of squared deviations from the median value we get a d^2 value of 4,794. This property, being the least squares estimate of central tendency, is a very useful one for the derivation of statistical tests of significance.

I should also note that I used a skewed distribution to show how the mode, median, and mean differ from each other because with a normal distribution these three measures of central tendency give the same value.

R note. The skewed distribution in Figure 1.14 comes from the "F" family of probability density distributions and is drawn in R using the `df()` density of "F" function.

```
plot(function(x)df(x,5,100),0,4,main="Measures of central
tendency")
```

The vertical lines were drawn with the `lines()` command. I used the `df()` function again to decide how tall to draw the lines and I used the `mean()` and `median()` commands with a data set drawn from this distribution to determine where on the x-axis to draw the mean and median lines.

```
lines(x = c(0.6,0.6), y = c(0,df(0.6,5,100)))
skew.data <- rf(10000,5,100)
lines(
```

```
       x = c(mean(skew.data),mean(skew.data)),
       y = c(0,df(mean(skew.data),5,100)))
lines(
       x = c(median(skew.data),median(skew.data)),
       y = c(0,df(median(skew.data),5,100)))
```

And finally, the text labels were added with the `text()` graphics command. I tried a couple of different x,y locations for each label before deciding on these.

```
text(1,0.75,labels="mode")
text(1.3,0.67,labels="median")
text(1.35,0.6,labels="mean")
```

Oh, and you might be interested in how I got the squared deviation d^2 values above. This illustrates how neatly you can do math in R. To square the difference between the mean and each data value in the vector I put the expression for the difference in `()` and then `^2` to square the differences. These then go inside the `sum()` function to add them up over the entire data vector. Your results will differ slightly because `skew.data` is a random sample from the F distribution and your random sample will be different from mine.

```
> sum((mean(skew.data)-skew.data)^2)
[1] 4570.231
> sum((median(skew.data)-skew.data)^2)
[1] 4794.141
```

We should probably also say something about the *weighted mean*. Suppose you asked someone to rate the grammaticality of a set of sentences, but you also let the person rate their ratings, to say that they feel very sure or not very sure at all about the rating given. These confidence values could be used as weights (w_i) in calculating the central tendency of the ratings, so that ratings given with high confidence influence the measure more than ratings given with a sense of confusion.

$$\bar{x} = \frac{\sum_{i=0}^{n} w_i x_i}{\sum_{i=0}^{n} w_i} \quad \text{weighted mean}$$

1.7 Measures of Dispersion

In addition to wanting to know the central point or most typical value in the data set we usually want to also know how closely clustered the data are around this central point – how dispersed are the data values away from the center of the distribution? The minimum possible amount of dispersion is the case in which every measurement has the same value. In this case there is no variation. I'm not sure what the maximum of variation would be.

A simple, but not very useful measure of dispersion is the *range* of the data values. This is the difference between the maximum and minimum values in the data set. The disadvantages of the range as a statistic are that (1) it is based on only two observations, so it may be sensitive to how lucky we were with the tails of the sampling distribution, and (2) range is undefined for most theoretical distributions like the normal distribution which extend to infinity.

I don't know of any measures of dispersion that use the median – the remaining measures discussed here refer to dispersion around the mean.

The average deviation, or the *mean absolute deviation*, measures the absolute difference between the mean and each observation. We take the absolute difference because if we took raw differences we would be adding positive and negative values for a sum of about zero no matter how dispersed the data are. This measure of deviation is not as well defined as is the standard deviation, partly because the mean is the least squares estimator of central tendency – so a measure of deviation that uses squared deviations is more comparable to the mean.

Variance is like the mean absolute deviation except that we square the deviations before averaging them. We have definitions for variance of a population and for a sample drawn from a larger population.

$$\sigma^2 = \sum(x_i - \mu)^2/N \qquad \text{population variance}$$

$$s^2 = \sum(x_i - \bar{x})^2/(n-1) \qquad \text{sample variance}$$

Notice that this formula uses the Sum of Squares (SS, also called d^2 above, the sum of squared deviations from the mean) and by dividing by N or $n - 1$, we get the Mean Squares (MS, also called s^2 here). We will see these names (SS, and MS) when we discuss the ANOVA later.

We take $(n - 1)$ as the denominator in the definition of s^2, sample variance, because $\bar{x}$ is not μ. The sample mean $\bar{x}$ is only an estimate of μ, derived from the x_i, so in trying to measure variance we have to keep in mind that our estimate of the central tendency $\bar{x}$ is probably wrong to a certain extent. We take this into account by giving up a "degree of freedom" in the sample formula. Degree of freedom is a measure of how much precision an estimate of variation has. Of course this is primarily related to the number of observations that serve as the basis for the estimate, but as a general rule the degrees of freedom decrease as we estimate more parameters with the same data set – here estimating both the mean and the variance with the set of observations x_i.

The variance is the average squared deviation – the units are squared – to get back to the original unit of measure we take the square root of the variance.

$\sigma = \sqrt{\sigma^2}$ population standard deviation

$s = \sqrt{s^2}$ sample standard deviation

This is the same as the value known as the RMS (root mean square), a measure of deviation used in acoustic phonetics (among other disciplines).

$$s = \sqrt{\frac{\sum(x_i - \bar{x})^2}{(n - 1)}} \quad \text{RMS = sample standard deviation}$$

1.8 Standard Deviation of the Normal Distribution

If you consider the formula for the normal distribution again, you will note that it can be defined for any mean value μ, and any standard deviation σ. However, I mentioned that this distribution is used to calculate probabilities, where the total area under the curve is equal to 1, so the area under any portion of the curve is equal to some proportion of 1. This is the case when the mean of the bell-shaped distribution is 0 and the standard deviation is 1. This is sometimes abbreviated as N(0,1) – a normal curve with mean 0 and standard deviation 1.

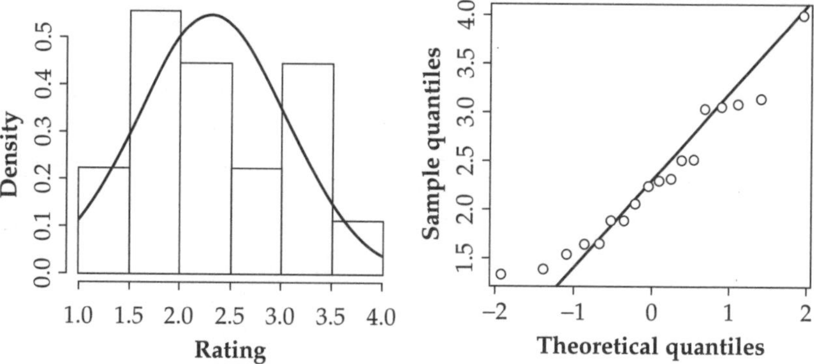

Figure 1.15 Histogram and Q-Q plot of some sample rating data.

$$f_x = \frac{1}{\sqrt{2\pi}} e^{-x^2/2} \quad \text{the normal distribution: N(0,1)}$$

I would like to make two points about this.

First, because the area under the normal distribution curve is 1, we can state the probability (area under the curve) of finding a value larger than any value of x, smaller than any value of x, or between any two values of x.

Second, because we can often approximate our data with a normal distribution we can state such probabilities for our data given the mean and standard deviation.

Let's take an example of this from some rating data (Figure 1.15). Listeners were asked to rate how similar two sounds were on a scale from 1 to 5 and their average ratings for a particular condition in the experiment ("How different do [d] and [ɾ] sound?") will be analyzed here. Though the histogram doesn't look like a smooth normal curve (there are only 18 data points in the set), the Q-Q plot does reveal that the individual data points do follow the normal curve pretty well (r = 0.97). Now, how likely is it, given these data and the normal curve that they fall on, that an average rating of less than 1.5 would be given? The area to the left of 1.5 under the normal curve in the histogram plot is 0.134, so we can say that 13% of the distribution covers rating values less than 1.5, so that if we are drawing more average rating values from our population – ratings given by speakers of Latin

American Spanish – we could predict that 13% of them would have average ratings less than 1.5.

R note. Figure 1.15 comes from the following commands (assuming a vector of data). This is all pretty familiar by now.

```
par(mfrow = c(1,2))
hist(data, freq=F)
plot(function(x)dnorm(x,mean=mean(data),sd=sd(data)),1,4,
add=T)
qqnorm(data)
qqline(data)
```

I calculated the probability of a rating value less than 1.5 by calling the `pnorm()` function.

```
pnorm(1.5,mean=mean(data),sd=sd(data))
[1] 0.1340552
```

`Pnorm()` also gives the probability of a rating value greater than 3.5 but this time specifying that we want the probability of the upper tail of the distribution (values greater than 3.5).

```
pnorm(3.5,mean=mean(data),sd=sd(data),lower.tail=F)
[1] 0.05107909
```

How does this work? We can relate the frequency distribution of our data to the normal distribution because we know the mean and standard deviation of both. The key is to be able to express any value in a data set in terms of its distance in standard deviations from the mean.

For example, in these rating data the mean is 2.3 and the standard deviation is 0.7. Therefore, a rating of 3 is one standard deviation above the mean, and a rating of 1.6 is one standard deviation below the mean. This way of expressing data values, in standard deviation units, puts our data on the normal distribution – where the mean is 0 and the standard deviation is 1.

I'm talking about *standardizing* a data set – converting the data values into *z-scores*, where each data value is replaced by the distance between it and the sample mean where the distance is measured as the number of standard deviations between the data value and the mean. As a result of "standardizing" the data, *z*-scores always have a mean

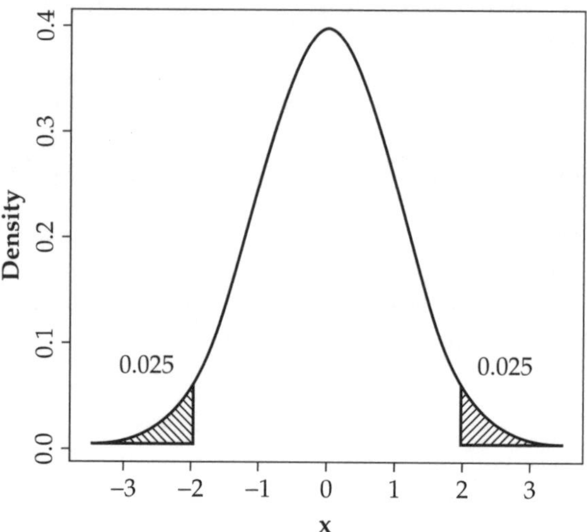

Figure 1.16 95% of the area under the normal distribution lies between –1.96*s* and 1.96*s*. 97.5% is above –1.96*s* and 97.5% is less than 1.96*s*.

of 0 and a standard deviation of 1, just like the normal distribution. Here's the formula for standardizing your data:

$$z_i = \frac{x_i - \bar{x}}{s} \quad z\text{-score standardization}$$

With standardized values we can easily make probability statements. For example, as illustrated in Figure 1.16, the area under the normal curve between –1.96 and 1.96 is 0.95. This means that 95% of the values we draw from a normal distribution will be between 1.96 standard deviations below the mean and 1.96 standard deviations above the mean.

EXERCISES

1 Open a dictionary of any language to a random page. Count the number of words that have 1, 2, 3, 4, etc. syllables. What kind of distribution do you get?

2 On the same page of the dictionary, count the number of instances of the different parts of speech – noun, verb, adjective, function word.

What kind of variable is part of speech and why can't you draw a reasonable distribution of part of speech?

3 Calculate the average number of syllables per word on this page. You can do this as a weighted mean, using the count as the weight for each syllable length.
4 What is the standard deviation of the average length in syllables? How do you calculate this? Hint: The raw data have one observation per word, while the count data have several words summarized for each syllable length.
5 Are these data an accurate representation of word length in this language? How could you get a more accurate estimate?
6 Using your word length data from question 1 above, produce a quantile-quantile (Q-Q) plot of the data. Are these data approximately normally distributed? What is the correlation between the normal curve quantiles (the theoretical quantiles) and the observed data?
7 Make a histogram of the data. Do these data seem to follow a normal distribution? Hint: Plotting the syllable numbers on the x-axis and the word counts on the y-axis (like Figure 1.1) may be a good way to see the frequency distribution.
8 Assuming a normal distribution, what is the probability that a word will have more than three syllables? How does this relate to the observed percentage of words that have more than three syllables in your data?

2 Patterns and Tests

In this chapter, I will present two key strategies in the quantitative analysis of linguistic data. We will come back to these in several different contexts in later chapters, so this is supposed to provide a foundation for those later discussions of how to apply hypothesis testing and regression analysis to data.

2.1 Sampling

But first I would like to say something about sampling. In Chapter 1, I made the distinction between a population parameter (Greek letter symbols like μ, σ, σ^2) and sample statistics (Roman letter symbols like $\bar{x}$, s, s^2). These differ like this: If we take the average height of everyone in the room, then the mean value that we come up with is the population parameter μ, of the population "everyone in the room." But if we would like to think that this group of people is representative of a larger group like "everyone at this university" or "everyone in this town," then our measured mean value is a sample statistic $\bar{x}$ that may or may not be a good estimate of the larger population mean.

In the normal course of events as we study language, we rely on samples to represent larger populations. It isn't practical to directly measure a population parameter. Imagine trying to find the grammaticality of a sentence from everyone who speaks a language! So we take a small, and we hope, representative sample from the population of ultimate interest.

So, what makes a good sample? To be an adequate representation of a population, the sample should be (1) large enough, and (2) random. Small samples are too sensitive to the effects of the occasional "odd" value, and nonrandom samples are likely to have some bias (called sampling bias) in them.

To be random it must be the case that every member of the population under study has an equal chance of being included in the sample. Here are two ways in which our linguistic samples are usually nonrandom.

1 We limit participation in our research to only certain people. For example, a consultant must be bilingual in a language that the linguist knows, college students are convenient for our listening experiments, we design questionnaires and thereby require our participants to be literate.
2 We observe linguistic performance only in certain restricted contexts. For example, we make tape recordings while people are reading a list of words or sentences. We ask for sentence judgments of sentences in a particular order on a questionnaire.

Obviously, it is pretty easy to violate the maxims of good sampling, but what should you do if your sample isn't representative of the population that you would most like to study? One option is to try harder to find a way to get a more random, representative sample. For instance you might collect some data from monolingual speakers and compare this with your data drawn from bilingual speakers. Or you might try conducting a telephone survey, using the listing of people in the phone book as your "population." And to address the context issue, you might try asking people meaningful questions in a natural context, so that they don't know that you are observing their speech. Or you might simply reverse the order of your list of sentences on the questionnaire.

In sum, there is a tradeoff between the feasibility of research and the adequacy of the sample. We have to balance huge studies that address tiny questions against small studies that cover a wider range of interesting issues. A useful strategy for the discipline is probably to encourage a certain amount of "calibration" research that answers limited questions with better sampling.

2.2 Data

Some of this discussion may reveal that I have a particular attitude about what linguistic data are, and I think this attitude is not all that unusual but worth stating explicitly. The data in linguistics are any observations about language. So, I could observe people as they speak or as they listen to language, and call this a type of linguistic data. Additionally, a count of forms used in a text, whether it be modern newspaper corpora or ancient carvings, is data. I guess you could say that these are observations of people in the act of writing language and we could also observe people in the act of reading language as well. Finally, I think that when you ask a person directly about language, their answers are linguistic data. This includes native speaker judgments, perceptual judgments about sounds, and language consultants' answers to questions like "what is your word for finger?"

Let's consider an observation and some of its variables.

The observation is this: A native speaker of American English judges the grammaticality of the sentence "Josie didn't owe nobody nothing" to be a 3 on a 7-point scale.

There are a large number of variables associated with this observation. For example, there are some static properties of the person who provided the judgment – gender, age, dialect, socioeconomic status, size of vocabulary, linguistic training. Additionally, aspects of the situation in which the judgment occurs may influence the participant. One common factor is what prior judgments were given already in this session. Perhaps we can't try all possible orderings of the sentences that we want to test, but we should pay attention to the possibility that order matters. Additionally, the person's prior experience in judging sentences probably matters. I've heard syntacticians talk about how their judgments seem to evolve over time and sometimes reflect theoretical commitments.

The task given to the participant may also influence the type of answer we get. For example, we may find that a fine-grained judgment task provides greater separation of close cases, or we may find that variance goes up with a fine-grained judgment task because the participant tends to focus on the task instead of on the sentences being presented.

We may also try to influence the participant's performance by instructing them to pay particular attention to some aspect of the stimuli or approach the task in a particular way. I've done this to no effect (Johnson, Flemming, & Wright, 1993) and to startling effect (Johnson, Strand, & D'Imperio, 1999). The participants in Johnson, Flemming, & Wright gave the same answers regardless (so it seemed) of the instructions that we gave them. But the "instruction set manipulation" in Johnson, Strand, & D'Imperio changed listeners' expectations of the talker and thus changed their performance in a listening experiment. My main point here is that how we interact with participants may influence their performance in a data collection situation.

An additional, very important task variable is the list of materials. The context in which a judgment occurs influences it greatly. So if the test sentence appears in a list that has lots of "informal" sentences of the sort that language mavens would cringe at, it may get a higher rating than if it appeared in a list of "correct" sentences.

The observation "3 on a 7-point scale" might have been different if we had changed any one of these variables. This large collection of potentially important variables is typical when we study complex human behavior, especially learned behavior like language. There are too many possible experiments. So the question we have to address is: Which variables are you interested in studying and which would you like to ignore? You have to ignore variables that probably could affect the results, and one of the most important elements of research is learning how to ignore variables.

This is a question of research methods which lies beyond the scope of this chapter. However, I do want to emphasize that (1) our ability to generalize our findings depends on having a representative sample of data – good statistical analysis can't overcome sampling inadequacy – and (2) the observations that we are exploring in linguistics are complex with many potentially important variables. The balancing act that we attempt in research is to stay aware of the complexity, but not let it keep us from seeing the big picture.

2.3 Hypothesis Testing

Now, keeping in mind the complexities in collecting representative samples of linguistic data and the complexities of the data themselves, we come to the first of the two main points of this chapter – hypothesis testing.

We often want to ask questions about mean values. Is this average voice onset time (VOT) different from that one? Do these two constructions receive different average ratings? Does one variant occur more often than another? These all boil down to the question is $\bar{x}$ (the mean of the data x_i) different from $\bar{y}$ (the mean of the data y_i)?

The smarty-pants answer is that you just look at the numbers, and they either are different or they aren't. The sample mean simply is what it is. So $\bar{x}$ is either the same number as $\bar{y}$ or it isn't. So what we are *really* interested in is the population parameter estimated by $\bar{x}$ and $\bar{y}$ – call them μ_x and μ_y. Given that we know the sample mean values $\bar{x}$ and $\bar{y}$, can we say with some degree of confidence that μ_x is different from μ_y? Since the sample mean is just an estimate of the population parameter, if we could measure the error of the sample mean then we could put a confidence value on how well it estimates μ.

2.3.1 *The central limit theorem*

A key way to approach this is to consider the sampling distribution of $\bar{x}$. Suppose we take 100 samples from a particular population. What will the distribution of the means of our 100 samples look like?

Consider sampling from a uniform distribution of the values 1 . . . 6, i.e. roll a dice. If we take samples of two (roll the dice once, write down the number shown, roll it again, and write down that number), we have 6^2 possible results, as shown in Table 2.1. Notice that the average of the two rolls is the same for cells in the diagonals. For example, the only way to average 6 is to roll 6 in both trials, but there are two ways to average 5.5 – roll a 6 and then a 5 or a 5 and then a 6. As you can see from Table 2.1, there are six ways to get an average of 3.5 on two rolls of the dice. Just to drive the point home, excuse the excess of this, the average of the following six two dice trials is 3.5 – (6,1), (5,2), (4,3), (3,4), (2,5), and (1,6). So, if we roll two dice, the probability of having an average number of dots equal to 3.5 is 6 times out of 36 trials (6 of the 36 cells in table 2.1).

In general the frequency distribution of the mean for two rolls of a dice has a shape like the normal distribution – this is shown in Figure 2.1. This is the beginning of a proof of the central limit theorem, which states that as the number of observations in each sample increases, the distribution of the means drawn from these samples tends toward the normal distribution. We can see in this simple example that even

Table 2.1 The possible outcomes of rolling a dice twice – i.e. samples of size two from a uniform distribution of the integers 1 . . . 6. The number of the first roll is indicated by the row number and the number of the second roll is indicated by the column number.

	1	**2**	**3**	**4**	**5**	**6**
1	1,1	1,2	1,3	1,4	1,5	1,6
2	2,1	2,2	2,3	2,4	2,5	2,6
3	3,1	3,2	3,3	3,4	3,5	3,6
4	4,1	4,2	4,3	4,4	4,5	4,6
5	5,1	5,2	5,3	5,4	5,5	5,6
6	6,1	6,2	6,3	6,4	6,5	6,6
$\bar{x}$	4	4.5	5	5.5	6	

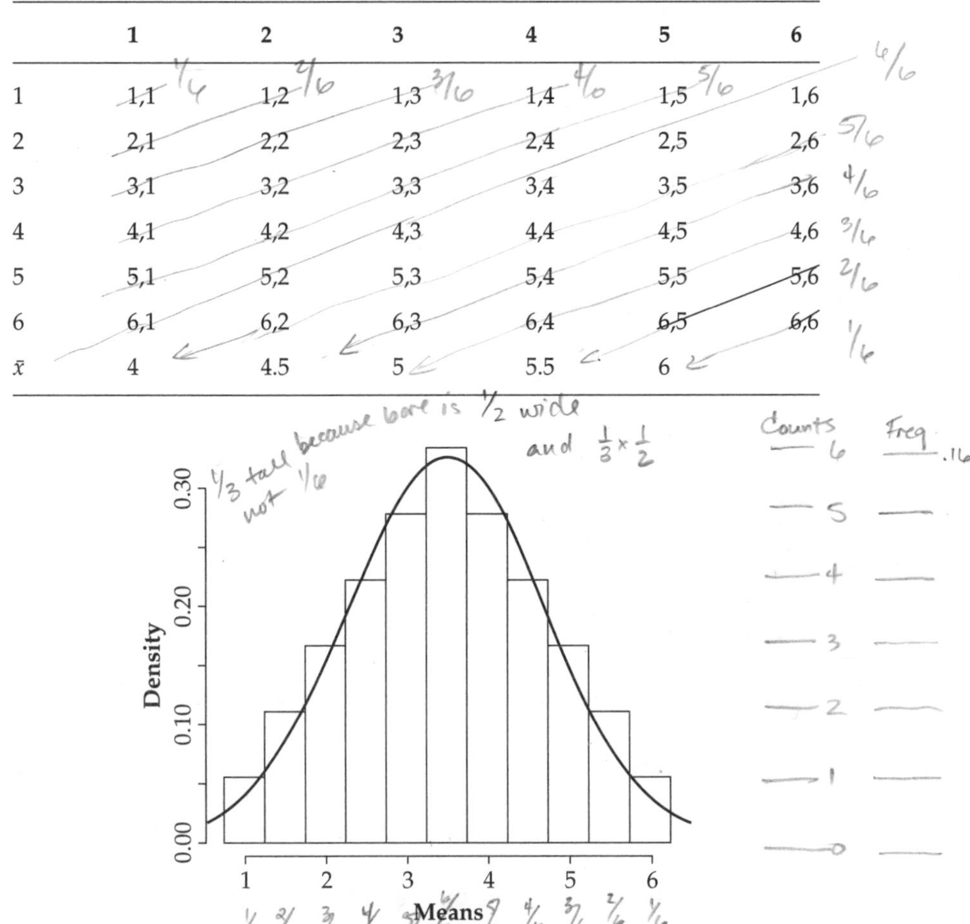

Figure 2.1 The frequency distribution of the mean for the samples illustrated in Table 2.1.

though the observations (dice throws) come from a uniform distribution in which each number on the dice has an equal probability of 1/6, the distribution of the means of just two observations looks remarkably like a normal distribution.

R note. Here's how I made Figure 2.1. First I entered a vector "means" that lists the mean value of each cell in Table 2.1. Then I entered a vector "b" to mark the edges of the bars that I want in the histogram. Then I plotted the histogram and best-fitting normal curve.

```
means = c(1, 1.5,1.5, 2,2,2, 2.5,2.5,2.5,2.5, 3,3,3,3,3,
3.5,3.5,3.5,3.5,3.5,3.5, 4,4,4,4,4, 4.5,4.5,4.5,4.5,
5,5,5, 5.5,5.5, 6)
b = c(0.75,1.25,1.75,2.25,2.75,3.25,3.75,4.25,4.75,
5.25,5.75,6.25)
hist(means,breaks=b,freq=F)
plot(function(x)dnorm(x,mean=mean(means), sd=sd(means)),
0.5,6.5, add=T)
```

Before we continue with this discussion of the central limit theorem we need step aside slightly to address one question that arises when you look at Figure 2.1. To the discriminating observer, the vertical axis doesn't seem right. The probability of averaging 3.5 dots on two rolls of the dice is 6/36 = 0.1666. So, why does the vertical axis in Figure 2.1 go up to 0.3? What does it mean to be labelled "density" and how is probability density different from probability?

Consider the probability of getting exactly some particular value on a continuous measurement scale. For example, if we measure the amount of time it takes someone to respond to a sound, we typically measure to some chosen degree of accuracy – typically the nearest millisecond. However, in theory we could have produced an arbitrarily precise measurement to the nanosecond and beyond. So, on a continuous measurement scale that permits arbitrarily precise values, the probability of finding exactly one particular value, say exactly 500 ms, is actually zero because we can always specify some greater degree of precision that will keep our observation from being exactly 500 ms – 500.00000001 ms. So on a continuous dimension, we can't give a probability for a specific value of the measurement variable. Instead we can only state the probability of a region under the cumulative distribution curve. For instance, we can't say what the probability of a measurement of 500 is, but we can say for example that about 16% of the cumulative distribution in Figure 2.2 falls to the left of 500 ms – that given a population like this one (mean = 600, standard deviation

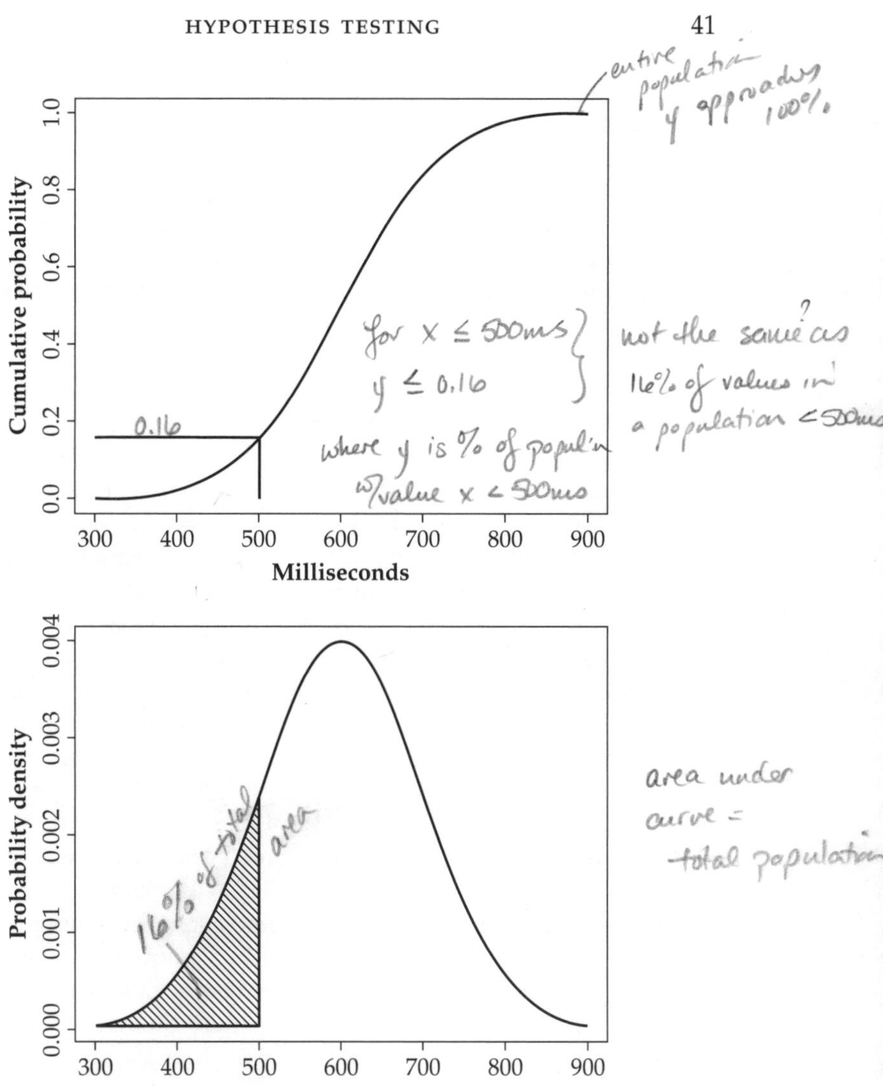

Figure 2.2 The cumulative probability function of the normal curve steadily increases from 0 to 1, while the probability density function (pdf) takes the familiar bell-shaped curve.

= 100) we expect 16% of the values in a representative sample to be lower than 500.

The probability density curve in the bottom panel of Figure 2.2 shows this same point, but in terms of the area under the curve instead of the value of the function at a particular point. In the probability density function, the area under the curve from 0 to 500 ms is 16% of the total area under the curve, so the value of the cumulative density function at 500 ms is 0.16. This relationship is illustrated in figure 2.2.

The probability density that we see in Figures 2.1 and 2.2 indicates the amount of change in (the derivative of) the cumulative probability function. If $f(x)$ is the probability density function, and $F(x)$ is the cumulative probability function then the relationship is:

$\frac{d}{dx}F(x) = f(x),$ the density function from the cumulative probability function

The upshot is that we can't expect the density function to have the values on the y-axis that we would expect for a cumulative frequency curve, and what we get by going to the trouble of defining a probability density function in this way is a method for calculating probability for areas under the normal probability density function.

Let's return now to the main point of Figure 2.1. We have an equal probability in any *particular trial* of rolling any one of the numbers on the dice – a *uniform distribution* – but the frequency distribution of the *sample mean*, even of a small sample size of only two rolls, follows the *normal distribution*. This is only approximately true with an n of 2. As we take samples of larger and larger n the distribution of the means of those samples becomes more and more perfectly normal. In looking at this example of two rolls of the dice, I was struck by how normal the distribution of means is for such small samples. This property of average values – that they tend to fall in a normal distribution as n increases – is called the *central limit theorem*. The practical consequence of the central limit theorem is that we can use the normal distribution (or, as we will see, a close approximation) to make probability statements about the mean – like we did with z-scores – even though the population distribution is not normal.

Let's consider another example this time of a skewed distribution. To produce the left side of Figure 2.3, I started with a skewed population distribution as shown in the figure and took 1,000 random samples from the distribution with a sample size of 10 data points per sample. I calculated the mean of each of the 1,000 samples so that now I have a set of 1,000 means. These are plotted in a histogram and theoretical curve of the histogram that indicate that the frequency distribution of the mean is a normal distribution. Also, a Q-Q plot (not shown) of these

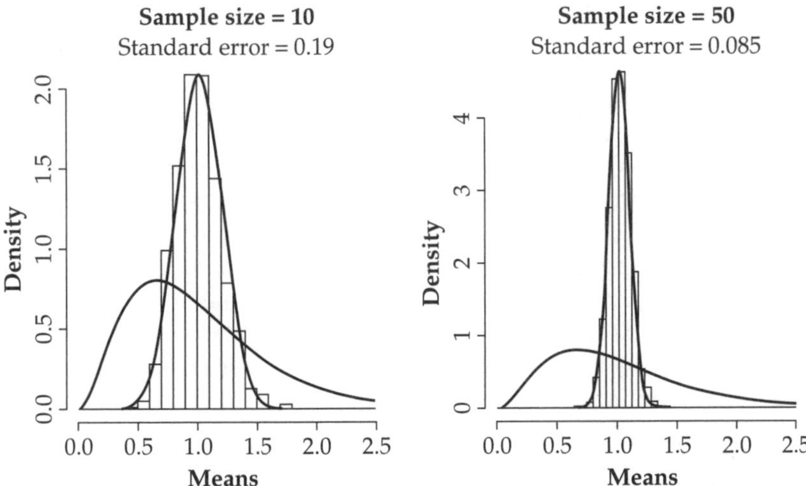

Figure 2.3 The sampling distribution of the mean taken from 1,000 samples that were drawn from a skewed population distribution when the sample size was only 10 observations, and when the sample size was 50 observations.

has a correlation of 0.997 between the normal distribution and the sampling distribution of the mean.

The panel on the right side of Figure 2.3 shows a similar situation except that each of the 1,000 samples had 50 observations in it instead of 10. Again the frequency distribution of the mean is normal (the Q-Q correlation was 0.998) and the fit to the normal curve is a little better than it was when we took samples of size 10 from this skewed distribution.

Notice in Figure 2.3 that I report the "standard error" of the 1,000 means in each panel. By standard error I mean simply the standard deviation of the sample of 1,000 means. As is apparent from the pictures, the standard deviation of the means is smaller when we take samples of 50 than when we take samples of 10 from the skewed distribution. This is a general feature. We are able to get a more accurate estimate of the population mean with a larger sample. You can see that this is so if we were to limit our samples to only one observation each. In such a case, the standard error of the mean would be the same as the standard deviation of the population being sampled. With larger samples the effects of observations from the tails of the distribution are dampened by the more frequently occurring observations from the middle of the distribution.

In fact, this value, the standard deviation of a sample of means, tells us just that – how accurately we can measure the mean of our raw data population. If you take a bunch of different samples and find that their means are really different from each other, then you have to wonder how accurate any one particular mean is when it comes to estimating the true mean of the population. Clearly one factor that matters is the size of the sample. The means drawn from samples of size 10 were much more spread out than were the means drawn from samples of size 50. Next we'll look at another factor that determines how accurately we can measure the population mean from samples drawn from that population.

R note. To explore the central limit theorem I wrote a function in R called `central.limit()`. Then to produce the graphs shown in Figure 2.3 all I had to do was type:

```
source("central.limit")
par(mfrow=c(1,2)) # to have one row with two graphs
central.limit(10) # to make the first graph
central.limit(50) # to make the second graph
```

I also made it so we can look at a Q-Q plot of the distribution of the means by changing the function call slightly.

```
central.limit(10,qq=TRUE)
```

I put a little effort into this `central.limit()` function so that I could change the shape of the population distribution, change the sample size, and the number of samples drawn, and to add some information to the output. Here's the definition of `central.limit()` that I stored in a text file called "central.limit" and that is read into R with the `source()` command above.

```
#-------- central.limit --------------
#
# The input parameters are:
#       n - size of each sample
#       m - number of samples of size n to select
#       qq - TRUE means show the Q-Q plots
```

```
#      df1, df2 - the df of the F() distribution from which
#      samples are drawn
#      xlow, xhigh - x-axis limits for plots

central.limit = function(n=15,m=1000,qq=FALSE,
df1=6,df2=200,xlow=0,xhigh=2.5) {
      means = vector() # I hereby declare that "means" is a
#     vector

      for (i in 1:m) { # get m samples from a skewed
            distribution
            data= rf(n,df1,df2) # the F() distribution is
      #     nice and skewed
            means[i] = mean(data) # means is our array of means
      }
      if (qq) { # call with TRUE and it makes the q-q plots
            x=qqnorm(means)$x
            qqline(means)
            caption = paste("n =",n,", Correlation = ",
               signif(cor(means,x),3))
            mtext(caption)
      } else { # the default behavior
            title = paste("Sample size = ",n)
            hist(means, xlim = c(xlow,xhigh),main=title,
               freq=F)
            plot(function(x)dnorm(x,mean=mean(means),
               sd=sd(means)), xlow, xhigh, add=T)
            plot(function(x)df(x,df1,df2),xlow,xhigh,add=T)
            caption = paste("Standard error = ",
               signif(sd(means),3))
            mtext(caption)
      }
}
```

This looks pretty complicated, I know, but I really think it is worth knowing how to put together an R function because (1) being able to write functions is one of the strengths of R, and (2) having a function that does exactly what you want done is extremely valuable. I do a number of new things in this function, but I also do a number of things that we saw in Chapter 1. For example, we saw earlier how to sample randomly from the *F*-distribution using the `rf()` command, and we saw how to plot a histogram together with a normal distribution curve. We also saw earlier how to draw Q-Q plots. So really, this function just puts together a number of things that we already know how to do.

There are only three new R capabilities that I used in writing the `central.limit()` function:

`function()`. The first is that `central.limit()` shows how to create a new command in R using the `function()` command. For example, this line:

```
>square = function(x) {return(x*x)}
```

creates, or defines, a function called `square()` that returns the square (x times x) of the input value. So now if you enter:

```
->square(1532)
```

R will return with the number "`2347024`". Note that in my definition of "central.limit()" I gave each input parameter a default value. This way the user doesn't have to enter values for these parameters, but can instead pick and choose which variable names to set manually. Because I set default values for the input variables in the central limit function, `central.limit(df1=3)` is a legal command that works so that the default values are used for each input parameter except `df1`. You can save function definitions in text files and use the `source()` command to read them into R and make them available for use.

`for (i...)`. The `central.limit()` function shows how to use a "for loop" to do something over and over. I wanted to draw lots (m) of random samples from the skewed *F*-distribution, store all of the means of these samples and then make a histogram of the means. So, I used a "for loop" to execute two commands over and over:

```
data= rf(n,df1,df2)
means[i] = mean(data)
```

The first one draws a new random sample of n data points from the *F*-distribution, and the second one calculates the mean of this sample and stores it in the *i*th location in the "means" vector. By putting these two commands inside the following lines we indicate that we want the variable i to start with a value of 1 and we want to repeat the commands bracketed by {...} counting up from $i = 1$ until $i = m$. This gives us a vector of m mean values stored in means[1]... means[m].

```
for (i in 1:m) {
        # my repeated stuff here
}
```

if (). Finally, `central.limit()` shows how to use an "if statement" to choose to do one set of commands or another. I wanted to have the option to look at a histogram and report the standard deviation, or to look at a Q-Q plot and report the correlation with the normal distribution. So, I had `central.limit()` choose one of these two options depending on whether the input parameter "qq" is TRUE or FALSE.

```
if (qq) {
        # do this if "qq" is TRUE
    else {
        # do this if "qq" is not TRUE
}
```

I made a new version of `central.limit()` that I decided to call `central.limit.norm()` because instead of sampling from a skewed population distribution, I sampled from a normal distribution. In all other regards `central.limit.norm()` is exactly like `central.limit()`. Figure 2.4 shows the population distribution (notice that now it is a normal distribution), a histogram of 5,000 means drawn from the population, and a normal curve fit to the histogram of means. The panels on the left had a population standard deviation (σ) of 1, while the panels on the right had a σ of 0.6. The top panels had a sample size (n) of 15, while for the bottom panels $n = 50$.

We saw in Figure 2.3 that our estimate of μ was more accurate (the standard deviation of $\bar{x}$ was smaller) when the sample size increased. What we see in Figure 2.4 is that the error of our estimates of μ are also smaller when the standard deviation of the population (σ) is smaller. In fact, figure 2.4 makes it clear that the standard error of

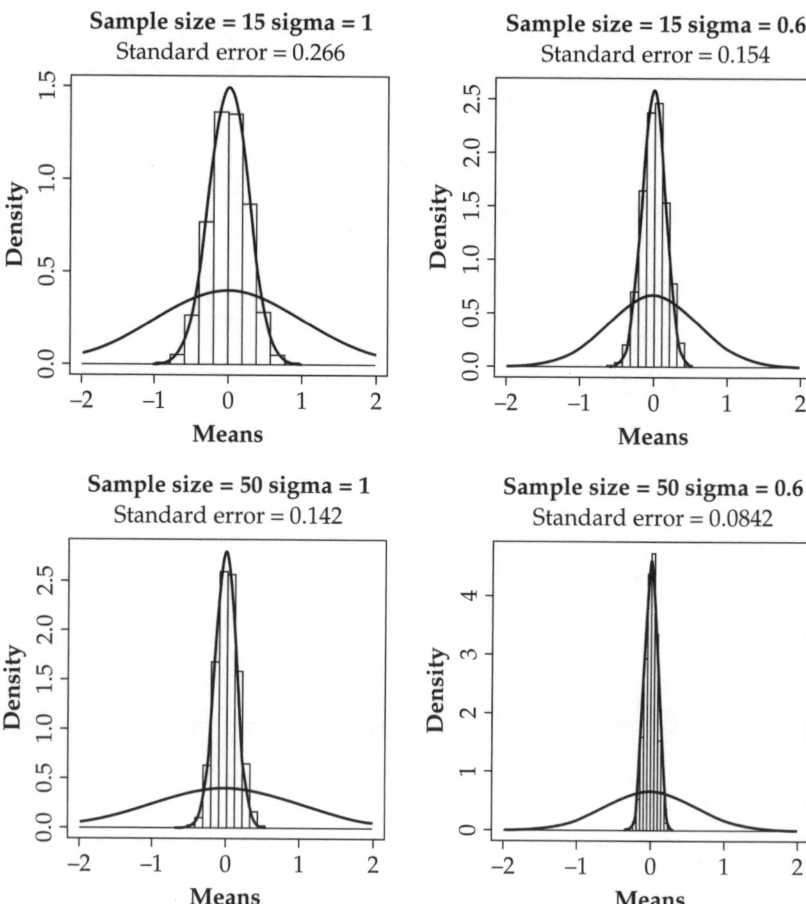

Figure 2.4 The sampling distribution of the mean of a normal distribution is a function of sample size and the population standard deviation (σ). Right panels: the population distribution has a σ of 1. Left panels: σ is 0.6. Top panels: Sample size (n) was 15. Bottom panels: n is 50.

the mean depends on both sample size and σ. So, we saw earlier in Figure 2.3 that the distribution of sample means $\bar{x}$ is more tightly focused around the true population mean μ when the sample n is larger. What we see in Figure 2.4 is that the distribution of sample means is also more tightly focused around the true mean when the population distribution is smaller.

Check this out. Let's abbreviate the standard error of the mean to *SE* – this is the standard deviation of $\bar{x}$ values that we calculate from successive samples from a population and it indicates how accurately we can estimate the population mean μ from a random sample of data drawn from that population. It turns out (as you might expect from the relationships apparent in Figure 2.4) that you can measure the standard error of the mean from a single sample – it isn't necessary to take thousands of samples and measure *SE* directly from the distribution of means. This is a good thing. Can you imagine having to perform every experiment 1,000 times so you can measure *SE* directly? The relationship between *SE* and σ (or our sample estimate of σ, *s*) is:

$$SE = s_{\bar{x}} = \frac{\sigma}{\sqrt{n}} \quad \text{standard error of the mean: population}$$

$$SE = s_{\bar{x}} = \frac{s_x}{\sqrt{n}} \quad \text{standard error of the mean: sample}$$

You can test this out on the values shown in Figure 2.4:

$$\frac{\sigma}{\sqrt{n}} = \frac{1}{\sqrt{15}} = 0.258 \quad \frac{\sigma}{\sqrt{n}} = \frac{0.6}{\sqrt{15}} = 0.155$$

$$\frac{\sigma}{\sqrt{n}} = \frac{1}{\sqrt{50}} = 0.141 \quad \frac{\sigma}{\sqrt{n}} = \frac{0.6}{\sqrt{50}} = 0.0849$$

The calculated values are almost exactly the same as the measured values of the standard deviation of the sets of 5,000 means.

2.3.2 *Score keeping*

Here's what we've got so far about how to test hypotheses regarding means.

1 You can make probability statements about variables in normal distributions.
2 You can estimate the parameters of empirical distributions as the least squares estimates of $\bar{x}$ and *s*.
3 Means themselves, of samples drawn from a population, fall in a normal distribution.
4 You can estimate the standard error (SE) of the normal distribution of $\bar{x}$ values from a single sample.

What this means for us is that we can make probability statements about means.

2.3.3 H_0: $\mu = 100$

Recall that when we wanted to make probability statements about observations using the normal distribution, we converted our observation scores into z-scores (the number of standard deviations different from the mean) using the z-score formula.

So, now to test a hypothesis about the population mean (μ) on the basis of our sample mean and the standard error of the mean we will use a very similar approach.

$$z = \frac{x_i - \bar{x}}{s} \quad z\text{-score}$$

$$t = \frac{\bar{x} - \mu}{s_{\bar{x}}} \quad t\text{-value}$$

However, we usually (almost always) don't know the population standard deviation. Instead we estimate it with the sample standard deviation, and the uncertainty introduced by using s instead of σ means that we are off a bit and can't use the normal distribution to compare $\bar{x}$ to μ. Instead, to be a little more conservative, we use a distribution (or family of distributions), called the t-distribution that takes into account how certain we can be about our estimate of σ. Just as we saw that a larger sample size gives us a more stable estimate of the population mean, so we get a better estimate of the population standard deviation with larger sample sizes. So the larger the sample size, the closer the t-distribution is to normal. I show this in Figure 2.5 for the normal distribution and t-distributions for three different sample sizes. So we are using a slightly different distribution to talk about mean values, but the procedure is practically the same as if we were using the normal distribution. Nice that you don't have to learn something totally new.

To make a probability statement about a z-score you refer to the normal distribution, and to make a probability statement about a t-value you refer to the t-distribution. It may seem odd to talk about comparing the sample mean to the population mean because we we can easily calculate the sample mean but the population mean is not a value that we can know. However, if you think of this as a way to

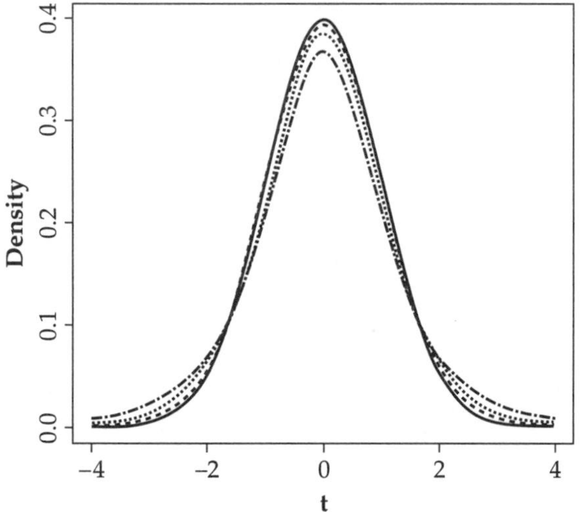

Figure 2.5 The normal distribution (solid line) and t-distributions for samples of size $n = 21$ (dash), $n = 7$ (dot) and $n = 3$ (dot, dash).

test a hypothesis, then we have something. For instance, with the Cherokee VOT data, where we observed that $\bar{x} = 84.7$ and $s = 36.1$ for the stops produced in 2001, we can now ask whether the population mean μ is different from 100. Let's just plug the numbers into the formula:

$$t = \frac{\bar{x}_i - \mu}{s_{\bar{x}}} = \frac{84.7 - 100}{36.1/\sqrt{26}} = \frac{-15.3}{7.08} = -2.168$$

So we can use the formula for t to find that the t-value in this test is −2.168. But what does that mean? We were testing the hypothesis that the average VOT value of 84.7 ms is not different from 100 ms. This can be written as H_0: $\mu = 100$. Meaning that the null hypothesis (the "no difference" hypothesis H_0) is that the population mean is 100. Recall that the statistic t is analogous to z – it measures how different the sample mean $\bar{x}$ is from the hypothesized population mean μ, as measured in units of the standard error of the mean. As we saw in Chapter 1, observations that are more than 1.96 standard deviations away from the mean in a normal distribution are pretty unlikely – only 5% of the area under the normal curve. So this t-value of −2.168 (a little more

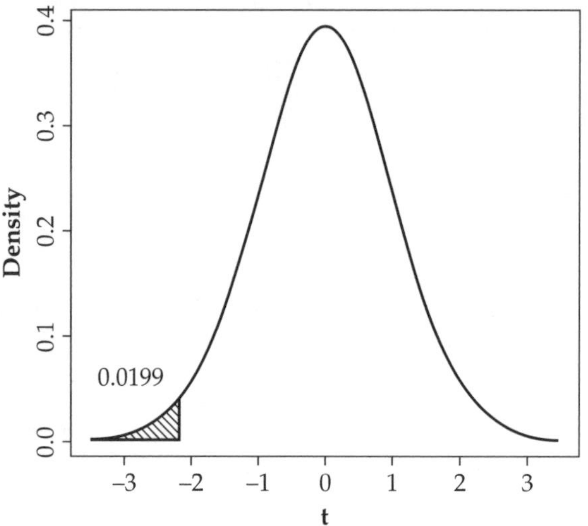

Figure 2.6 The probability density function of t with 25 degrees of freedom. The area of the shaded region at $t < -2.168$ indicates that only a little over 2% of the area under this curve has a t-value less than –2.168.

than 2 standard errors less than the hypothesized mean) might be a pretty unlikely one to find if the population mean is actually 100 ms.

How unlikely? Well, the probability density function of t with 25 degrees of freedom (since we had 26 observations in the VOT data set) shows that only 2% of all t-values in this distribution are less than –2.16 (Figure 2.6). Recall that we are evaluating the null hypothesis that $\mu = 100$. Therefore, this probability value says that if we assume that $\mu = 100$ it is pretty unlikely (2 times in 100) that we would draw a sample that has an $\bar{x}$ of 84.7. The more likely conclusion that we should draw is that the population mean is less than 100.

R note. I wrote a script to produce t probability density functions with shaded tails such as the one in Figure 2.6. The function is called "shade.tails" (check for it in the "Data sets and scripts" part of the book web page), and to produce Figure 2.6, I entered the t-value we calculated above, the degrees of freedom for the t-distribution, and indicated that we want the probability of a lower *t*-value. The key functions in shade.tails are `pt()`, the probability of getting a smaller or larger *t*-value, and `dt()` the density functon of *t*. For example, the probability of finding a smaller *t*-value, given 25 degrees of freedom is calculated by the `pt()` function.

```
> shade.tails(2.16,tail="lower",df=25)
> pt(-2.168,25)
[1] 0.01994047
```

This hypothesis test – using the mean, standard deviation, and hypothesized population mean (μ) to calculate a *t*-value, and then look up the probability of the *t*-value – is a very common statistical test. Therefore, there is a procedure in R that does it for us.

```
> vot01 = c(84, 82, 72, 193, 129, 77, 72, 81, 45, 74, 102, 77,
187, 79, 86, 59, 74, 63, 75, 70, 106, 54, 49, 56, 58, 97)
> vot71 =c(67, 127, 79, 150, 53, 65, 75, 109, 109, 126, 129,
119, 104, 153, 124, 107, 181, 166)
> t.test(vot01,mu=100,alternative="less")

  One Sample t-test

data: vot01
t = -2.1683, df = 25, p-value = 0.01993
alternative hypothesis: true mean is less than 100
95 percent confidence interval:
  -Inf 96.74298
sample estimates:
mean of x
  84.65385
```

In this call to `t.test()`, I entered the name of the vector that contains my data, the hypothesized population mean for these data, and that I want to know how likely it is to have a lower *t*-value.

2.3.4 *Type I and type II error*

We seek to test the hypothesis that the true Cherokee VOT in 2001 (μ) is 100 ms by taking a sample from a larger population of possible measurements. If the sample mean ($\bar{x}$) is different enough from 100 ms, then we reject this hypothesis; otherwise we accept it.

The question is, how different is different enough? We can quantify the difference between the sample mean and the hypothesized population mean in terms of a probability. As we saw above, if the population mean is 100 ms, then in only 2 times in 100 could we get a sample mean of 84.7 or less. Suppose that we decide then that this is a big enough difference – the probability of a sample of 84.7 mean coming from a population that has a mean of 100 ms is pretty darn low – so we reject the hypothesis that $\mu = 100$ (let's label it H_0), and instead accept the alternative hypothesis that $\mu < 100$ (call this H_1 and note that this is only one of several possible alternative hypotheses).

H_0: $\mu = 100$ Reject
H_1: $\mu < 100$ Accept

We have to admit, though, that 2 times out of 100 this decision would be wrong. It may be unlikely, but it is still possible that H_0 is correct – the population mean really could be 100 ms even though our sample mean is a good deal less than 100 ms. This error probability (0.02) is called the probability of making a type I error. A type I error is that we incorrectly reject the null hypothesis – we claim that the population mean is less than 100, when actually we were just unlucky and happened to draw one of the 2 out of 100 samples for which the sample mean was equal to or less than 84.7.

No matter what the sample mean is, you can't reject the null hypothesis with certainty because the normal distribution extends from negative infinity to positive infinity. So, even with a population mean of 100 ms we could have a really unlucky sample that has a mean of only 5 ms. This probably wouldn't happen, but it might. So we have to go with our best guess.

In practice, "going with your best guess" means choosing a type I error probability that you are willing to tolerate. Most often we are willing to accept a 1 in 20 chance that we just got an unlucky sample that leads us to make a type I error. This means that if the probability of the *t*-value that we calculate to test the hypothesis is less than 0.05, we are willing to reject H_0 ($\mu = 100$) and conclude that the sample mean comes from a population that has a mean that is less than 100 ($\mu < 100$). This criterion probability value ($p < 0.05$) is called the "alpha" (α) level of the test. The α level is the acceptable type I error rate for our hypothesis test.

Table 2.2 The decision to accept or reject the null hypothesis may be wrong in two ways. An incorrect rejection, a type I error, is when we claim that the means are different but in reality they aren't, and an incorrect acceptance, a type II error, is when we claim that the means are not different but in reality they are.

		Reality	
		H_0 is true	H_0 is false
Decision	accept H_0	correct	Type II error
	reject H_0	Type I error	correct

Where there is a type I error, there must be a type II error also (see Table 2.2). A type II error occurs when we incorrectly accept the null hypothesis. Suppose that we test the hypothesis that the average VOT for Cherokee (or at least this speaker) is 100 ms, but the actual true mean VOT is 95 ms. If our sample mean is 95 ms and the standard deviation is again about 35 ms we are surely going to conclude that the null hypothesis (H_0: $\mu = 100$) is probably true. At least our data is not inconsistent with the hypothesis because 24% of the time ($p = 0.24$) we can get a *t*-value that is equal to or less than −0.706.

$$t = \frac{\bar{x} - \mu}{s_{\bar{x}}} = \frac{95 - 100}{36.1/\sqrt{26}} = \frac{-5}{7.08} = -0.706 \quad \text{testing for a small difference}$$

Nonetheless, by accepting the null hypothesis we have made a type II error. Just as we can choose a criterion α level for the acceptable type I error rate, we can also require that our statistics avoid type II errors. The probability of making a type II error is called β, and the value we are usually interested in is $1 - \beta$, the *power* of our statistical test. As my example illustrates, to avoid type II errors you need to have statistical tests that are sensitive enough to catch small differences between the sample mean and the population mean – to detect that 95 really is different from 100. With only 26 observations ($n = 26$) and a standard deviation of 36.1, if we set the power of our test to 0.8 (that is, accept type II errors 20% of the time with $\beta = 0.2$) the difference between the hypothesized mean and the true population mean would have to be 18 ms before we could detect the difference. To detect a smaller difference like 5 ms we would have to increase the power of the hypothesis test.

You'll notice that in the calculation of *t* there are two parameters other than the sample mean and the population mean that affect the *t*-value. These are the standard deviation of the sample (*s*) and the size of the sample (*n*). To increase the power of the *t*-test we need to either reduce the standard deviation or increase the number of observations. Sometimes you can reduce the standard deviation by controlling some uncontrolled sources of variance. For example, in this VOT data I pooled observations from both /t/ and /k/. These probably do have overall different average VOT, so by pooling them I have inflated the standard deviation. If we had a sample of all /k/ VOTs the standard deviation might be lower and thus the power of the *t*-test greater. Generally, though, the best way to increase the power of your test is to get more data. In this case, if we set the probability of a type I error at 0.05, the probability of a type II error at 0.2, and we want to be able to detect that 95 ms is different from the hypothesized 100 ms, then we need to have an *n* of 324 observations (see the R note for the magic).

R note. The R function `power.t.test()` provides a way to estimate how many observations you need to make in order to detect differences between means of any specified magnitude with α and β error probabilities controlled. In the call below, I specified that I want to detect a difference of 5 ms (`delta=5`), that I expect that the standard deviation of my observations will be 36.1 (`sd=36.1`), and that we are testing whether the sample mean is less than the hypothesized mean, not just different one way or the other (`alternative = "one.sided"`). With $\alpha = 0.05$ (`sig.level=0.05`) and $\beta = 0.2$ (`power=0.8`), this function reports that we need 324 (`n = 323.6439`) observations to detect the 5 ms difference.

```
power.t.test(power=0.8,sig.level=0.05,delta=5,sd=36.1,
type="one.sample",alternative="one.sided")
One-sample t test power calculation
   n = 323.6439
```

```
delta = 5
sd = 36.1
sig.level = 0.05
power = 0.8
alternative = one.sided
```

Of course, collecting more data is time consuming, so it is wise to ask, as Ilse Lehiste once asked me, "sure it is significant, but is it important?" It may be that a 5 ms difference is too small to be of much practical or theoretical importance, so taking the trouble to collect enough data so that we can detect such a small difference is really just a waste of time.

2.4 Correlation

So far we have been concerned in this chapter with the statistical background assumptions that make it possible to test hypotheses about the population mean. This is the "tests" portion of this chapter on "Patterns and tests." You can be sure that we will be coming back to this topic in several practical applications in chapters to follow. However, because this chapter is aiming to establish some of the basic building blocks that we will return to over and over in the subsequent chapters, I would like to suspend the "tests" discussion at this point and turn to the "patterns" portion of the chapter. The aim here is to explain some of the key concepts that underlie studies of relationships among variables – in particular to review the conceptual and mathematical underpinnings of correlation and regression.

One way to explore the relationship between two variables is by looking at counts in a contingency table. For example, we have a data set of two measurements of the lowest vocal tract resonance frequency – the first formant (F1). We have F1 values for men and women for the vowels /i/, /e/, /a/, /o/, and /u/ in four different languages (see the data file "F1_data.txt"). Women tend to have shorter vocal tracts than men and thus to have higher resonance frequencies. This is the case in our data set, where the average F1 of the women is 534.6 Hz and the average F1 for men is 440.9. We can construct a contingency table by counting how many of the observations in this data set fall

Table 2.3 A 2 × 2 contingency table showing the number of F1 values above or below the average F1 for men and women in the small "F1_data.txt" data set.

		Female F1	
		below	above
Male F1	above	0	6
	below	12	1

above or below the mean on each of the two variables being compared. For example, we have the five vowels in Sele (a language spoken in Ghana) measured on two variables – male F1 and female F1 – and we are interested in studying the relationship or correlation between male and female F1 frequency. The contingency table in Table 2.3 then shows the number of times that we have a vowel that has female F1 above the average female F1 value while for the same vowel in the same language we have male F1 above the male F1 average – this "both above" condition happens six times in this small data set. Most of the other vowels (twelve) have both male and female F1 falling below their respective means, and in only one vowel was there a discrepancy, where the female F1 was above the female mean while the male F1 was below the male F1.

So, Table 2.3 shows how the F1 values fall in a two by two (2 × 2) contingency table. This table shows that for a particular vowel in a particular language (say /i/ in Sele), if the male F1 falls below the average male F1, then the female F1 for that vowel will probably also fall below the average F1 for female speakers. In only one case does this relationship not hold.

I guess it is important to keep in mind that Table 2.3 didn't have to come out this way. For instance, if F1 was not acoustically related to vowel quality, then pairing observations of male and female talkers according to which vowel they were producing would not have resulted in matched patterns of F1 variation.

Contingency tables are a useful way to see the relationship, or lack of one, between two variables, and we will see in Chapter 5 that when the counts are a good deal larger than these – particularly when we have more than 5 or 10 observations even in the smallest cell of the table – we can test the strength of the relationship using the χ^2 distribution. However, we threw away a lot of information by constructing this contingency table. From Table 2.3 all we know is that if the male F1 is above average so is the female F1, but we don't know whether they tend to be the same amount above average or if sometimes the amount above average for males is much more than it is for females. It would be much better to explore the relationship of these two variables without throwing out this information.

In Figure 2.7 you can see the four cells of Table 2.3. There are 6 data points in the upper right quadrant of the graph, 12 data points in the lower left, and 1 that just barely ended up in the lower right quadrant. These quadrants were marked in the graph by drawing a dashed line at the mean values for the male (441 Hz) and female (535 Hz) talkers. As you can see, the relationship between male and female F1 values goes beyond simply being in one quadrant of the graph or not. In fact,

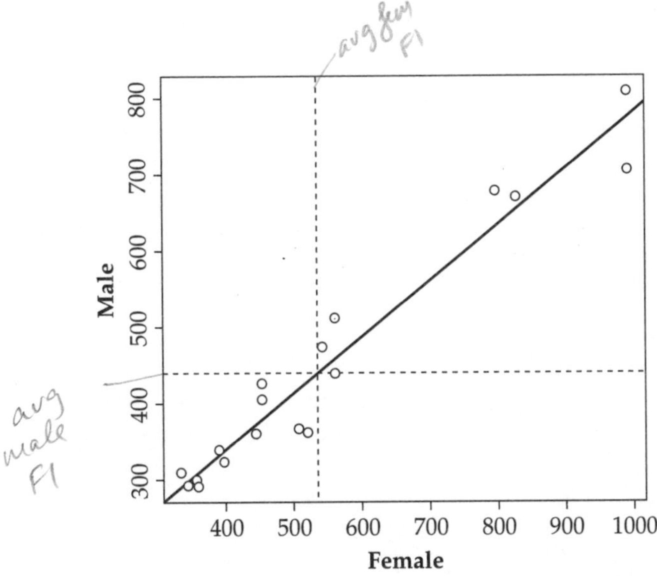

Figure 2.7 Nineteen pairs of male and female F1 values drawn from four different languages and 4 or 5 vowels in each language. The grid lines mark the average female (vertical line) and male (horizontal line) F1 values. The diagonal line is the best-fitting straight line (the linear regression) that relates female F1 to male F1.

it looks as though if we divided the lower left and the upper right quadrants into quadrants again we would still have the relationship, higher male F1 is associated with higher female F1. We need a measure of association that will give us a consistent indication of how closely related two variables are.

R note. For the example in Table 2.3 and Figure 2.7, I used data that are stored in a data file that I called "F1_data.txt". This is laid out like a spread sheet, but it is important to keep in mind that it is a text file. So, if you are preparing data for import into R you should be sure to save your data file as a ".txt" file (actually R doesn't care about the file name extension, but some programs do). The first three lines of my data file look like this:

```
female  male  vowel  language
391     339   i      W.Apache
561     512   e      W.Apache
......
```

The first row contains the names of the variables, and the following rows each contain one pair of observations. For example, the first row indicates that the vowel [i] in Western Apache has an F1 value of 391 Hz for women and 339 Hz for men. I used the `read.delim()` function to read my data from the file into an R `data.frame` object.

```
f1data = read.delim("F1_data.txt")
```

This object `f1data` is composed of four vectors, one for each column in the data file. So, if I would like to see the vector of female F1 measurements I can type the name of the data frame followed by a dollar sign and then the name of the vector within that data frame.

```
> f1data$female
 [1] 391 561 826 453 358 454 991 561 398 334 444 796 542 333
[15] 343 520 989 507 357
```

The command `summary()` is a useful one for verifying that your data file has been read correctly.

```
> summary(f1data)
    female           male        vowel  language
 Min.   :333.0  Min.   :291.0  a:4    CA English:5
 1st Qu.:374.5  1st Qu.:317.5  e:4    Ndumbea   :5
 Median :454.0  Median :367.0  i:4    Sele      :5
 Mean   :534.6  Mean   :440.9  o:4    W.Apache  :4
 3rd Qu.:561.0  3rd Qu.:493.0  u:3
 Max.   :991.0  Max.   :809.0
```

It is a bit of a pain to keep typing `f1data$female` to refer to a vector, so the `attach()` command is useful because once a data frame has been attached you don't have to mention the data frame name.

```
attach(f1data)
```

Now, having read in the data, here are the commands I used to produce Figure 2.7 (I'll discuss the diagonal line later):

```
plot(female,male)
lines(x=c(mean(female),mean(female)),y=c(200,900),lty=2)
lines(x=c(200,1100),y=c(mean(male),mean(male)),lty=2)
```

Finally, as you might expect, R has built-in functions to calcluate the covariance and correlation between two variables.

```
> cov(female,male)
[1] 33161.79
> cor(female,male)
[1] 0.9738566
```

2.4.1 *Covariance and correlation*

The key insight in developing a measure of association between two variables is to measure deviation from the mean $(x_i - \bar{x})$. As we saw in Figure 2.7, the association of male F1 and female F1 can be captured by noticing that when female F1 (let's name this variable x) was higher than the female mean, male F1 (y) was also higher than the male mean. That is, if $x_i - \bar{x}$ is positive then $y_i - \bar{y}$ is also positive. What is more, the association is strongest when the magnitudes of these deviations are matched – when x_i is quite a bit larger than the x mean and y_i is also quite a bit larger than the y mean. We can get an overall sense of how strong the association of two variables is by multiplying the deviations of x and y and summing these products for all of the observations.

$$\sum_{i=0}^{n}(x_i - \bar{x})(y_i - \bar{y}) \quad \text{sum of product of deviations}$$

Notice that if x_i is much larger than the mean and y_i is also much larger than the mean then the product will be greater than if y_i is only a little larger than the mean. Notice also that if x_i is quite a bit less than the mean and y_i is also quite a bit less than the mean the product will again be a large positive value.

The product of the deviations will be larger as we have a larger and larger data set, so we need to normalize this value to the size of the data set by taking the average of the paired deviations. This average product of the deviations is called the covariance of X and Y.

$$\frac{\sum_{i=0}^{n}(x_i - \bar{x})(y_i - \bar{y})}{n} \quad \text{covariance of X and Y}$$

Of course, the size of a deviation from the mean can be standardized so that we can compare deviations from different data sets on the same measurement scale. We saw that deviation can be expressed in units of standard deviation with the z-score normalization. This is commonly done when we measure association too.

$$\frac{\sum_{i=0}^{n}\left(\frac{x_i - \bar{x}}{s_x}\right)\left(\frac{y_i - \bar{y}}{s_y}\right)}{n} = \frac{\sum_{i=0}^{n}(z_x)(z_y)}{n} = r_{xy} \quad \text{correlation of X and Y}$$

The main result here is that the correlation coefficient r_{xy} is simply a scaled version of the sum of the product of the deviations using the idea that this value will be highest when x and y deviate from their means in comparable magnitude. Correlation is identical to covariance, except that correlation is scaled by the standard deviations. So covariance can have any value, and correlation ranges from 1 to –1 (perfect positive correlation is 1 and perfect negative correlation is –1).

2.4.2 *The regression line*

Notice in Figure 2.7 that I put a diagonal line through the data points that shows generally the relationship between female and male F1. This line was not drawn by hand, but was calculated to be the best fitting straight line that could possibly be drawn. Well, let's qualify that by saying that it is the best-fitting least-squares estimate line. Here the squared deviations that we are trying to minimize as we find the best line are the differences between the predicted values of y_i, which we will write as y_i hat ($\hat{y}_i$), and the actual values. So the least-squares estimate will minimize $\sum(y_i - \hat{y}_i)^2$. The difference between the predicted value and the actual value for any observation of y_i is called the "residual."

Here's how to find the best-fitting line. If we have a perfect correlation between x and y then the deviations z_x and z_y are equal to each other for every observation. So we have:

$$\frac{y_i - \bar{y}}{s_y} = \frac{x_i - \bar{x}}{s_x} \quad \text{deviations are equivalent if } r_{xy} = 1$$

So, if we solve for y_i to get the formula for the predicted $\hat{y}_i$ if the correlation is perfect, then we have:

$$\hat{y}_i = \frac{s_y}{s_x}(x_i - \bar{x}) + \bar{y} \quad \text{predicting } y_i \text{ from } x_i \text{ when } r_{xy} = 1$$

Because we want our best prediction even when the correlation isn't perfect and the best prediction of z_y is r_{xy} times z_x, then our best prediction of y_i is:

$$\hat{y}_i = r_{xy}\frac{s_y}{s_x}(x_i - \bar{x}) + \bar{y} \quad \text{predicting } y_i \text{ from } x_i \text{ when } r_{xy} \neq 1$$

Now to put this into the form of an equation for a straight line ($\hat{y}_i = A + Bx_i$) we let the slope of the line $B = r_{xy}(s_x/s_y)$ and the intercept of the line $A = \bar{y} - B\bar{x}$.

R note. Let's return to the male versus female vowel F1 data and see if we can find the slope and intercept of the best-fitting line that relates these two variables. Note that we are justified in fitting a line to these data because when we look at the graph, the relationship looks linear.

Using the correlation function cor() and the standard deviation function sd(), we can calculate the slope of the regression line.

```
cor(male,female)
[1] 0.9738566
sd(male)
[1] 160.3828
sd(female)
[1] 212.3172
B = cor(male,female)*(sd(male)/sd(female))
A = mean(male) - B*mean(female)
A
[1] 47.59615
B
[1] 0.7356441
```

Now we have values for A and B, so that we can predict the male F1 value from the female F1:

male F1 = 0.736 * female F1 + 47.6

Consider, for example, what male F1 value we expect if the female F1 is 700 Hz. The line we have in Figure 2.7 leads us to expect a male F1 that is a little higher than 550 Hz. We get a more exact answer by applying the linear regression coefficients:

```
> B*700 + A
[1] 562.547
```

2.4.3 *Amount of variance accounted for*

So now we have a method to measure the association between two continuous variables giving us the Pearson's product moment correlation (r_{xy}), and a way to use that measure to determine the slope and intercept of the best-fitting line that relates x and y (assuming that a linear relationship is correct).

So what I'd like to present in this section is a way to use the correlation coefficient to measure the percent of variance in y that we can correctly predict as a linear function of x. Then we will see how to put all of this stuff together in R, which naturally has a function that does it all for you.

So, we have a statistic r_{xy} that ranges from –1 to 1 that indicates the degree of association between two variables. And we have a linear function $\hat{y}_i = A + Bx_i$ that uses r_{xy} to predict y from x. What we want now is a measure of how much of the variability of y is accurately predicted by this linear function. This will be the "amount of variance accounted for" by our linear model.

Is it a model or just a line? What's in a name? If it seems reasonable to think that x might cause y we can think of the linear function as a model of the causal relationship and call it a "regression model." If a causal relationship doesn't seem reasonable then we'll speak of the correlation of two variables.

As it turns out, you can simply square the correlation coefficient to get the amount of variance in y that the line $A + Bx$ accounts for. I hope that it will add some insight to look at how we come to this conclusion.

$r^2 = r_{xy}r_{xy}$ r-squared, the amount of variance accounted for

The variance of y is s_y^2. We are trying to measure how much of this variance can be accounted for by the line $\hat{y}_i = A + Bx_i$. The amount of variance that is predicted by this "linear regression function" is $s_{\hat{y}}^2$. Which means that the unpredicted variance is the variance of the deviation between the actual y_i values and the predicted values $\hat{y}_i$. Call this unpredicted, or residual, variance $s_{y-\hat{y}}^2$. Because we used the optimal rule (the least-squares criterion) to relate x and y, $s_{\hat{y}}^2$ and $s_{y-\hat{y}}^2$ are not correlated with each other, therefore

$$s_y^2 = s_{\hat{y}}^2 + s_{y-\hat{y}}^2.$$

In words that is: The total variance of y is composed of the part that can be predicted if we know x and the part that is independent of x.

If we consider this same relationship in terms of z-scores instead of in terms of the raw data ($s_{z_y}^2 = s_{z_{\hat{y}}}^2 + s_{z_y - z_{\hat{y}}}^2$) we can equivalently talk about it in terms of proportion of variance because the variance s_z^2 of the normal distribution is equal to one. Then instead of dividing the total amount of variance into a part that can be predicted by the line and a part that remains unpredicted we can divide it into a proportion can be predicted and a remainder.

In terms of z-scores the line equation $\hat{y} = A + Bx$ is $\hat{z}_y = rz_x$ and from the definition of variance, then,

Removing the intercept from regression equations is not standard practice.

$$s^2_{\hat{z}_y} = \frac{\sum(rz_x)^2}{n} = r^2\frac{\sum(z_x^2)}{n} = r^2 \quad \text{proportion of variance accounted for is } r^2$$

I guess, in deciphering this it helps to know that $\sum z_x^2 = n$ because the standard deviation of z is 1.

The key point here is that r^2 is equivilent to $s^2_{\hat{z}_y}$, the proportion of total variance of y that can be predicted by the line.

R note. We return once again to the male and female vowel F1 data. Earlier we calculated the regression coefficients from the standard deviations and the correlation of male and female F1 values. What I'd like to do here is to introduce the function `lm()`. This function calculates a linear model in which we try to predict one variable from another variable (or several).

In this example, I ask to see a summary of the linear model in which we try to predict male F1 from female F1. You can read "`male~female`" as "male as a function of female".

```
> summary(lm(male~female))

Call:
lm(formula = male ~ female)

Residuals:
    Min       1Q  Median      3Q     Max
-70.619  -18.170   3.767  26.053  51.707

Coefficients:
            Estimate  Std. Error  t value  Pr(>|t|)
(Intercept) 47.59615    23.85501    1.995    0.0623  .
female       0.73564     0.04162   17.676  2.23e-12  ***
---
Signif. codes: 0 `***' 0.001 `**' 0.01 `*' 0.05 `.' 0.1 ` ' 1

Residual standard error: 37.49 on 17 degrees of freedom
Multiple R-Squared: 0.9484,  Adjusted R-squared: 0.9454
F-statistic: 312.4 on 1 and 17 DF, p-value: 2.230e-12
```

Notice that this summary statement gives us a report on several aspects of the linear regression fit. The first section of the report is on the residuals ($y_i - \hat{y}_i$) that shows their range, median, and quartiles. The second section reports the coefficients. Notice that `lm()` calculates the same A and B coefficients that we calcuated in explicit formulas above. But now we also have a *t*-test for both the intercept and the slope.

Finally, `lm()` reports the r^2 value and again tests whether this amount of variance accounted for is greater than zero – using an *F*-test. The line $F1_{male} = 47.596 + 0.7356*F1_{female}$ accounts for almost 95% of the variance in the male F1 values.

The *t*-tests for A and B (the regression coefficients) above indicate that the slope (labeled `female`) is definitely different from zero but that the `intercept` may not be reliably different from zero. This means that we might simplify the predictive formula by rerunning `lm()` specifying that we don't want the equation to have an intercept value. When I did this using the command `lm(male ~ female-1)`, where adding "-1" to the formula means "leave out the intercept (A) parameter," the regression accounted for 99% of the male F1 variance by simply multiplying each paired female F1 value by 0.813. That is, the regression formula was $F1_{male} = 0.813*F1_{female}$. The two regression analyses (with and without the intercept coefficient) are shown in Figure 2.8.

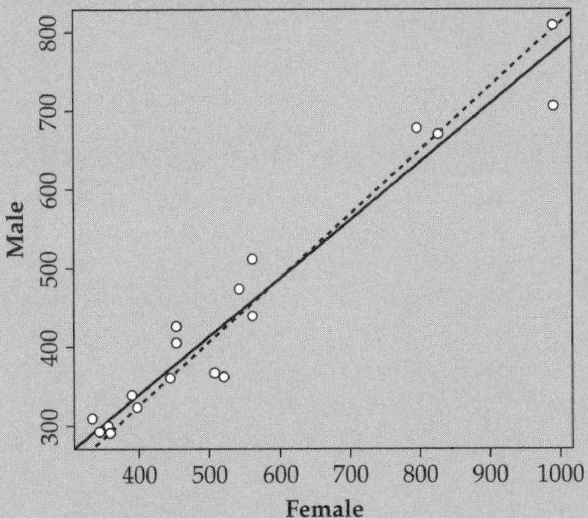

Figure 2.8 Regression lines at $y = 47.5 + 0.736x$ (solid line) and $y = 0.81x$ (dashed line).

EXERCISES

1 Given a skewed distribution (Figure 2.3) what distribution of the mean do you expect for samples of size $n = 1$?

2 I used the custom R function `central.limit()` to draw Q-Q plots for samples from this skewed distribution for samples of size $n = 1$ through $n = 8$. Here are the correlations between the normal distribution and the distribution of the means for samples of these sizes:

n	1	2	3	4	6	8
correlation	0.965	0.981	0.988	0.991	0.993	0.997

What do these values indicate about the distribution of the mean? Where was the biggest change in the correlation?

3 We test the hypothesis that the mean of our data set ($\bar{x} = 113.5$, $s = 35.9$, $n = 18$) is no different from 100, and find that the t is 1.59, and the probability of finding a higher t is 0.065. Show how to get this t-value and this probability from the t-distribution. What do you conclude from this t-test?

4 Calculate the covariance and correlation of the following data set by hand (well, use a calculator!). Plot the data and notice that the relationship is such that as Y gets bigger X gets smaller. How do your covariance and correlation values reflect this "down going" trend in the data?

X	Y
90	−7
82	−0.5
47	8
18	32
12	22
51	17
46	13
2	31
48	11
72	4
18	29
13	32

5 `Source()` the following function and explore the χ^2 distribution. It is said that the expression $(n - 1)s^2/\sigma^2$ is distributed in a family of distributions (one slightly different distribution for each value

of n) that is analogous to the t-distribution. Try this function out with different values of n, and different population standard deviations. Describe what this function does in a flow chart or a paragraph – whatever makes most sense to you. What is the effect of choosing samples of different size ($n = 4, \ldots, 50$)?

```
#--------- chisqu ---------------
#
#The input parameters are:
#       n - size of each sample
#       m - number of samples of size n to select
#       mu, sigma - the mean and sd the normal distribution from
        which samples are drawn

chisq = function(n=15,m=5000,mu=0,sigma=1) {

        sigsq=(sigma*sigma)
        xlow = 0
        xhigh = 2*n

        vars = vector() # I hereby declare that "vars" is a vector

        for (i in 1:m) { # get m samples
              data= rnorm(n,mu,sigma) # sample the normal dist
              vars[i] = var(data) # vars is our array of variances
        }
        title = paste("Sample size = ",n, "df = ",n-1)
        hist((n-1)*vars/sigsq,
           xlim=(xlow,xhigh),main=title,freq=F)
        plot(function(x)dchisq(x,df=(n-1)),xlow,xhigh,add=T)
}
```

6 Is the population mean (μ) of the 1971 Cherokee VOT data (Chapter 1, Table 1.1) 100 ms? How sure are you?

7 You want to be able to detect a reaction time difference as small as 20 ms between two conditions in a psycholinguistic experiment. You want your t-test to have a criterion type I error rate of 0.05 and you want the type II error rate to be 0.2. The standard deviation in such experiments is typically about 60 ms, so how many observations do you have to make in order to detect a 20 ms difference? Try this with the type of comparison being "paired" instead of "two. sample" and with the standard deviation of the differences being 20 ms. Which method do you prefer – two independent samples, or paired observations?

3 Phonetics

Phoneticians have a long tradition of quantifying their observations of pronunciation and hearing. In this history both hypothesis testing and regression techniques have been extensively used. Obviously the full range of methods used in the quantitative analysis of phonetic data cannot be covered in a short chapter on the topic, however I do hope to extend the discussion of *t*-test and regression in interesting ways here, and to introduce factor analysis.

3.1 Comparing Mean Values

We saw in Chapter 2 that we can test the hypothesis that a sample mean value $\bar{x}$ is the same as or different from a particular hypothesized population mean μ. Sometimes, this is a test that we are interested in. For example, we might want to know if the observed, sample mean $\bar{x}$ is reliably different from zero, but, in many cases the $\bar{x}$-μ comparison is not really what we want because we are comparing two sample means.

For example, the key question of interest with the Cherokee 1971/2001 data is the comparison of two sample means. Is the mean VOT in 1971 different from the mean VOT in 2001, as the boxplot in Figure 3.1 suggests? This comparison will be the focal example of this section.

3.1.1 *Cherokee voice onset time:* $\mu_{1971} = \mu_{2001}$

We want to test whether the average VOT in 1971 was equal to the average VOT in 2001, because we think that for this speaker there may have been a slow drift in the aspiration of voiceless stops as a result of language contact. This question provides us with the null

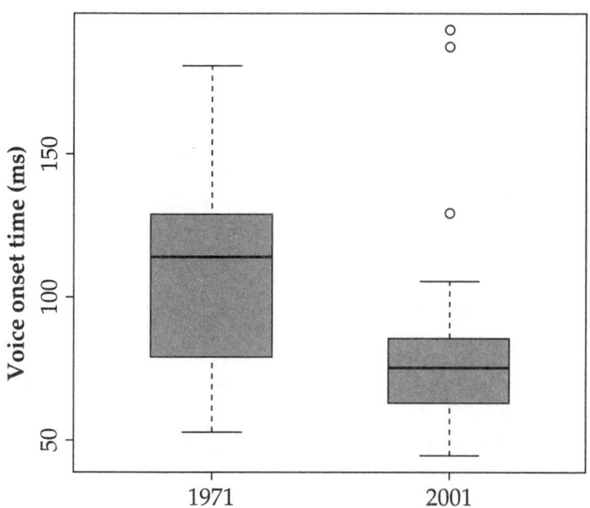

Figure 3.1 A boxplot of voice onset time measurements for Cherokee voiceless stops /t/ and /k/ produced by speaker DF in 1971 and in 2001.

hypothesis that there was no reliable difference in the true, population, means for these two years – that is: H_0: $\mu_{1971} = \mu_{2001}$.

We can test this hypothesis with a *t*-test similar to the "one sample" *t*-test that was discussed in Chapter 2. In that discussion, just to review, we tested the null hypothesis: H_0: $\mu_{1971} = \mu_{hyp}$, where we supplied the hypothesized population mean. Recall that the idea with the *t*-test is that we expect the difference between means to be zero – the null hypothesis is that there is no difference – and we measure the magnitude of the observed difference relative to the magnitude of random or chance variation we expect in mean values (the standard error of the mean). If the difference between means is large, more than about two standard errors (a *t*-value of 2 or –2), we are likely to conclude that the sample mean comes from a population that has a different mean than the hypothesized population mean.

$t = \frac{\bar{x} - \mu}{SE}$ the *t*-statistic is the difference between observed and expected mean, divided by standard error of the observed mean

So in testing whether the mean VOT in 1971 is different from the mean VOT in 2001 for this talker we are combining two null hypotheses:

H0: $\mu_{1971} = \mu$
H0: $\mu_{2001} = \mu$
H0: $\mu_{1971} = \mu_{2001}$

The expected mean value of the 1971 sample is the same as the expected value of the 2001 sample, so just as with a one-sample *t*-test the expected value of the difference is 0. Therefore we can compute a *t*-statistic from the difference between the means of our two samples.

$$t = \frac{\bar{x}_{1971} - \bar{x}_{2001}}{SE} \quad \text{the two-sample } t\text{-value}$$

There is one little complication when we compare the two means in this computation of *t*. We have two samples of data, one from 1971 and one from 2001 and therefore we have two estimates of the standard error of the mean (SE). So, in calculating the *t*-statistic we need to take information from both the 1971 data set and the 2001 data set when we compute the SE for this test.

R note. Before running *t*-tests on the Cherokee data we need to read the data from a text file. The Cherokee data are in "cherokeeVOT.txt" and are arranged in three columns (I made this text file in a spreadsheet program using the "save as" command to save the data as "tab delimited text"). The first column has the VOT measurement in milliseconds, the second column indicates that this VOT measurement is from a 1971 recording or a 2001 recording, and the third column indicates that the measurement comes from either a /k/ or a /t/. Use `read.delim()` to read the data file. I usually type the name of the data frame to see the column names and data values to be sure that the file was read correctly – here I show only the first five lines of the printout.

```
> vot <- read.delim("cherokeeVOT.txt")
> vot
  VOT  year Consonant
1  67  1971         k
2 127  1971         k
3  79  1971         k
4 150  1971         k
5  53  1971         k
```

Everything is apparently fine, but when we look at a `summary()` to get some descriptive statistics of the variables we see a problem. This R function is convenient when you have a large data file and you want to quickly verify that your data have been read correctly.

```
summary(vot)
      VOT              year       Consonant
Min.   : 45.00  Min.   :1971  k:21
1st Qu.: 71.50  1st Qu.:1971  t:23
Median : 81.50  Median :2001
Mean   : 96.45  Mean   :1989
3rd Qu.:120.25  3rd Qu.:2001
Max.   :193.00  Max.   :2001
```

The data `summary()` indicates a problem because I intended "year" to be a nominal variable that has only two levels "2001" and "1971." R, quite naturally, saw that the column was filled with numbers and so treated the variable as continuous (either a ratio or interval variable). This needs to be changed explicitly by instructing R to treat the "year" column as a `factor()`. After entering the `factor()` command "year" shows up as a nominal variable with 18 data points from 1971 and 26 data points from 2001.

```
> vot$year <- factor(vot$year)
> summary(vot)
      VOT           year    Consonant
Min.   : 45.00  1971:18  k:21
1st Qu.: 71.50  2001:26  t:23
Median : 81.50
Mean   : 96.45
3rd Qu.:120.25
Max.   :193.00
```

If you wish to add a new column to the data.frame that has the factorized "year", rather than changing "year" in place, you can type the command as: `>vot$fyear <- factor(vot$year)`.

Use `attach(vot)` to instruct future commands to look in the "vot" spreadsheet/data.frame for the variables that we mention (this is so we can refer to "year" instead of "vot$year"). Now we can use mean() and sd() to get the means and standard deviations for the 1971 and 2001 data.

```
> mean(VOT[year=="1971"])
[1] 113.5
> mean(VOT[year=="2001"])
[1] 84.65385
> sd(VOT[year=="1971"])
[1] 35.92844
> sd(VOT[year=="2001"])
[1] 36.08761
```

The notation VOT[year=="1971"] specifies a subset of the VOT values for which the variable year is equal to "1971."

Oh, by the way. I made Figure 3.1 with the boxplot() command. A boxplot is a very good way to see the central tendency and the range of variability of the data.

```
> boxplot(VOT~year,data=vot,col="lightgrey",
    ylab = "Voice Onset Time (ms)")
```

3.1.2 *Samples have equal variance*

So we are testing the null hypothesis that one Cherokee speaker's average VOT was the same in 1971 and 2001. That is: H_0: $\mu_{1971} = \mu_{2001}$. We have two samples of data, one from each year and we want to use our sample data to calculate a value of t that will tell us whether it is likely that the null hypothesis is true.

$$t = \frac{\bar{x}_{1971} - \bar{x}_{2001}}{SE} \quad t \text{ from the deviation between sample means}$$

Our sample estimates of the means are easy – $\bar{x}_{1971}$ and $\bar{x}_{2001}$ are the least squares estimates of these parameters. What is our estimate of the standard error of the mean? With only one sample we used the standard deviation or the variance of the sample to estimate the standard error:

$$SE = \frac{s}{\sqrt{n}} = \sqrt{\frac{s^2}{n}} \quad \text{the usual definition of sample standard error of the mean}$$

With two samples, there are two estimates of variance, s^2_{1971} and s^2_{2001}. If we can assume that these two represent essentially the same value then we can pool them by taking the weighted average as our best estimate of SE.

Before pooling the variances from our 1971 and 2001 samples we need to test the hypothesis that they do not differ (i.e. H0: $s^2_{1971} = s^2_{2001}$). This hypothesis can be tested using the *F*-distribution – a theoretical probability distribution that gives probabilities for ratios of variances. Incidentally, this distribution is named after the eminent statistician Ronald Fisher, inventor of ANOVA and maximum likelihood. We'll come back to *F* in later chapters, so here we will only note that the expected value of *F* is 1 if the null hypothesis is true. Because the two estimates of variance are based on independent samples, *F* is actually a family of distributions, the exact shape of which depends on the degrees of freedom of both variances. One caveat about using the *F*-distribution to compare variances is that it is quite sensitive to whether the population distributions are normal (Hays 1973: 450–1).

So, if we want to know if the two estimates of variance are equal to each other we can simply take their ratio and test the probability of this ratio, given the degrees of freedom that went into each variance estimate. We do this with the *F*-distribution because this distribution lets us specify degrees of freedom for the numerator and the denominator of the ratio.

$$F = \frac{s^2_{2001}}{s^2_{1971}} = \frac{36.0876^2}{35.9284^2} = \frac{1302.32}{1290.85} = 1.0089 \quad \text{F-test of equality of variance}$$

It is pretty obvious that the variances are not very different from each other (36.1 ms versus 35.9 ms), so the variances are also very similar in magnitude and thus the *F*-ratio is close to one. We look up the probability of getting an *F* of 1.0089 or higher using the R `pf()` function:

```
> pf(1.0089,25,17,lower.tail=F)
[1] 0.5034847
```

In this function call I specified the degrees of freedom of the numerator ($n_{2001} - 1 = 25$) and of the denominator ($n_{1971} - 1 = 17$) for the two estimates of variance that went into the *F*-ratio. I also specified that we are looking at the upper tail of the *F*-distribution because, as is usually done, I put the larger of the two variances as the numerator. The probability of getting an *F* value of 1.0089 or higher when the variances

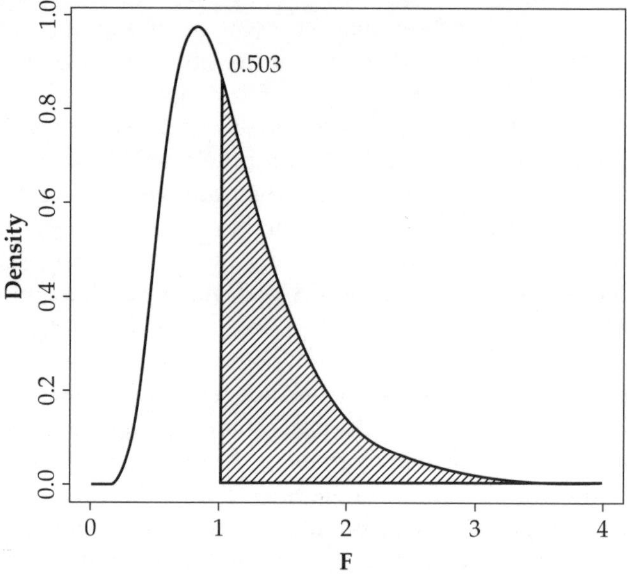

Figure 3.2 The *F* probability density distribution for 25 and 17 degrees of freedom showing that 0.503 of the area under the curve lies above the *F*-value found by taking the ratio of variances from 2001 and 1971 in the Cherokee data.

are in fact equal is quite high, p = 0.5, so we have no reason to believe that the variance of the 1971 data is any different from the variance of the 2001 data. Thus, because the sample variances in 2001 and 1971 are about the same, we can estimate SE for our test of whether VOT was different in 2001 than it was in 1971 by pooling the two sample variances. This is done using the weighted average of the variances where each variance is weighted by its degrees of freedom.

$$s_p^2 = \frac{(n_a - 1)s_a^2 + (n_b - 1)s_b^2}{(n_a - 1) + (n_b - 1)}$$ pooled variance, when the variances are roughly equal

The pooled variance for our Cherokee VOT data is thus 1297.7 and hence the pooled standard deviation is $s = 36.02$. We will also use the denominator in this weighted mean formula as the degrees of freedom for the *t*-statistic that we calculate next.

The *t*-statistic that we use then to compare two means uses the pooled variance from the two samples to estimate *SE* – the standard error of the mean(s) – and *t* is a ratio of (1) the difference between the two means

$(\bar{x}_a - \bar{x}_b)$ with (2) *SE* calculated from the pooled variance. If the means differ from each other by much more than you would expect (the standard error) then we are likely to declare that the two samples (VOT 2001, and VOT 1971) have different means.

$$t = \frac{\bar{x}_a - \bar{x}_b}{\sqrt{s_p^2/(n_a + n_b)}}$$

This works out to be $t = 2.6116$ for our data, and the degrees of freedom is $(18 - 1) + (26 - 1) = 42$. So the probability of getting a *t*-value this big if there is actually no difference between mean VOT in 1971 and 2001 (as compared with the hypothesis that VOT in 2001 was less than it was in 1971) is less than 1 in 100 ($p < 0.01$). So we conclude that this speaker's VOT was shorter in 2001 than it was in 1971. This in itself is an interesting finding – perhaps indicating a gradual phonetic change that may be due to language contact. Of course this result, based on one talker, doesn't really tell us anything about Cherokee as a whole.

R note. I specified the *t*-test contrasting Cherokee VOT in 1971 and 2001 with the command given below. I used the subset notation `VOT[year=="1971"]` to say that I wanted all of the VOT values for which the variable `year` is equal to "1971." I specified that the variance in the 1971 data is equivalent to the variance in the 2001 data with `var.equal=T`, and I specified that I expected VOT to be greater in 1971 than in 2001 because I hypothesized that this would be the direction of change if there was an impact of English on Cherokee.

```
> t.test(VOT[year=="1971"],VOT[year=="2001"], var.equal=T,
    alternative="greater")

Two Sample t-test
data: VOT[year == "1971"] and VOT[year == "2001"]
t = 2.6116, df = 42, p-value = 0.006223
alternative hypothesis: true difference in means is greater
than 0 95 percent confidence interval:
10.2681  Inf
sample estimates:
mean of x mean of y
113.50000 84.65385
```

3.1.3 *If the samples do not have equal variance*

What if we find that the variances of our two samples are not equal? Instead of using the pooled variance, we calculate the standard error of the mean as:

$$SE = \sqrt{(s_a^2/n_a + s_b^2/n_b)}$$ standard error of the mean for unequal variances

The t-value calculated with this estimated standard error ($t^* = (\bar{x}_a - \bar{x}_b)/SE$) follows the normal distribution if both samples have greater than 30 data points ($n_a > 30$ & $n_b > 30$). For smaller samples the t distribution is used with a degrees of freedom equal to:

$$df = \frac{U^2}{V^2/(n_a - 1) + W^2/(n_b - 1)} - 2$$

where

$V = s_a^2/n_a$, the Welch correction of degrees of freedom
$W = s_b^2/n_b$,

and

$$U^2 = V + W$$

By adusting the degrees of freedom, this correction puts us on a more conservative version of the t-distribution. Recall that t is a family of distributions and that the tails of the distribution grow as the df decreases – see Figure 2.5. The Welch correction is done by default for two-sample t-tests in R, so that in order to conduct the test with the assumption that the variances are equal you have to actually declare that `var.equal=TRUE`. In my experience, I've not noticed much difference between the two ways of calculating t, but maybe I haven't really dealt yet with a situation where the variances are strongly unequal.

R note. Below is the `t.test()` call when we do not assume that the variance in 2001 equals the variance in 1971. In this call, I used the function notation rather than specifying two vectors of numbers. You read the expression `VOT~year` as "VOT varies as a function of year." In formula notation, the "dependent variable" or the "criterion variable" appears on the left of the tilde (~) and the "independent variables" or the "predictive factors" appear on the right side of the tilde. Because `year` only has two levels in this data set (1971 and 2001) we can use this notation to describe the desired *t*-test.

This test reports that the Welch correction of degrees of freedom was used (notice that we now have df = 36.825, instead of df = 42). The *t*-statistic is also slightly different because the SE used in calculating *t* was different in this test than in the one for equal variance. The conclusion that we draw from this test is the same as the conclusion we arrived at when we assumed equal variances ($s^2_{1971} = s^2_{2001}$).

```
> t.test(VOT ~ year, alternative="greater")
Welch Two Sample t-test
data: VOT by year
t = 2.6137, df = 36.825, p-value = 0.006448
alternative hypothesis: true difference in means is greater
than 0
95 percent confidence interval:
10.22436  Inf
sample estimates:
mean in group 1971 mean in group 2001
  113.50000           84.65385
```

3.1.4 *Paired* t-*test: Are men different from women?*

There is a particularly powerful and easy-to-use kind of *t*-test if you have observations that are meaningfully paired. What "meaningfully paired" means is that the observations naturally come in pairs. For example, there is no rational way to pair VOT measurements from 1971 with measurements taken in 2001. We could suggest that VOTs taken from /t/ should be matched with each other, but there is no meaningful way to choose which 2001 /t/ VOT should be paired with the first /t/ VOT on the 1971 list, for example. Now, if we had measurements from the same words spoken once in 1971 and again in 2001 it would be meaningful to pair the measurements for each of the words.

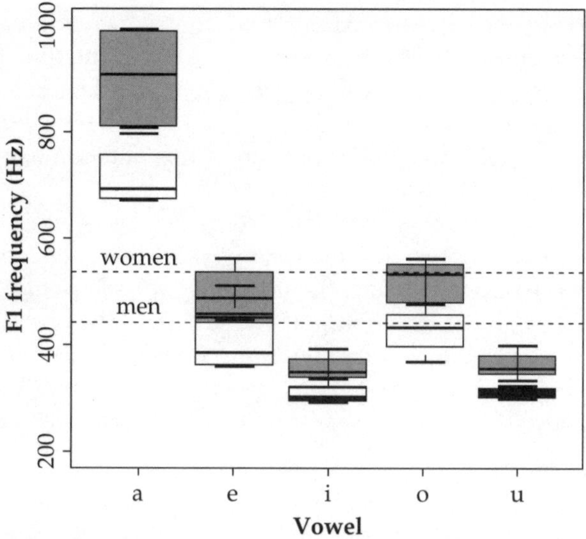

Figure 3.3 Boxplot comparing male (white boxes) and female (gray boxes) vowel F1 frequencies for five different vowels. The overall average F1 values for men and women are plotted with dashed lines.

In Chapter 2 though, we looked at a data set for which the observations *are* meaningfully paired. The first formant data in "F1_data.txt" was given for men and women for each language and vowel in the data set, so that it is natural to match, for example, the male F1 of /a/ in Sele with the female F1 of /a/ in Sele, the male F1 of /i/ in Sele with the female F1 of /i/ in Sele, and so on. Figure 3.3 shows that men and women tend to have systematically different vowel F1 frequency, but that the difference between vowels can be bigger than the overall male/female difference. To have a sensitive test of the male/female difference we need to control for the vowel differences. Pairing male/female differences by vowel provides just such control.

With paired observations we can then define a derived variable – the difference between the paired observations

$d_i = x_{ai} - x_{bi}$ the difference between paired observations

then calculate the mean and variance of the difference as we would for any other variable:

$$\bar{d} = \frac{\sum d_i}{n}, \; s_d^2 = \frac{\sum (d_i - \bar{d})^2}{n-1} \quad \text{the mean and variance of the differences}$$

Now we test the null hypothesis that there is no difference between the paired observations, i.e. that H_0: $\bar{d} = 0$. The *t*-value, with degrees of freedom $n - 1$, is:

$$t = \frac{\bar{d}}{\sqrt{s_d^2/n}} \quad \text{does } \bar{d} \text{ differ from zero?}$$

The beauty of the paired *t*-test is that pairing the observations removes any systematic differences that might be due to the paired elements. For example, this measure of F1 difference is immune to any vowel or language influences on F1. So, if F1 varies as a function of language or vowel category these effects will be automatically controlled by taking paired F1 measurements from the same vowels spoken by speakers of the same language. In some other situations we are most interested in letting each person serve as his/her own control, because if we sample from a population of people, each of whom may differ from other members of the population in some systematic way, paired observations from the same person provide a control over individual sources of variation. Consequently, the paired *t*-test tends to be much more sensitive (powerful) than the two-sample *t*-test.

The increased power of the paired *t*-test is seen in a comparison of "independent samples" and "paired comparisons" tests of the null hypothesis that male F1 frequencies are no different from female F1 frequencies. We'll contrast this hypothesis with the H_1, suggested by years of research, that female F1 is higher than male F1.

The independent samples comparison suggests that men and women are not reliably different from each other [t(36) = 1.5, $p = 0.067$], while the paired comparison results in a much higher *t*-value [t(18) = 6.1, $p < 0.01$] showing a much more reliable difference. Evidently, in the independent samples comparison, the gender difference was swamped by variation due to vowel and perhaps language differences, and when we control for these sources of variation by contrasting men's and women's F1 values for matched vowels and languages, the gender difference is significant. Note that in this report of the results I'm using a standard style for reporting *t*-test results: put the *t*-value and its associated degrees of freedom and probability value in square brackets. The degrees of freedom is in parentheses after the letter "t," and the probability is reported as $p = 0.067$ if the value is above the

Type I error criterion α(0.01), or if the probability of *t* is less than α then you should report $p < 0.01$. It is preferable to round off *t* to one or two places after the decimal point.

R note. The two *t*-tests contrasting vowel F1 frequencies for men and women in the "F1_data.txt" data set are shown below.

```
> f1 <-read.delim("F1_data.txt")
> attach(f1)

> t.test(female,male,alternative="greater",var.equal = T)

      Two Sample t-test

data: female and male
t = 1.5356, df = 36, p-value = 0.0667
alternative hypothesis: true difference in means is greater
than 0
95 percent confidence interval:
-9.323753  Inf
sample estimates:
mean of x mean of y
534.6316 440.8947

> t.test(female,male,paired=T,alternative="greater")

      Paired t-test

data: female and male
t = 6.1061, df = 18, p-value = 4.538e-06
alternative hypothesis: true difference in means is greater
than 0
95 percent confidence interval:
67.11652  Inf
sample estimates:
mean of the differences
         93.73684
```

3.1.5 *The sign test*

A quick and easy variant of the paired *t*-test works with the signs of the differences – no calculation of the mean or standard deviation of the differences, just coding whether the difference for each pair is positive or negative. But keep in mind that the "sign test" is only valid if you have 25 or more pairs.

Here's how it works. Mark each paired observation according to whether d_i is greater than zero or less than zero. Let n^+ be the number of pairs with d_i greater than zero, and n^- be the number of pairs with d_i less than zero. The probability of the null hypothesis $\bar{x}_a = \bar{x}_b$ is given by the probability of having a smaller or larger (two-tailed) *z*-score:

$$z = \frac{|n^+ - n^-| - 1}{\sqrt{n^+ + n^-}} \quad \text{z-score used in the sign test}$$

3.2 Predicting the Back of the Tongue from the Front: Multiple Regression

Suppose that you have a method for tracking the locations of three or four small gold pellets or electromagnetic transducers that are glued onto the upper surface of the tongue. Phoneticians do this (X-ray microbeam, EMMA). Such a point-tracking system provides some very valuable information about speech production, but the root of the tongue is not represented.

Now, suppose that data about the location of points on the top surface of the tongue could be used to predict the location of a point on the root of the tongue. It seems to be reasonable that we could do this. After all, we are dealing with a physical structure with extrinsic tongue muscles that move the tongue up, front, and back as whole. Additionally, because the tongue is an incompressible mass, the intrinsic tongue muscles that reshape the tongue produce predictable effects (like squeezing a water balloon – squeeze the back of the tongue and the top goes up).

So the nature of the tongue suggests that we might be able to make good guesses about the root of the tongue (which can't be tracked in the current systems) from the information that we have about the front of the tongue. Multiple regression is the key.

We saw in Chapter 2 that we can define a regression line $y = a + bx$ that captures whatever linear relationship might exist between two variables, and that we can measure the strength of linear association between two variables with the Pearson's product moment correlation coefficient r.

Now we will extend this idea to consider regression equations that have more than one predictor variable, e.g. $y = a + b_1x_1 + b_2x_2 + \ldots + b_nx_n$. Such equations have some valuable practical applications in phonetics, one of which we will explore, but they also provide a formal basis for building models of causal relationships in many domains of scientific inquiry.

3.2.1 *The covariance matrix*

We have some data that shows the top of the tongue as well as the root (Johnson, Ladefoged, & Lindau 1993). So we might be able to use this data to develop a regression equation that will let us predict the location of the back of the tongue from the front. A chain of 15 small gold pellets was draped over the tongue of one of the talkers in Johnson et al. (1993). This talker, unlike the others, was able to tolerate having the chain go very far back in the mouth extending back over the root of the tongue. X-ray images were taken of the tongue position during 11 different vowels, and Figure 3.4 shows the tongue shape that

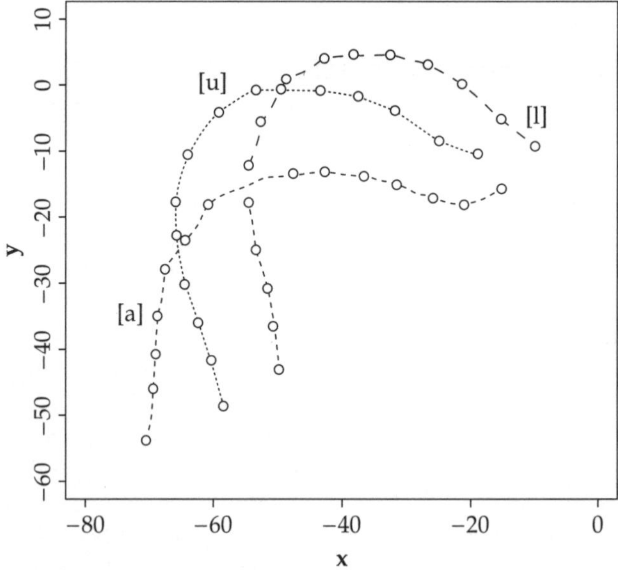

Figure 3.4 A chain of 15 small gold pellets was draped over the tongue and the positions of the pellets were recorded from X-ray scans.

was recorded in the x and y locations of the pellets for the corner vowels [i], [a], and [u].

The 15 pellets in the chain each have an x and a y location in space, so we have 30 variables in this data set. Some of them are highly correlated with each other. For example, the vertical (y) location of the fifteenth pellet is correlated with the y location of the fourteenth pellet with $r = 0.9986$. So with a regression formula we can predict 99.7% of the variance of pellet 14's y location if we know the y location of pellet 15. There is some indication also that it may be possible to predict the xy location of one of the back pellets from one of the front pellets. For example, the correlation between the y locations of pellet 1 and pellet 14 is $r = 0.817$. However, the highest correlation between the x location of pellet 14 and any of the front pellets is with the y location of pellet 6 ($r = 0.61$).

We could explore this data set for quite some time calculating correlations among the 30 variables, but with so many correlations to look at (435 r-values) and with so many of them falling at approximately the same level, it isn't clear how to pick and choose among the correlations to highlight comparisons that are especially meaningful. Of course we could show all 435 of the r-values in a table, but that would be mean and a waste of paper.

R note. Perhaps it is mean and a waste of paper to show all 435 of the correlations among 30 variables in a table, but it sure is easy to produce such a table in R! In the data set "chaindata.txt," I named the x location of pellet 1, `x1`, and so on. `subset()` is used to extract data for talker PL1 (there are five other talkers in the data file, though only PL1 had 15 points in the chain of gold pellets – the others didn't tolerate the chain as far back on the tongue). If you use `subset()` to extract data for any of the other talkers you will need to specify which of the 30 variables to extract more laboriously (e.g. `x1:x12,y1:y12`) than I did in this command where I could specify x_1 through y_{15} with `x1:y15`.

The correlation matrix is produced by `cor()`. Note that $x1$ is perfectly correlated ($r = 1$) with itself. Note also that the matrix is symmetrical – the correlation of x_1 and x_2 is the same in row x_2, column x_1 as it is in row x_1, column x_2 ($r = 0.9972439$).

```
> chain <- read.delim("chaindata.txt")
> PL1 <- subset(chain,talker=="PL1",x1:y15)
> cor(PL1)
           x1        x2        x3        x4        x5        x6
x1  1.0000000 0.9972439 0.9586665 0.9727643 0.9485555 0.9313837
x2  0.9972439 1.0000000 0.9737532 0.9839730 0.9647815 0.9452476
x3  0.9586665 0.9737532 1.0000000 0.9911912 0.9933240 0.9844554
x4  0.9727643 0.9839730 0.9911912 1.0000000 0.9939075 0.9706192
x5  0.9485555 0.9647815 0.9933240 0.9939075 1.0000000 0.9791682
x6  0.9313837 0.9452476 0.9844554 0.9706192 0.9791682 1.0000000
x7  0.8826467 0.9045604 0.9676897 0.9444815 0.9590505 0.9857084
x8      .....
```

The covariance matrix is also easy to produce, using `cov()`. Note that both of these functions (`cor()` and `cov()`) are able to work with `PL1` because in the subset command I extracted continuous numeric vectors into the subset leaving out the `talker` and `vowel` columns of the original data set. If I had used `subset(chain, talker=="PL1")` each row would have been labeled with a vowel label copied from the original spreadsheet. Then the `x1:y15` columns would have to be specified explicitly in `cor()` and `cov()`.

```
> cov(PL1)
           x1        x2        x3        x4        x5        x6
x1  18.688494 20.257932 19.559742  20.71310 18.317303 16.912481
x2  20.257932 22.080714 21.595530  22.77404 20.251032 18.657079
x3  19.559742 21.595530 22.274955  23.04179 20.941653 19.516232
x4  20.713102 22.774042 23.041793  24.26056 21.867947 20.081253
x5  18.317303 20.251032 20.941653  21.86795 19.953692 18.372171
x6  16.912481 18.657079 19.516232  20.08125 18.372171 17.643432
x7  16.101781 17.936760 19.272782  19.63106 18.078109 17.471889
x8      .....
```

The patterns of interrelatedness, and perhaps causal relationships in the data are implicit in the correlation and covariance matrices and there are several techniques that can be used to discover and visualize these patterns (one of which will be the topic of section 3.3). In the remainder of this section, though, we will examine a stepwise method to find the best linear combination of variables that can be used to predict the value of a criterion variable. In this case we want to predict the location of the root of the tongue (which is hard to observe directly) from the locations of pellets on the top of the tongue (which can be tracked without too much trouble).

3.2.2 *More than one slope: The* β_i

The best way to predict the *y* location of pellet 15 on the root of the tongue from the locations of pellets 2 through 6 on the top of the tongue is with the following formula:

$$y_{15} = -16.81 + 1.28y_2 + 3.85y_6 - 4.11x_5 + 1.47x_6 - 1.15x_5$$

This formula, a linear combination of some of the tongue pellet *xy* variables, produces an estimate of y_{15} that accounts for 98% of the variance of the *y* location of pellet 15.

Similarly, we can predict the *x* location of pellet 15 from the front pellets with this formula:

$$x_{15} = -51.69 - 0.97y_5 + 1.05x_2 - 4.04x_6 + 4.66x_4 + 0.61y_2 - 3.69x_3 + 2.66x_5 + 1.48y_4$$

This linear equation predicts 99% of the variance of the *x* location of pellet 15. With these two equations we should be able to make pretty good guesses about the location of the root of the tongue based on our knowledge of the top of the tongue. Of course, this could be a very valuable bit of knowledge as we attempt to model processes of speech articulation on the basis of X-ray microbeam, or EMMA data.

Now the method for coming up with these linear equations is not exactly magic, but it is still pretty neat.

First, let's recall that the equation for the regression line with one variable ($\hat{y} = A + Bx$) can be expressed as $\hat{z}_y = rz_x$ using the standardized *z*-scores. Then from this we get the slope *B* from the correlation *r* and the ratio of standard deviations: $B = r(s_x/s_y)$. In determining the β coefficients in the multiple regression equation $\hat{z}_y = \beta_1 z_{x_1} + \beta_2 z_{x_2} \ldots \beta_n z_{x_n}$ we must take into account the correlations of the *x* predictor coefficients as well as the correlation between *x* and *y*. Unlike our calculation for *r* which is based on the product of *z*-scores, values from the correlation matrix are used to compute the β values. The coefficient for predictor variable x_1 is based, naturally enough, on the correlation between variable x_1 and the variable (*y*) that we are trying to predict.

But, the formula for β_1 removes from r_{y1} an amount that is based on how much x_2 can predict y and how closely correlated x_1 and x_2 are to each other.

$$\beta_1 = \frac{r_{y1} - r_{y2}r_{12}}{1 - r_{12}^2} \quad \text{the coefficient that relates } x1 \text{ to } y$$

This formula, and others like it for coefficients in larger models, are called beta weights and because they are coefficients for the standardized variables z_y, z_{x1}, z_{x2}, etc. they indicate the relative strength of an x variable in predicting the y variable. To get the non-standardized coefficients, like those that I used in the predictive formulas for y_{15} and x_{15} above, you scale the β weights by the ratio of predicted and predictor standard deviations just like we did when there was only one b to be calculated.

$$b_i = \beta_i \frac{s_y}{s_i} \quad \text{scaling by ratio of standard deviations to get } b \text{ from } \beta$$

R note. The R function `lm()` finds the regression coefficients in linear models. For example, I used the following command to find the coefficients for the equation for y_{15} that started this section. Please read down the "Estimate" column and compare these numbers with the b_i values in the formula for y_{15}.

```
> summary(lm(y15 ~ y2 + y6 + y5 + x6 + x5, data = PL1))

Coefficients:
             Estimate  Std. Error  t value  Pr(>|t|)
(Intercept) -16.8100      6.8275   -2.462   0.05708  .
y2            1.2785      0.1937    6.599   0.00120  **
y6            3.8458      0.6110    6.294   0.00149  **
y5           -4.1140      0.6104   -6.740   0.00109  **
x6            1.4703      0.8134    1.808   0.13048
x5           -1.1467      0.8165   -1.404   0.21919
---
Signif. codes: 0 `***' 0.001 `**' 0.01 `*' 0.05 `.' 0.1 ` ' 1
Residual standard error: 1.304 on 5 degrees of freedom
Multiple R-Squared: 0.9826,  Adjusted R-squared: 0.9652
F-statistic: 56.46 on 5 and 5 DF, p-value: 0.0002130
```

Similarly, the coefficients of the x_{15} model are given by a call to lm().

```
> summary(lm(x15 ~ y5 + x2 + x6 + x4 + y2 + x3 + x5 + y4, data = PL1))

Coefficients:
             Estimate Std. Error t value Pr(>|t|)
(Intercept) -51.6910      8.7933  -5.878  0.02774  *
y5           -0.9702      0.5103  -1.901  0.19767
x2            1.0540      0.4120   2.558  0.12482
x6           -4.0357      0.3624 -11.135  0.00797  **
x4            4.6618      0.7939   5.872  0.02780  *
y2            0.6083      0.2932   2.075  0.17370
x3           -3.6891      0.5072  -7.273  0.01838  *
x5            2.6555      0.8803   3.017  0.09456  .
y4            1.4818      0.7193   2.060  0.17559
---
Signif. codes: 0 `***' 0.001 `**' 0.01 `*' 0.05 `.' 0.1 ` ' 1

Residual standard error: 0.5194 on 2 degrees of freedom
Multiple R-Squared: 0.9989,  Adjusted R-squared: 0.9943
F-statistic: 220.1 on 8 and 2 DF, p-value: 0.00453
```

The printout given by summary() reports t-tests for each of the coefficients in the linear equation. The test compares the given coefficient value with zero and in general we want to include in the regression equation only coefficients that are reliably different from zero. However, the method that I used to select the regression models shown here relies on a measure of the effectiveness of the overall model, and not just on the t-tests of the coefficients. So, we have one case (x3 as a predictor of y15) of a coefficient that is not significantly different from zero on one test, but which is a reliable predictor when we compare different possible models with each other.

3.2.3 *Selecting a model*

So, in general that is how the regression coefficients (the b_i values in the regression equation $y = a + b_1x_1 + b_2x_2 + \ldots + b_nx_n$) are found. There is an art, though, to selecting a model. I restricted the model search for predicting the root of the tongue from the top of the tongue to models that use some combination of the *x* and *y* locations of pellets 2, 3, 4, 5, and 6. I felt that pellet 1 was sometimes not actually on the surface of the tongue (see the low back vowel [a] in Figure 3.4), and I didn't want to go back further than pellet 6. Even with this restriction, though, there are 10 variables in the predictor set (5 pellets, *x* and *y* dimensions), so there are 2^{10} possible regression models. Choosing the best one from this set of possibilities is the subject of this section.

The procedure that is illustrated here is only one of several approaches that exist. These different approaches have their advocates and a discussion of the pros and cons of them is beyond the scope of this chapter – though we will return to this later. Perhaps one lesson to draw from the fact that there is more than one way to do this is that choosing the correct model is a bit of an art. The balancing act in this art is between high within-dataset accuracy on the one hand, and high predictive accuracy for new data on the other. So, with enough parameters you can account for all of the variation that is present in a set of data – particularly a tiny data set like the one we are looking at in this illustration of multiple regression. However, such "over-fitted" models are brittle and tend to break down when confronted with new data. So we are looking for a model that will use only a few parameters to fit the data – get as good a fit as possible with a minimum of predictive variables. For this, the `step()` function in R uses the Akaike Information Criterion (AIC). This criterion uses a log-likelihood measure of how well the model fits the data and adds a penalty for each new parameter (regression variable) that is added to the model. So, to overcome the "added parameter" penalty the model predictions have to improve by a substantial amount. Tiny improvements don't make the cut.

Log-likelihood is a way of measuring model fit that is analogous to least-squares. We call the arithmetic average the least-squares estimate of central tendency because this measure minimizes the squared deviations. A log-likelihood estimate seeks to maximize likelihood of the model and is a bit like an information measure. At this point, that's about all I'm going to say about it, but we will be returning to this topic in the sociolinguistics chapter.

For now, I present the the formula for AIC acknowledging that it has a magical part L(M) the likelihood of model M. Realizing that this is a measure of model fit we can see that AIC is composed of two terms, the first is related to model fit and the second is related to model size, where n_m is the number of coefficients in the regression equation.

$$AIC = -2\log L(M) + 2n_M \quad \text{Akaike Information Criterion}$$

R note. I used `step()` to select a model to predict the y location of pellet 15 in the `PL1chain` data set (which is assumed because of an earlier `attach(PL1chain)` command). The initial model has only one parameter – the intercept value. This is specified with y15~1. The largest model I want to consider has the *xy* locations for pellets 2, 3, 4, 5, and 6.

```
> summary(y.step <- step(lm(y15 ~ 1,data=PL1),y15~ x2+y2 +
    x3+y3+ x4+y4 + x5+y5+ x6+y6))
Start: AIC= 43.74
 y15 ~ 1

        Df  Sum of Sq     RSS    AIC
+ y2     1     400.03   88.79  26.97
+ y3     1     323.32  165.50  33.82
+ y6     1     315.23  173.59  34.35
+ y4     1     301.93  186.90  35.16
+ y5     1     296.26  192.56  35.49
+ x4     1     121.77  367.06  42.58
+ x2     1     114.65  374.18  42.80
+ x5     1     105.75  383.08  43.05
+ x3     1      93.55  395.28  43.40
<none>                 488.82  43.74
+ x6     1      56.78  432.05  44.38
```

What the printout shows is the first step in the stepwise search for the best combination of variables to include in the model. A plus sign in the first column indicates that the program considered what would happen if the variable named on that row was added to the model. The result of adding y_2 for example is that the sum of squared variance accounted for would go up leaving a small residual sum of squares and a smaller AIC value. The decision to add y_2 to the model at this step is taken because this model (with y_2 added) results in the lowest AIC as compared with any other model that is considered at this step. In particular, adding this variable reduces the AIC when compared with no change in the model <none>. So, the program adds y_2 and considers adding other variables.

```
Step: AIC= 26.97
 y15 ~ y2

         Df  Sum of Sq     RSS    AIC
+ y3      1      20.84   67.95  26.03
+ y4      1      15.87   72.92  26.81
<none>                   88.79  26.97
+ y5      1      10.68   78.11  27.56
+ x2      1       2.83   85.96  28.62
+ y6      1       2.10   86.69  28.71
+ x4      1       1.78   87.01  28.75
+ x3      1       0.93   87.86  28.86
+ x6      1       0.61   88.18  28.90
+ x5      1       0.50   88.29  28.91
- y2      1     400.03  488.82  43.74
```

So, the starting point for this step is the y15 ~ y2 model, and the printout shows that the best possible thing to do now is to add y_3 to the model, and the worst possible thing to do is to remove y_2 (the row marked "- y2"). The "do nothing" approach <none> is also less good than adding y_3. One thing to notice here is that the ordering of the variables has changed from step 1 to step 2. At step 1 the second best thing we could have done would have been to add not y_6 to the model. At this step y_6 appears in sixth place on the list. Evidently the correlation between y_2 and y_6 has resulted in a situation that when we add y_2 to the model now y_6 doesn't make such a large unique contribution in predicting the value of y_{15}. Ready for step 3.

```
Step: AIC= 26.03
 y15 ~ y2 + y3

         Df  Sum of Sq     RSS    AIC
+ y6      1     32.429  35.525 20.896
+ y5      1     11.557  56.397 25.980
<none>                  67.954 26.030
- y3      1     20.836  88.790 26.972
```

```
+ x2     1     3.243  64.711 27.492
+ y4     1     3.049  64.905 27.525
+ x5     1     2.612  65.342 27.599
+ x4     1     2.292  65.662 27.653
+ x3     1     2.175  65.779 27.672
+ x6     1     1.706  66.248 27.751
- y2     1    97.548 165.502 33.822
```

Now we can add y_6! Notice that the option to remove y_3 is pretty far up the list. One other thing to notice is that by optimizing AIC we give up on having the smallest possible residual error from our model. The idea is that we are seeking a stable model that produces a good fit to the data, and the AIC approach scores stability in terms of the information gain, per coefficient added to the model. This tends to keep out weak, unstable coefficients so that we avoid modeling the randomness of the data set and instead only capture robust relationships.

This process of adding variables, considering the possibility of making no change to the model, or even of removing variables that had been added at a previous step, is continued until the <none> option appears at the top of the list. Here's a summary of the steps that were taken on this run:

step 1 + y2
step 2 + y3
step 3 + y6
step 4 + y5
step 5 + x6
step 6 −y3 (remove y3)
step 7 + x5
step 8 <none> (finished)

The resulting model, with the variables that survived the process of adding and removing variables (`y15 ~ y2 + y6 + y5 + x6 + x5`), is declared the winner because it produced the lowest AIC value.

The procedure for finding the best predictive model of x_{15} is exactly comparable to this.

```
> summary(x.step <- step(lm(x15 ~ 1,data=PL1),x15~ x2+y2 +
x3+y3+ x4+y4 + x5+y5+ x6+y6))
```

How good is 99% variance accounted for? There are only 11 different vowels in the PL1 chain data, and we are using eight parameters to estimate the 11 x_{15} data values and six parameters to estimate the 11 y_{15} values. So it isn't too surprising that we can get very high variance accounted for in these cases. A more robust and realistic use of multiple regression would draw on many more observations providing presumably more variance to be accounted for and more variance in the values of the predictor variables as well.

Despite these caveats regarding this tongue position example, I decided to try the regression equations for predicting the location of pellet 15 by using the average pellet locations for pellets 2, 3, 4, 5, and 6 to predict pellet 15 (Figure 3.5). Though the regression never saw the average tongue shape, it does an excellent job of predicting the average location of pellet 15 from the top of the tongue pellets.

This is a very informal evaluation of a model fit, more like a "gee whiz" demo. What is really needed is a dataset large enough to split into two pieces. Then the first piece could be used to produce the fit

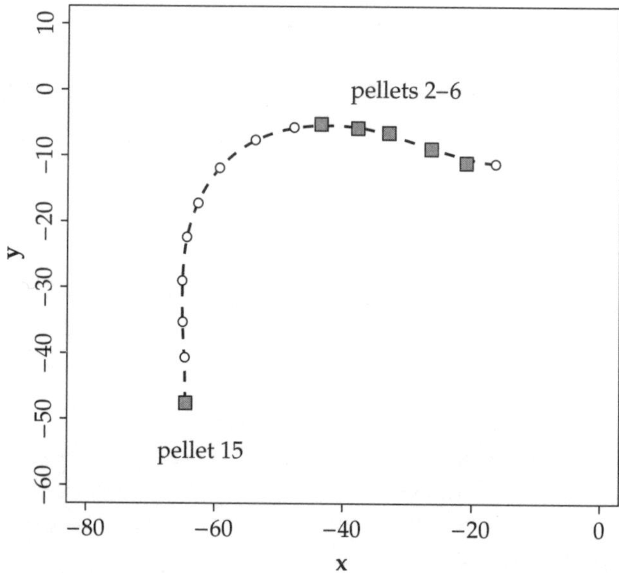

Figure 3.5 The average pellet locations, averaged across 11 vowels. The locations of five pellets on the top of the tongue were used to predict the location of pellet 15.

and the remainder could be used to make predictions and evaluate the model by measuring the differences between the predicted and the actual locations of pellet 15 for tokens that weren't used to build the model (see Chapter 7 for an example of this method).

What about the other pellets? If we can predict the location of pellet 15, why not use the same method to predict 14, 13, 12, etc.? In other words, doesn't the covariance matrix contain information that would make it possible for us to characterize all of the pellets at once?

The answer is "yes" and this leads us to principal components analysis.

3.3 Tongue Shape Factors: Principal Components Analysis

One of the primary aims of quantitative analysis in phonetics, as well as in other subareas in linguistics, is to discover underlying factors that in some sense "cause" the pattern of data that we observe in our studies.

As we saw in section 3.2, adjacent points on the tongue are not physically or statistically independent of each other. The natural next question is: how many independent parameters of tongue movement are there? To answer this question we will use principal components analysis (PCA) to extract independent factors of tongue movement from the covariance matrix.

The main idea with PCA is to use the correlations of raw data variables to define abstract components of correlated variation. With tongue motion, we want to find the main components of tongue shape variation. As we saw earlier, the second point and the third point on the tongue are highly correlated with each other, suggesting that we could account for both of these variables and probably others by a single abstract factor. The linguistic analysis of tongue position in vowels suggests that there may be only two factors – tongue height and tongue backness.

I think of PCA as a series of multiple regression analyses. We saw that in regression we can describe the relationship between two variables as a line so that for any one location on the regression line you know the value for both of the correlated variables that define the line. This is a kind of data reduction technique because we go from two axes, x and y, to one derived line, a new axis F. So, imagine (see Figure 3.6) that our derived factor F is a line that captures the correlation between

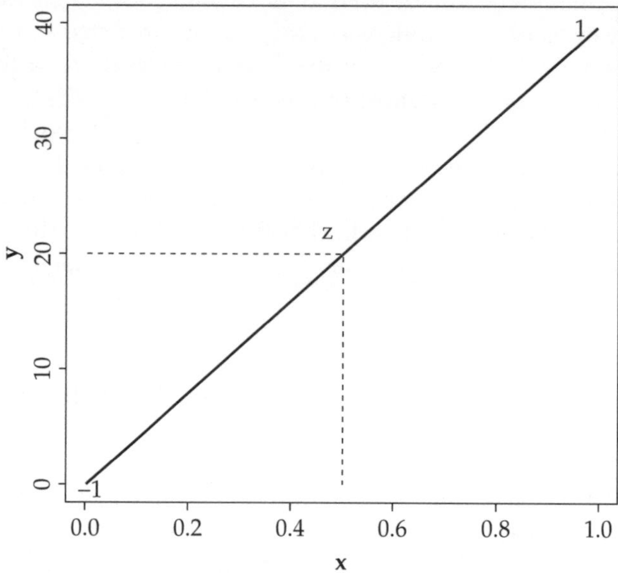

Figure 3.6 A derived factor is a line that relates x and y to each other. By knowing one value on the factor axis (z) you know two values (x and y) in the raw data.

x and y, and we let values on this line range from –1 to 1. When we say that an observation has a value (z) on the factor axis – the regression line – we can expand this into a statement about the x and y values of this observation. In Figure 3.6, I put the value of z at 0 on the factor axis (halfway between –1 and 1). This corresponds to an x value of 0.5 and a y value of 20. In this way, principal components analysis uses correlations among raw data variables to define the main components of variation in our data set and reduce the dimensions of description from many variables to only a few principal components of variation.

How it works. With two variables, x and y, it is fairly easy to imagine how principal components analysis works. We rotate the two-dimensional space so that the slope of the best-fitting regression line is zero and the y intercept is zero. Now we have a horizontal line – our new derived axis replaces the two raw variables x and y. No further reduction of dimensions is possible because we have reduced from two dimensions (x and y) to one.

With a larger number of variables, such as the x and y locations of pellets on the tongue, it is harder to visualize the principal components. The strategy that I and others have taken with tongue shape data is to plot the principal components (the "loadings" matrix, as discussed below) in the original data dimensions. For example, the first principal component of tongue shape usually corresponds to the high/low distinction and the second principal component corresponds to the front/back distinction.

Because a component of variation is a way of describing deviation from the mean, we start with the average values of the x and y variables in our tongue shape data for talker PL1. We only have 11 vowel shapes to work with, so we can have no more than 11 variables in the input (recall that with 15 pellets in two-dimensional space we have 30 variables). Therefore, I choose five pellets to represent the general shape of the tongue. The average x and y locations of these five pellets is shown in Figure 3.7.

The correlations among the 10 input variables (xy locations of 5 pellets) are analyzed in `princomp()` and a principal components analysis is calculated. This model has 10 principal components but the

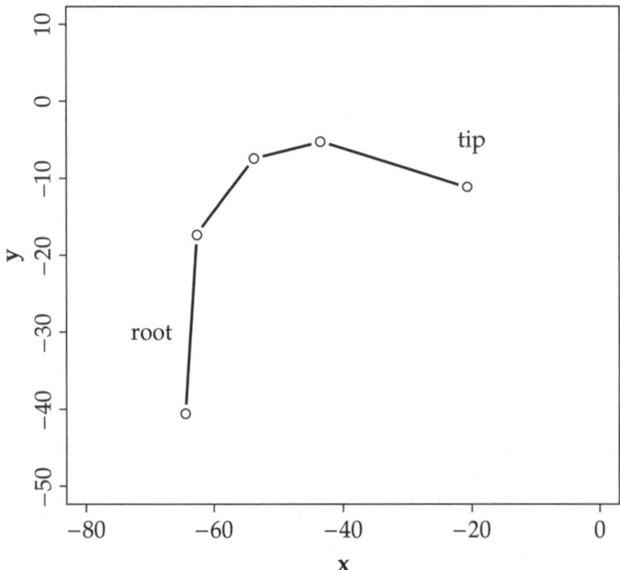

Figure 3.7 The average location of the five pellets that were analyzed.

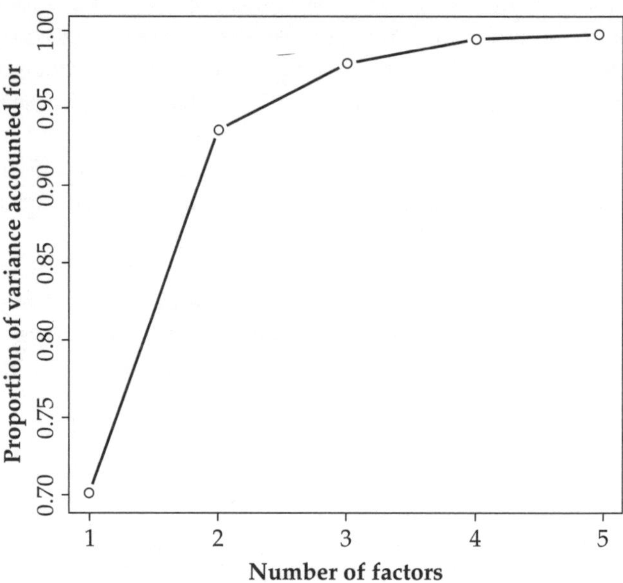

Figure 3.8 The cumulative proportion of variance accounted for by the first five principal components of tongue shape.

first 2 components account for most of the variance in the tongue shape data. As Figure 3.8 shows, the first principal component accounts for 66% of the variance and the first 2 components together account for 93% of the variance. Each additional component accounts for a very small amount of variance (5% for component 3, 2% for component 4, and less than 1% for all the others). Therefore, our most robust results are to be found in looking at the first 2 components. The higher components are likely to code minor quirks that are only present in these particular data that won't generalize to other similar data sets.

We are using principal components analysis to discover the main correlated patterns of variation that distinguish vowels in the tongue shape data set. We have found so far that the variation in these 10 variables can be described in terms of just two dimensions of variation. Another way of thinking about this is to say that any particular tongue shape in the data set can be described as a combination of two basic shapes – two "principal components" of variation. This is because principal components analysis decomposes the data matrix X into two matrices V and U, such that $X = V^T * U$, where V is the set of principal components (also called the "loadings" matrix), and U is the set of "scores" on those components for each observation. You can reconstruct the data values X from the scores and loadings. The loadings matrix is an abstraction over the data set that captures a few main patterns of correlation that are present in the data set, and the scores matrix indicates for each vowel how much of each principal component (positive or negative) can be found in the vowel's tongue shape. With two principal components each vowel will be represented with only two numbers – a score for principal component 1 and a score for principal component 2. The PCA loadings will translate these scores into detailed tongue shapes.

To visualize the two main principal components of tongue shape we will plot values from the loadings matrix to draw pictures of the tongue shape differences that are captured in the first and second principal components. PCA loadings are *z*-scores, so to visualize them you take loading times standard deviation, then add that to the variable's mean value to put the loading back into the original measurement units. For instance, if principal component 1 has a loading of 0.5 on data variable x_1, this means that if a vowel has a score of 1 for the first principal component then the predicted value of x_1 for that vowel is the average tongue position plus 0.5 times the standard deviation associated with the first principal component. The loadings for the first principal component (Table 3.1) are mainly on the *y* variables – this is a high/low component of tongue movement, while the second principal component loadings are mainly on the *x* variables – a front/back component.

We can visualize the principal components of tongue shape variation for this talker by graphing weighted deviations from the average

Table 3.1 Loadings of the tongue *x* and *y* variables on the first two principal components of variation. PC1 is an abbrevation of "principal component 1." Values near 0 are not listed in the table.

	x2	x6	x8	x10	x14	y2	y6	y8	y10	y14
PC1					.2	.47	.5	.45	.36	.37
PC2	.43	.37	.36	.44	.55		.12			–.15

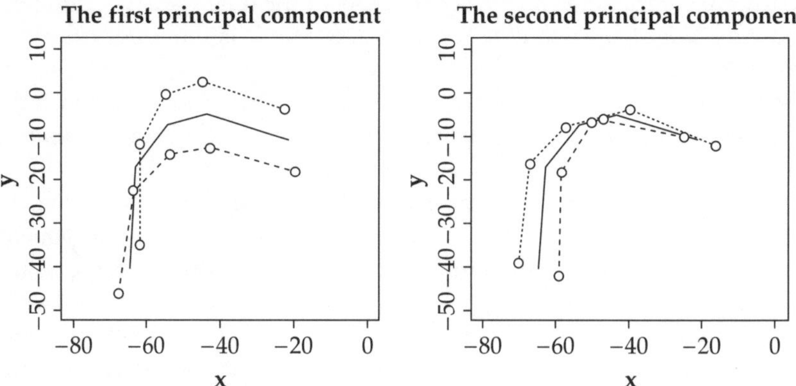

Figure 3.9 The first two principal components of variation in the tongue shape data of talker PL1.

tongue shape. The first two components are shown in Figure 3.9. The principal components analysis of tongue shapes "decomposes" all tongue shapes into some combination of these two basic tongue shape components, one for the front/back location of the tongue and one for the high/low location of the tongue. This two-component decomposition of tongue shape was not prespecified by me in setting up the analysis, but emerges from the data. To plot PC1 in that figure I took the average locations of the pellets and added the standard deviation of PC1 multiplied by the loading (written w in the formula below) to get one of the dotted lines and then subtracted the standard deviation times the loading to get the other dotted line. These lines show tongue shapes associated with the variation captured by PC1.

$x_{ji} = \bar{x}_i \pm s_j w_{ji}$ to visualize the variance of variable i encoded in PCj

R note. Computing the principal components analysis and plotting the results is actually pretty easy. We have some data in PL1 with *xy* locations of pellets on the tongue. I chose to use pellets 2, 6, 8, 10, and 14 for this analysis. Because the data set only has 11 vowels for this talker, we can analyze only 11 or fewer variables.

```
> summary(pc <- princomp(~ x2+x6+x8+x10+x14+y2+y6+y8+y10
    +y14, data = PL1))
Importance of components:
                           Comp.1    Comp.2     Comp.3     Comp.4      Comp.5
Standard deviation     15.3389055 9.6094120 4.13258604 2.48945962 1.230628457
Proportion of Variance  0.6664402 0.2615568 0.04837448 0.01755426 0.004289695
Cumulative Proportion   0.6664402 0.9279971 0.97637154 0.99392580 0.998215497
```

The summary produces an "Importance of components" printout. From this I used the standard deviations of components 1 and 2 in producing Figure 3.9 ($s_1 = 15.33$, and $s_2 = 9.6$). Additionally the proportion of variance accounted for is reported. I plotted the cumulative proportion of variance accounted for of the first five components in Figure 3.8.

The object pc contains a number of other results. For example, the values returned by pc$center are the average values for each of the variables ($\bar{x}_i$ in the formula above). I plotted the average values in Figure 3.7 and again as the solid lines in Figure 3.9.

```
> pc$center
        x2         x6         x8        x10        x14         y2
-20.911655 -43.554792 -53.972281 -62.819160 -64.590483 -11.240615
        y6         y8        y10        y14
 -5.194050  -7.400377 -17.428613 -40.752770
```

The factor loadings (the w_{ji} in the formula above) are saved in pc$center. I reported these in Table 3.1 and used them together with the averages and standard deviations to produce Figure 3.9.

```
> pc$loadings
Loadings:
    Comp.1 Comp.2
x2         -0.427
x6         -0.369
x8         -0.355
x10        -0.443
x14 -0.201 -0.549
y2  -0.472
y6  -0.498 -0.119
y8  -0.452
y10 -0.360
y14 -0.368  0.152
```

In particular, the plot commands for the left side of Figure 3.9 (of PC1) were:

```
> attach(pc)
> plot(center[1:5]+loadings[1:5,1]*15, center[6:10e+
      loadings[6:10,1]*15, ylim=c(-50,10),
      xlim=c(-80,0),xlab = "x", ylab = "y", type="b",lty=2)
> points(center[1:5]-loadings[1:5,1]*15, center[6:10]-
      loadings[6:10,1]*15, type="b",lty=2)
> lines(center[1:5],center[6:10])
```

To produce the right side of the figure (PC2), you replace the standard deviation 15 with the PC2 value 9.6, and refer to `loadings[,2]` instead of `loadings[,1]`.

EXERCISES

1 Pooled error variance. At one point I just declared that the pooled variance in the Cherokee VOT data is 1297.7. Show how this number was derived from the data. Why is this different from the overall variance of VOT in this data set (note: `sd(VOT)^2 = 1473.3`)?

2 Calculate the sign test contrasting male and female vowel first formant frequency from the data in "F1_data.txt."

3 Below is a matrix of correlations among three variables, x_1, x_2, and y. The standard deviations of these three variables are: $s_{x1} = 11.88$, $s_{x2} = 6.02$, and $s_y = 9.95$. Use these correlations and standard deviations to compute a regression formula to predict the value of y from x_1 and x_2. Show your calculations. Use the regression equation to predict the value of y when x_1 is 30 and x_2 is 6.

```
           y          x1         x2
y   1.000000   0.7623830 -0.8292570
x1  0.762383   1.0000000 -0.3596465
x2 -0.829257  -0.3596465  1.0000000
```

4 Variations on the `t.test()` command. Read the "cherokeeVOT.txt" data with `read.delim()` and try these variations on the `t.test()` command illustrated in this chapter.

```
t.test(VOT[year=="1971"],VOT[year=="2001"],
     alternative="greater")
```

```
t.test(VOT~year, alternative="greater")
t.test(VOT~year)
```

What changes in the results? What do these changes suggest, as regards the hypothesis being tested and the conclusions that you can reach with the test? Hint: you can look at the help page `>help(t.test)` to see a list of the options taken by the `t.test()` function. Do the default values always produce the most conservative test?

5 Use the data file "regression.txt." Read this data into a data.frame called `reg`. Look at the results of `plot(reg)` and compare the graph there to the correlation matrix given by `cor(reg)`. Use `lm()` to fit three models $y \sim x_1$, $y \sim x_2$, $y \sim x_1 + x_2$. Which do you prefer to account for variance in y? What is the regression equation? Use the regression equation to predict the value of y when x_1 is 30 and x_2 is 6.

6 Use the data file "chaindata.txt." Read this data into a data.frame called `chain`. Use `subset()` to extract the data for one of the other talkers in the data set (not PL1), and perform a principal components analysis of the tongue shape for this talker. How many factors seem to be needed to model the variance in this talker's productions? See if you can produce graphs of the principal components like those in Figure 3.9.

7 The F-distribution. I said that it is common to put the larger of two variances as the numerator in an F-ratio testing whether two variances are equal. Is this necessary or merely conventional? Use the function `shade.tails.df()`, which you will find on the book web page (don't forget to "source" the function), and find the F-value and probability of a more extreme F for these values:

$$s_a^2 = 300,\ s_b^2 = 1200,\ \mathrm{n_a} = 15,\ \mathrm{n_b} = 50$$

Do this once with $F = s_a^2/s_b^2$ and once with $F = s_b^2/s_a^2$.

4 Psycholinguistics

In psycholinguistic experiments, research factors such as word frequency, syntactic construction, or linguistic context are manipulated in a set of materials and then participants provide responses that can be scored on a continuous scale – such as reaction time, preference, or accuracy. The gold standard approach to the quantitative analysis of this type of data (continuous response measure, factorial experimental conditions) testing hypotheses about experimental factors is the analysis of variance (ANOVA).

Of course, psycholinguistics is not the only subdiscipline of lingusitics for which ANOVA is relevant. In fact, the structure of this book around particular subdisciplines of linguistics is a little artificial because most of the techniques find application in most of the subdisciplines. Nonetheless, multifactor experiments with analysis of variance hypothesis testing is the primary methodology in psycholinguistics.

We are returning to the two key ideas of Chapter 2 that I called "patterns" and "tests." In that chapter I introduced hypothesis testing and correlation. That was pass number one. In Chapter 3 we went further into the *t*-test, emphasizing that the *t*-test is a comparison (a ratio) of two estimates of variability, and we spent some time discussing how to find the right estimates of variation for use in the *t*-ratio. Then we dipped into the correlation matrix to see how to find data patterns using regression and principal components analysis. That was pass number two. In this chapter we are going to stay with hypothesis testing all the way – keeping our focus on analysis of variance. Then in the following chapter on sociolinguistics we will stay in pattern discovery for a chapter. The interesting thing is that by the end of all this we will have blurred the line between hypothesis testing and pattern analysis showing how the same basic statistical tools can be used in both, concluding that the difference lies primarily in your approach to research rather than in the quantitative methods you use.

4.1 Analysis of Variance: One Factor, More than Two Levels

With only two levels of a factor (for instance sex is male or female) we can measure an experimental effect with a *t*-test. However, as soon as we go from two to three levels the *t*-test is not available and we move to analysis of variance.

I will start the discussion (in this section and the next) with a set of data contributed by Mark Pitt, Professor of Psychology at Ohio State University. Pitt and Lisa Shoaf (2002) studied phonological priming in word perception. They were interested in knowing if the effect of phonological overlap between a prime word and the following target word would be the same throughout an experiment. They reasoned that if the priming effect changed as the experiment progressed then one might conclude that the priming effect has more to do with the listener's strategy in the experiment than with a necessary benefit (or impediment) of phonological overlap.

In a phonological priming study the listener hears a prime word, to which no response is given, and then a target word, which does recieve a response. The response measured by Pitt and Shoaf was "shadowing time" – that is, how long in milliseconds it took the listener to begin to repeat the target word. For example, in a 3-phone overlap trial the listener would hear the prime "stain" and then the target "stage" and then respond by saying "stage." In a 0-phone overlap trial the prime might be "wish" and the target "brain." Shadowing time was measured from the onset of the target to the onset of the listener's production of the target. Pitt and Shoaf had a large number of listeners in the study (96) and were able to compare the first occurence of a 3-phone overlap trial (after a long initial run of trials with zero overlap) with the last 3-phone overlap at the end of the experiment. We'll take advantage of their large subject pool to first explore analysis of variance with data sets that have a single observation per listener – reaction time from a single trial.

The simple models that we are starting with don't work for most psycholinguistics experiments because psycholinguists almost always use repeated measures (see section 4.3), so I'm using simple models to test subsets of the Pitt and Shoaf data where we have only a single observation per listener. Keeping our analysis for now confined to a single data point per person allows us to avoid the complications that arise when we examine data that involve multiple observations per person. Another characteristic of these initial datasets that makes it possible to use classical ANOVA is that we have an equal number of measurements in each cell.

A short note about models. The analysis of variance is a test of a statistical model of the data. "Model" is a pretty popular term and is used to mean different things in different research contexts, so let's step back and get clear about what a statistical model is. A computer simulation of a proposed neural circuit for processing language is a type of model, so is a box diagram of proposed stages of processing in some cognitive process, and so is a proposed account of social-mediated sound change. In each of these, the model embodies some assumptions or bits of knowledge about the components of a system and the nature of the modeler's task is to derive empirical predictions from the proposed model. A statistical model, on the other hand, is a proposed mathematical description of the data with no assumptions about the possible mechanisms that cause the data to be the way they are. For instance, if we include word frequency as an experimental factor and then test whether word frequency has a statistically reliable (non-zero) effect on the experimental results, the statistical test involves "modeling" the data, but at the end of the day all the statistical test tells us is whether or not word frequency seems to influence behavior in the experiment. The model does not explain why word frequency matters – that requires a model of the nonstatistical type (a theory).

Here's a simple statistical model of the sort we are considering in this section:

$$x_{ij} = \mu + \tau_i + \varepsilon_{ij} \quad \text{"treatments" model}$$

This statement says that we can describe an observed value x_{ij} (a response time, or accuracy measure, for example) as made up of three components: the overall mean μ, the average effect of the *i*th treatment effect (τ_i), and a random error component (ε_{ij}) that is unique to this particular observation *j* of treatment *i*. This statistical model assumes that the treatment effects (τ_i) which are the experimental factors or conditions in a psycholinguistic experiment are different from each other. When we find that the treatment effects are different from each other (see below) we can report that there was "a main effect of factor τ" (we'll get to interaction effects later). This means that the best-fitting statistical model includes this factor. The ANOVA compares the model with τ against the null hypothesis which says that we can just as accurately describe the data with a "no treatments" model:

$$x_{ij} = \mu + \varepsilon_{ij} \quad \text{"no treatments" model}$$

But, "describe the data" is the right way to characterize what these statistical models do. An explanatory account of why the treatment affects the response requires a theory that specifies the mechanism – the statistical model is good for testing whether there is any effect to be explained but does not provide the explanation.

The analyses that I will describe in this section and in section 4.2 assume that each observation in the data set is independent from the others. I selected data from Pitt and Shoaf's raw data files so that this would be true by following the sampling plan shown schematically in Table 4.1. Listener S1 provides a data point (x1) in the no-overlap, early position condition; listener S2 provides a data point in the no-overlap, mid position cell, and so on. With this sampling plan we know that observation x1 is independent of all of the other observations as assumed by the analysis of variance. It was possible to follow this data sampling plan because Pitt and Shoaf tested 96 listeners (16 in each column of Table 4.1) and this is a large enough sample to provide relatively stable estimates of shadowing time.

In this section we will discuss an analysis of variance that only has one factor and this factor has three levels, or in terms of the model outlined above we have three "treatments" that will be compared with each other – the reaction time when prime and target overlap by 3 phones at the beginning, middle, and end of a list of phonological priming trials. The measurements of reaction time (RT) for the beginning trial is modeled as:

Table 4.1 Data sampling plan with no repeated measures – one observation per listener.

	no overlap			3-phone overlap		
	early	**mid**	**late**	**early**	**mid**	**late**
S1	x1					
S2		x2				
S3			x3			
S4				x4		
S5					x5	
S6						x6

$$RT_{beg} = \mu + \tau_{beg} + \varepsilon_{beg,j}$$

$$RT_{beg} = 810 + 78 + \varepsilon_{beg,j}$$ our best guess for RT at the beginning of the list

where μ is estimated by the overall sample average (810 ms in this particular experiment) and τ_{beg} is estimated by the difference between the average RT for the beginning trial and the overall average (78 ms). The model predictions for the other list predictions are constructed in the same way. Now the test is whether the treatment effects, the τ_i, are reliably different from zero. Another way of stating this null hypothesis is to say that we are testing whether the treatment effects are the same, that is: $\tau_{beg} = \tau_{mid} = \tau_{end}$.

Now the treatment effects that we observe in the data (the differences between the means of reaction time at different positions and the overall mean) are undoubtably not exactly equal to each other – it would be odd indeed to take a random sample of observations and find the average values exactly match each other even if the treatments are actually not different – so the question we have to answer is this: Are the observed differences big enough to reject the null hypothesis?

The analysis of variance addresses this question by comparing a model with treatments specified to one with no treatments specified. If the null hypothesis is true in supposing that any observed differences among the treatment effects is a function of the random variation component ε_{ij} in a model which does not have treatment effects, then the magnitude of the differences between beginning, middle, and end positions, for example, should be comparable to the magnitude of the random component ε_{ij}.

So we have two ways to estimate the random, error variance. If variance measured from the τ_i is equivalent to variance measured from ε_{ij} (in the model with treatment effects), then we can assume that the null hypothesis is correct – the differences among the τ_i are due solely to error variance of ε_{ij} and the null hypothesis model is correct.

To calculate an estimate of error variance from the treatment means in the Pitt and Shoaf dataset we compare the means for 3-phone overlap trials from different list positions with the overall mean of the data set.

The overall average RT of the 96 measurements in our data set is 810 ms. We will symbolize this as $\bar{x}_{..}$ – read this as "x-bar, dot, dot." (Ninety-six measurements are for 32 listeners tested at each list position – beginning, middle, end. In this section we will take a subset of these data so that we have only one measurement from each listener.) The squared deviation between the means of the conditions (the "treatment" means) and the overall mean is calculated in Table 4.2 – 10,891 is the sum of squared deviations of the treatment means from the grand mean. To get sum of squared deviations per observation from this we multiply by the number of observations in each cell (in the formula below "r" is used as the number of observations per treatment). Thus, each mean in Table 4.2 stands for 18 observations and so represents 18 deviations of about this magnitude. We have then a sum of squared deviations due to differences among consonants ($SS_{treatment}$) of 347,155 (~32*10891). This measure is then converted to variance (the mean squared deviation) by dividing by the degrees of freedom of the estimate, which in this case is 2 (the number of treatments minus 1). This gives an estimate of the variance in our dataset of 173,577.

$SS_{treatment} = r\sum(\bar{x}_{i.} - \bar{x}_{..})^2$ sum of squares: treatment

$MS_{treatment} = \dfrac{SS_{treatment}}{df_{treatment}}$ mean square deviation (variance): treatment

If the differences among the means for different conditions are typical of the differences among the observations in the data set generally, then we expect the variance of the dataset to be 173,577. If you ignore condition differences entirely and just calculate the variance of

Table 4.2 Calculation of the sum of the squared deviations of the treatment means from the overall mean RT value in the Pitt_Shoaf1.txt data set.

	Beginning	Middle	End	Overall
$\bar{x}_{i.}$	889	805	741	$\bar{x}_{..} = 810$
$\bar{x}_{i.} - \bar{x}_{..}$	78	−4.6	−69	
$(\bar{x}_{i.} - \bar{x}_{..})^2$	6,111	21.1	4,759	sum = 10,891

the 96 numbers in the data set (recall that variance is the square of the standard deviation) you get a variance of 36,669. This is clearly much smaller than the estimate that comes from the differences between the list position averages, but it is still not a good estimate of variance in the data set because it includes the list position differences. We need to be able to remove variance that is due to position differences from our estimate of the random effect in the treatments model.

One way to partition out the treatment variance is to subtract the sum of squared deviation due to treatment differences from the total sum of squared deviations. The total sum of squared deviation is found by summing the squared deviations between each data point compared with the grand mean, without regard for which treatment the data point represents.

$$SS_{tot} = \sum(x_{ij} - \bar{x}_{..})^2 \quad SS_{total} \text{ is calculated from the grand mean}$$

This measure of the sum of squares total for the Pitt and Shoaf data set is 3,483,523. So we can estimate that the sum of squares that results from removing the treatment effect from the total is 3,136,368 (= 3,483,523 – 347,155). This is called the sum of squares of error, SS_{error}, or the residual sum of squares. It is a measure of how much random variation exists within each cell of the design. We calculated it by subtracting $SS_{treatment}$ from SS_{total}, but we could also have calculated it directly. For example, we could add the sum of squared deviations of the beginning reaction times from the average RT for beginning trials with the sum of squared deviations for middle RTs and for the end RTs. This somewhat direct approach measures how variable the items are within the set of RTs for trials at each position in the list.

Table 4.3 Analysis of variance table for reaction times in Pitt_Shoaf1.txt.

	Df	Sum of squares	Mean square	*F*-value	Pr (> F)
Treatment	2	347,155	173,577	5.15	< 0.01
Error	93	3,136,368	33,724		
Total	95	3,483,523			

I used this method to measure the SS_{error} for this dataset and found it to be 3,136,368. This divided by the degrees of freedom for the calculation (n – t = 96 – 3 = 93) yields an estimate of within-treatment variance of 33,724 (recall that the variance when we ignored treatment differences was 36,669).

$$SS_{error} = \sum(x_{ij} - \bar{x}_{i.})^2 \quad \text{calculated from the treatment means}$$

The partition of variance in our data set into the treatment and error components results in an analysis of variance (ANOVA) table – see Table 4.3. The model that we are assuming here is that each observation is composed of a treatment effect and some amount of random variation.

$$x_{ij} = \mu + \tau_i + \varepsilon_{ij} \quad \text{the model assumed in a one-way analysis of variance}$$

We have an estimate of variance from how widely the treatment means differ from each other (the treatment effect, τ_i) and from how variable the observations are when the treatment doesn't vary (random error, ε_{ij}). The ratio of these two estimates of variance ($MS_{treatment}/MS_{error}$) has a known distribution (named the "*F*-distribution") for the null hypothesis that the treatment effects are all equal to 0. In particular, if the treatment effects are all equal to 0 then the *F* ratio ($MS_{treatment}/MS_{error}$) should be close to 1. Because we are dealing with a sample of data from a larger population, we can estimate the probability that a particular *F*-value is drawn from a population where the treatment effects are all 0. The procedure for estimating this *F*-ratio probability distribution is analogous to the procedure used to derive the *t*-distribution. In essence though, the further an *F*-value is from 1, the less likely it is that the null hypothesis is correct. A "significant" *F*-value ($p < 0.05$) thus indicates that in all likelihood the best fitting statistical model is one that includes treatment effects – that is, that the treatments differ from each other.

H0: $\tau_{early} = \tau_{mid} = \tau_{late} = 0$ The null hypothesis

Table 4.3 shows the analysis of variance table for the Pitt and Shoaf reaction time data (one observation per listener). The *F*-value is the ratio between variance calculated from the treatment effects ($MS_{treatment}$) and the pooled variance of the observations within each treatment (MS_{error}). This value should be equal to 1 ($MS_t = MS_e$) if there are no treatment effects in the data. The observed *F*-value for this data set is so large that it is unlikely that these data could have been generated by a "no treatments" model – the differences between the treatments are too large to be the result of random differences.

The analysis of variance is based on several assumptions about the data. First, ANOVA assumes the equality of the variance within each treatment. We pool the variance among the early, mid, and late list positions voice onset times to get an estimate of the error variance on the assumption that variance in these treatments is approximately the same. We saw this same assumption in the *t*-test and discussed in Chapter 3 a method to compare variance before pooling. ANOVA also assumes that the error values ε_{ij} are normally distributed and independent from each other. In practice, these assumptions are approximately correct in psycholinguistic data, and when the assumptions aren't exactly met by psycholinguistic data, the mismatch between model assumptions and data isn't enough to cause concern (ANOVA is actually pretty robust in the face of assumption violations, except that the independence assumption turns out to be very important. We'll discuss this further in a later section).

R note. The data for this first illustration are in the file "Pitt_Shoaf1.txt." The reaction time measurements are in the column "rt," and the list position is indicated in column "position."

```
> ps1 <- read.delim("Pitt_Shoaf1.txt", sep=" ")
> attach(ps1)
```

There are 32 (r = 32) instances of each of 3 (t = 3) positions. I extracted this data from Pitt and Shoaf's larger data set by arbitrarily assigning the 96 listeners to either the early, mid, or late groups and then taking a single reaction time measurement from each listener's data. This arbitrary selection of data defeats Pitt and Shoaf's careful construction of test lists that put each word in each position an equal number of times. Later in the chapter we will use the full controlled data set in a repeated measures ANOVA. Although the data are more variable, taking one observation from each listener, the conclusions that we draw from them are the same.

Recall that the definition of variance is:

$$\text{var}(x) = \frac{\sum(x_{ij} - \bar{x}_{..})^2}{rt - 1}$$

where r is the number of observations in each treatment and t is the number of treatments.

The reason for dealing in squared deviations rather than variance in analysis of variance is that we can linearly partition the sum of squared deviations into deviations due to differences between the treatments (Table 4.3) and to deviation within treatment conditions without worrying about the divisors that are used in calculating variance. We are working here with squared deviations from the mean, and if you will recall, the variance of a data set is the average of the squared deviations from the mean – the sum of squared deviations divided by the number of observations in the data set. Therefore, if we know the variance in a data set we can calculate the sum of squared deviations by multiplying the variance times the degrees of freedom.

$$SS_{tot} = \sum(x_{ij} - \bar{x}_{..})^2 = (rt - 1)\text{var}(x)$$

I used this association between variance and sum of squared deviations (SS = variance * df) to calculate the SS_{error} for this VOT data set. It is:

```
> var(rt[position=="early"])*30 + var(rt[position==
    "mid"])*31 + var(rt[position=="late"])*32
[1] 3136368
```

The total sum of squared deviations (SS_{tot}) in the data set can also be calculated from the variance. There are 96 measurements in the data set, so the degrees of freedom is 95. You should notice that these two numbers are in table 4.3.

```
> var(rt)*95
[1] 3483523
```

Subtract SS_{error} from SS_{tot} to get $SS_{treatment}$ or calculate the treatment effect from Table 4.2. Either way we get about the same answer (the uneven number of observations in different list positions complicates this slightly).

Naturally, you don't have to do these calculations to do analysis of variance in R. There is a way of reporting or summarizing a linear equation model to give the analysis of variance table. This is the same `lm()` that we used to perform linear regression in the last chapter. It is clearly a very versatile function.

```
> anova(lm(rt~position,data=ps1))
Analysis of Variance Table

Response: rt
          Df  Sum Sq Mean Sq F value   Pr(>F)
position   2  347155  173577  5.1469 0.007586 **
Residuals 93 3136368   33724
---
Signif. codes: 0 '***' 0.001 '**' 0.01 '*' 0.05 '.' 0.1 ' ' 1
>
```

This result tells us that the shadowing time values at the beginning, middle, and end of the experiment are not all equal to each other. Given prior results we expect that the shadowing times at the beginning of the list will be longer. Prior expectation, based on theory or previous experience, justifies the use of planned comparisons (*t*-tests) to test particular contrasts. For these data, planned comparisons contrasting list positions find that shadowing time early in the list was longer than in the middle [$t(61) = 2.06$, $p < 0.05$], and end [$t(62) = 3.04$, $p < 0.01$]. Shadowing times from the middle and end of the list were not reliably different from each other [$t(63) = 1.3$, $p = 0.189$].

```
> t.test(rt[position=="early"],rt[position=="mid"],
   var.equal=T)
```

```
  Two Sample t-test

data: rt[position == "early"] and rt[position == "mid"]
t = 2.0621, df = 61, p-value = 0.04346
alternative hypothesis: true difference in means is not
equal to 0
95 percent confidence interval:
  2.509136 163.027154
sample estimates:
mean of x mean of y
888.5806 805.8125

> t.test(rt[position=="early"],rt[position=="late"],
    var.equal=T)

  Two Sample t-test

data: rt[position == "early"] and rt[position == "late"]
t = 3.0401, df = 62, p-value = 0.003462
alternative hypothesis: true difference in means is not
equal to 0
95 percent confidence interval:
  50.39623 243.91657
sample estimates:
mean of x mean of y
  888.5806 741.4242
```

4.2 Two Factors: Interaction

Now, the finding that reaction time is slower at the beginning of an experiment than at the end may simply suggest that listeners get better at the task, and thus has nothing to do with a response strategy. Pitt and Shoaf thought of this too and added a condition in which the prime and the target do not overlap at all. Contrasting this no-overlap condition at the beginning, middle, and end of the experiment with the 3-phone overlap condition that we examined above will give a clearer picture as to whether we are dealing with a practice effect (which should affect all responses) or a phonological priming effect (which should affect only the overlap trials).

Table 4.4 Two factors in a study of phonological priming.

	Early	Mid	Late	$\bar{x}$
0-phone	745	905	701	784
3-phone	910	820	691	807
$\bar{x}$	828	863	696	795

In particular, Pitt and Shoaf (2002) suggested that slower response times observed for 3-phone overlap trials (Table 4.4) may be due to the listener's strategy for completing rather than to any stable property of lexical processing. This conclusion is based on the interaction between the overlap factor (0- vs. 3-phones overlap between the prime and the target), and the list position factor (trials early, mid, and late in the experiment). Their argument was that if phonological overlap affects lexical processing in general then the effect of overlap should be seen throughout the experiment. Instead, Pitt and Shoaf found an interaction: that the overlap effect was only present in the first part of the trial list.

The model tested in this two-factor analysis is:

$$x_{ijk} = \mu + \alpha_i + \beta_j + \alpha_i\beta_j + \varepsilon_{ijk}$$

The α_i and β_j effects are exactly analogous with the τ_i (treatment) effect that we examined in the one-factor ANOVA of section 4.1. The estimated variance ($MS_{position}$ and $MS_{overlap}$ in our example) is derived by comparing treatment means (the row and column means in Table 4.4) with the grand mean. The sum of square total, SS_{tot}, is also caluclated exactly as in section 4.1. The interaction effect $\alpha_i\beta_j$, though, is new. This effect depends on the interaction of the two factors α and β.

A note on effects. In the two-factor analysis of variance, we have two main effects (a and b) and one interaction effect (ab). It is pretty easy to compute each one of the coefficients in the model directly off of the average values in Table 4.4. For example, the effect for 3-phone overlap is $\alpha_{[3]} = 807 - 795 = +12$, the difference between the RT of overlap trials and the overall average RT in the data set. The other main effect coefficients are calculated in the same way, subtracting the actual value from the predicted value. Note that the treatment effects coefficients for an effect sum to 0.

$\alpha_{[3]} = 807 - 795 = +11.6$
$\alpha_{[0]} = 784 - 795 = -11.6$
$\beta_{[early]} = 828 - 795 = +32.2$
$\beta_{[mid]} = 863 - 795 = +67.1$
$\beta_{[late]} = 696 - 795 = -99.3$

The interaction effects can also be easily calculated now that we have the main effects. For instance, given our main effects for position and overlap we expect the RT for early 3-phone overlapped trials to be 839 – the overall mean (795 ms) plus the effect for overlap (+11.6 ms), plus the effect for being early in the list (+32.2 ms). The actual average RT of 3-phone overlapped trials early in the list was 910 ms, thus the interaction term $\alpha_{[3]}\beta_{[beg]}$ is 910 – 839 = 71 ms.

$$
\begin{aligned}
RT_{[3][beg]k} &= \mu + \alpha_{[3]} + \beta_{[beg]} + \alpha_{[3]}\beta_{[beg]} + \varepsilon \\
&= 795 + 12 + 32 + 71 + \varepsilon \\
&= 910 + \varepsilon
\end{aligned}
$$

It is useful to look at the size of the effects like this. The position effect is larger than the overlap effect while the interaction is the largest effect of all. You can work out the other interaction effect terms to see how symmetrical and consistently large they are.

The shadowing time data distributions are shown in Figure 4.1. As we saw when we looked at the 3-phone overlap data, shadowing times seem to be longer in the 3-phone overlap trials early in the experiment but not later. Now comparing data from a control condition – trials that have no overlap between the prime and the target – we can test whether the faster shadowing times that we see in the later 3-phone overlap trials are a result of a general improvement over the course of the experiment. According to the general improvement hypothesis we would expect the no-overlap data to pattern with the 3-phone overlap

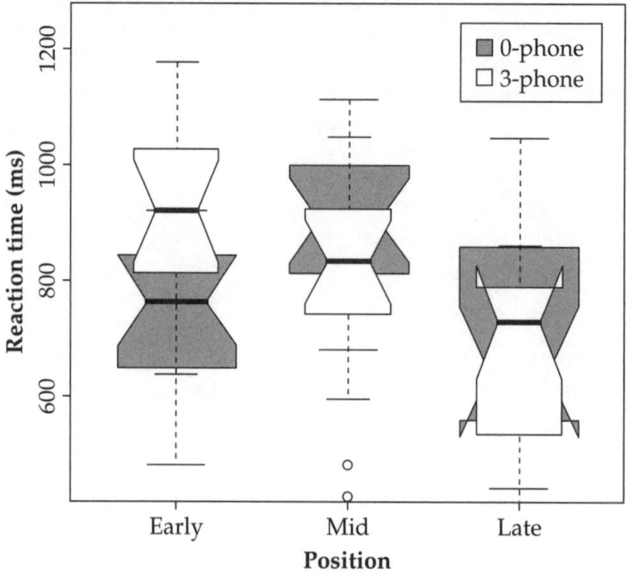

Figure 4.1 Shadowing time for no-overlap (gray) and 3-phone overlap (white) phonological priming, as a function of list position (a subset of data from Pitt & Shoaf, 2002, experiment 2).

data. This is a test of an interaction – do the factors list **position** and **overlap** interact with each other? The "general improvement" hypothesis predicts that there will be no interaction – the overlap conditions will show the same pattern over the different list positions. The "something is going on with overlap" hypothesis predicts that the pattern over list positions will be different for the no-overlap and 3-phone overlap trials. This means that the interaction terms $\alpha_{[3]}\beta_{[beg]}$, $\alpha_{[3]}\beta_{[mid]}$, $\alpha_{[3]}\beta_{[end]}$, etc. will be different from each other, that the best-fitting statistical models should include the interaction terms.

The analysis of variance (Table 4.5) of this subset of the Pitt and Shoaf (2002, experiment 2) data suggests that there is a reliable interaction. We find a significant main effect of position [$F(2,90) = 8.3$, $p < 0.01$] and more importantly for the test distinguishing our two hypotheses we find a reliable interaction between position and overlap [$F(2,90) = 4.98$, $p < 0.01$]. This crucial interaction is shown in Figure 4.1. A set of planned comparisons between the no-overlap "control" data and the 3-phone overlap phonological priming data indicate that the 3-phone overlap

Table 4.5 Two-factor analysis of variance of the "Pitt_Shoaf2.txt" data set. The R command to produce this table was: `anova(lm(rt~position*overlap, data=ps2))`.

```
Analysis of Variance Table
Response: rt
                  Df  Sum Sq Mean Sq F value    Pr(>F)
position           2  476184  238092  8.3465 0.0004729 ***
overlap            1   10592   10592  0.3713 0.5438308
position:overlap   2  284302  142151  4.9832 0.0088608 **
Residuals         90 2567333   28526
---
Signif. codes: 0 '***' 0.001 '**' 0.01 '*' 0.05 '.' 0.1 ' ' 1
```

pairs were shadowed more slowly than the no-overlap prime-target pairs at the beginning of the experiment [t(26.7) = –3.4, p < 0.01], while the no-overlap and 3-phone overlap conditions did not differ from each other in the middle of the experiment [t(29.2) = 1.4, p = 0.18] and at the end of the experiment [t(30) = 0.29, p = 0.78].

R note. The data for this section are in the file "Pitt_Shoaf2.txt." As with Pitt_Shoaf1.txt, I took only a single reaction time measurement from each listener in the experiment for the data set in Pitt_Shoaf2.txt. We have six groups (3 positions x 2 overlaps), each of which is made up of 16 listeners. The selection of which listeners would be in each group was done arbitrarily.

```
> detach(ps1)
> ps2 <- read.delim("Pitt_Shoaf2.txt", sep=" ")
> attach(ps2)
```

The `factor()` function is used to put the levels of the "position" factor into a sensible (nonalphabetic) order so Figure 4.1 will look right.

```
> ps2$position <- factor(ps2$position,levels=c("early",
   "mid","late"))
```

Figure 4.1 was created using the `boxplot()` procedure. The first call plots the gray boxes for the subset of shadowing times where there was no phonological overlap between prime and target. The second call adds narrower white boxes plotting the distributions of times when the overlap was 3 phones.

```
> boxplot(rt~position,data=ps2,notch=T, col="gray",
    subset=overlap=="zero", boxwex=0.7, ylim=c(450,1250))
> boxplot(rt~position,data=ps2,notch=T, col="white",
    subset=overlap=="three", boxwex=0.5, add=T)
> legend(2.8,1225,c("zero","three"),fill=c("lightgray",
    "white"))
```

`Boxplot()` produces a "box and whisker" summary of the data distributions. The box has a notch at the median and covers the first and third quartiles of the distribution. This means that 50 percent of the data points lie within the box. The whiskers extend out to the largest and smallest data values unless they are beyond 1.5 times the length of the box away from the box, in which case the outlier data values are plotted with dots. So what we see in Figure 4.1 is a representation of six distributions of data.

The planned comparisons that explore the position X overlap interaction are illustrated below. Note that I used the subset syntax to select RT measurements to include in the tests. For example, `rt[position=="early" & overlap=="zero"]` selects the reaction times for the 16 listeners who were selected to represent the no-overlap, early condition.

```
> t.test(rt[position=="early" & overlap=="zero"],
    rt[position=="early" & overlap=="three"])

    Welch Two Sample t-test

data: rt[position == "early" & overlap == "zero"] and
rt[position == "early" & overlap == "three"]
t = -3.4015, df = 26.669, p-value = 0.002126
alternative hypothesis: true difference in means is not
equal to 0
95 percent confidence interval:
  -278.23698 -68.78802
sample estimates:
mean of x mean of y
  744.6875 918.2000
```

4.3 Repeated Measures

As I mentioned in section 4.1, the analyses described in sections 4.1 and 4.2 assume that each observation in the data set is **independent** from the others, and I made it this way by selecting data from Pitt and Shoaf's raw data files following the sampling plan shown in Table 4.1.

This sampling plan gives us a data set that meets the independence assumption of the analysis of variance, but this type of sampling is disadvantageous for two main reasons. First, it requires that we test many more subjects than are actually necessary. And second, it keeps us from using each subject as his/her own control. Table 4.6 expands on this second point. Here we see a data sampling plan with repeated measures. In this scheme, which was used by Pitt and Shoaf in their study, we collect six reaction time values from each listener. Recall that I said that the "no-overlap" condition was added as a control to help guide our interpretation of the 3-phone overlap condition. In the independent observations scheme of Table 4.1 listeners S1, S2, and S3 provide the control reaction times which will then be compared with the reaction times given by listeners S4, S5, and S6. Thus, any individual differences between the listeners (alertness level, motivation, etc.) contribute to random unexplained variation among the conditions. When we compare listener S1's reaction times in the six conditions, though, we have a somewhat more sensitive measure of the differences among

Table 4.6 Data sampling plan using repeated measures – six observations per listener.

	no overlap			**3-phone overlap**		
	early	**mid**	**late**	**early**	**mid**	**late**
S1	x1	x2	x3	x4	x5	x6
S2	x7	x8	x9	x10	x11	x12
S3		and so on . . .				
S4						
S5						
S6						

the conditions because presumably his/her alertness and motivation is relatively constant in the test session.

The statistical complication of the repeated measures sampling scheme is that now the individual observations are not independent of each other (e.g. x1–6 were all contributed by S1), so the standard analysis of variance cannot be used.

We saw in Chapter 3 that if you have two measurements from each person you can use a paired *t*-test instead of an independent samples *t*-test and the test is much more powerful because each person serves as his/her own control. Recall, in the paired *t*-test the overall level for a person may be relatively high or low, but if people with slow reaction times show a difference between conditions and people with fast reaction times also show a difference, then the overall difference between people doesn't matter so much – the paired comparison tests the difference between conditions while ignoring overall differences between people.

That's what repeated measures analysis of variance does too. However, just as standard ANOVA lets us look at factors that have more than two levels, and lets us look at interactions among factors for independent observations, so repeated measures ANOVA extends the concept of matched comparisons to more complicated designs.

In a data set with more than one observation per person, the observations all from one person (within subject) are often more highly correlated with each other than they are with observations of other people. For example, in reaction time experiments subjects typically differ from each other in their average reaction time. One person may be a bit faster while another is a bit slower. It may be that despite this overall difference in reaction time an experimental manipulation does impact behavior in a consistent way for the two subjects.

Here's an illustration using hypothetical data to show how repeated measures analysis of variance works. If we want to know if an effect is consistently present among the participants of a study we need to look at the subjects individually to see if they all show the same pattern. This is shown in the comparison of two hypothetical experiments in Figures 4.2 and 4.3. In these hypothetical data we have two experiments that resulted in the same overall mean difference between condition A and condition B. In condition A the average response was 10 and in condition B the average response was 20. However, as the figures make clear, in experiment 1 the subjects all had a higher response

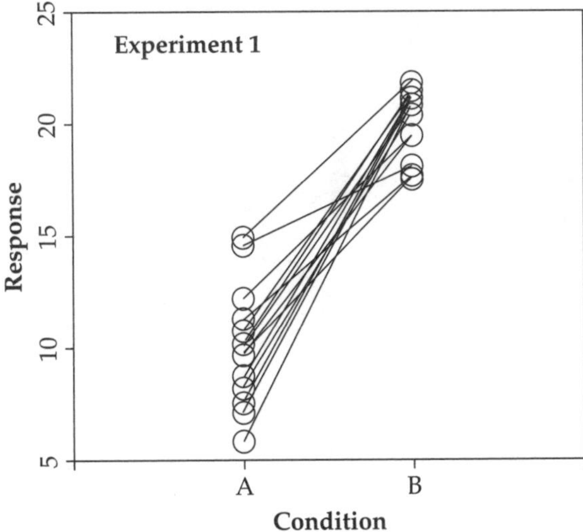

Figure 4.2 The average response in condition A was 10, and the average response in condition B was 20. In this hypothetical experiment the subjects (each of which is plotted individually) showed the same basic tendency to have a higher response in condition B. Thus the condition by subjects interaction is relatively small.

for condition B than condition A, while in experiment 2 some subjects showed this effect and some didn't.

If we act as if the observations in the data sets are independent of each other – as if we did not have repeated measures – then analysis of variance shows a significant difference between condition A and condition B in both experiments. The *F*-value for experiment 1 in this independent observations ANOVA was $F(1,30) = 212$, $p < 0.01$, and for experiment 2 it was $F(1,30) = 13.2$, $p < 0.01$. However, when we conduct the ANOVA with repeated measures we find that the difference between conditions A and B was significantly greater than chance in experiment 1 [$F(1,15) = 168$, $p < 0.01$] while this distinction was less reliable in experiment 2 [$F(1,15) = 7$, $p = 0.018$]. The inconsistency among subjects in realizing the A/B contrast results in a lower likelihood that we should conclude that there is a real difference between A and B in this population, even though the average difference is the same.

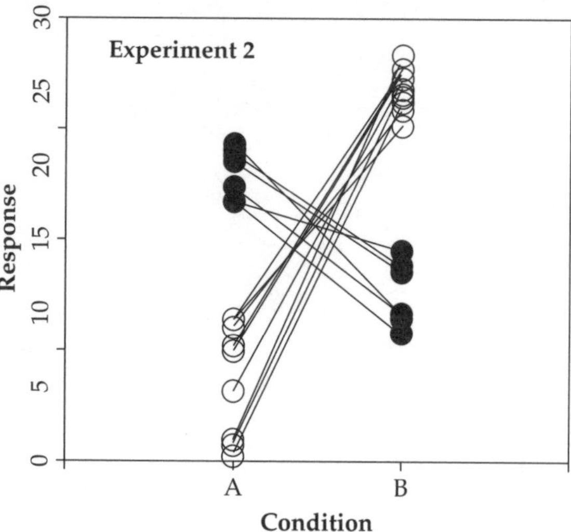

Figure 4.3 In this experiment the average response in condition A was again 10 and the average response in condition B was 20, but this time there was a subset of subjects (marked with filled symbols) who showed the opposite trend from that shown by the majority of the subjects.

R note. The comparison of the hypothetical experiments 1 and 2 (Figures 4.2 and 4.3) was done with the following R commands.

```
e12 <- read.delim("exp1versusexp2.txt") # read the data
e12$subj <- factor(e12$subj) # treat subject as a nominal
variable
e1 <- subset(e12,experiment=="exp1") # get the exp1 data
e2 <- subset(e12,experiment=="exp2") # get the exp2 data

# an incorrect analysis of variance - yes R lets you make
mistakes
anova(lm(response~condition,data=e1)) # incorrect!!!!
```

To see what is happening in the repeated measures analysis – the correct analysis with (subj) as the error term in the test of the condition main effect – look at these three ANOVA tables. First, we have a test of `lm(response~condition, data=e2)`.

```
             Df   Sum Sq  Mean Sq  F value     Pr(>F)
condition     1   736.80   736.80   13.261  0.001012  **
Residuals    30  1666.85    55.56
```

The *F*-value here is 736.8 divided by 55.6. The error term, 55.6, is the variance of the data values around the means of conditions A and B, incorrectly treating each observation as if it is independent of all the others. We saw in Figure 4.3 that the subjects were not consistent in their responses to the A/B contrast, so we might expect the interaction between condition and subject to be large in this data set. The table produced by `lm(response~condition*subj)` shows a pretty large MS value (variance) attributable to the condition:subj interaction, as we would expect because the subjects showed different patterns from each other.

```
                Df   Sum Sq  Mean Sq  F value  Pr(>F)
condition        1   736.80   736.80
subj            15    89.38     5.96
condition:subj  15  1577.47   105.16
Residuals        0     0.00
```

To test whether the condition main effect was consistent across subjects we use the MS for the `condition:subj` interaction as the denominator (error term) in the F ratio. In this case that means that we would take F(1,15) = 736.8/105.16 = 7. Note that the variance due to condition is the same in both the repeated measures analysis (with condition:subj as the error term) as it is in the non-repeated measures analysis (with the residual mean square as the error term). The only change is in the selection of the error term. The correct error term is selected automatically in R using `aov()` with `subject` specified as the error variable, and that we have repeated measures over the factor `condition`.

```
> summary(aov(response~condition+Error(subj/condition),
    data=e2))
Error: subj
           Df  Sum Sq  Mean Sq  F value  Pr(>F)
Residuals  15  89.382    5.959

Error: Within
           Df   Sum Sq  Mean Sq  F value    Pr(>F)
condition   1   736.80   736.80   7.0062  0.01830  *
Residuals  15  1577.47   105.16
```

This analysis uses the MS for the condition:subj interaction as the error term (denominator) in the F ratio testing whether there was a reliable or consistent effect of condition. And in general the key method in repeated measures analysis of variance, then, is to test the significance of an effect with the effect:subjects interaction as the error term in the F ratio. The `aov()` function with its option to specify the Error term simplifies the analysis of complicated designs in which we have several within-subjects factors (for which we have repeated measures over each participant) and between-subjects factors (for which there were different groups of people).

4.3.1 *An example of repeated measures ANOVA*

Now, at long last, we can analyze Pitt and Shoaf's (2002) data. Figure 4.4 shows the shadowing time data for all of the critical trials at the beginning, middle, and end of the experimental session, for no-overlap prime/target pairs and for 3-phone overlap pairs. The pattern that we saw in sections 4.1 and 4.2 is now quite clear. Responses in the early 3-phone overlap trials are longer than any of the other responses which are centered around 860 ms. We found with a subset of these data that there was an interaction between position and overlap and it looks like that will be the case again, but how to test for it?

Following the procedure for a repeated measures analysis of variance that was just described, we can construct an ANOVA (Table 4.7) with three experimental variables – position, overlap, and subject. Notice from the analysis of variance table produced with this model (rt ~ position*overlap*subj) that there are no *F*-values. This is because all of the variance in the data set is covered by the variables – by the time we get to the early, no-overlap reaction time produced by subject S1 there is only one value in the cell – and thus no residual variance between the model predictions and the actual data values.

This is just as well, because the analysis of variance table in Table 4.7 is incorrectly based on the assumption that the observations in the data set are independent of each other. We need to perform a repeated measures analysis. At this point we can either use the values in Table 4.7 to compute the repeated measures statistics by hand, or

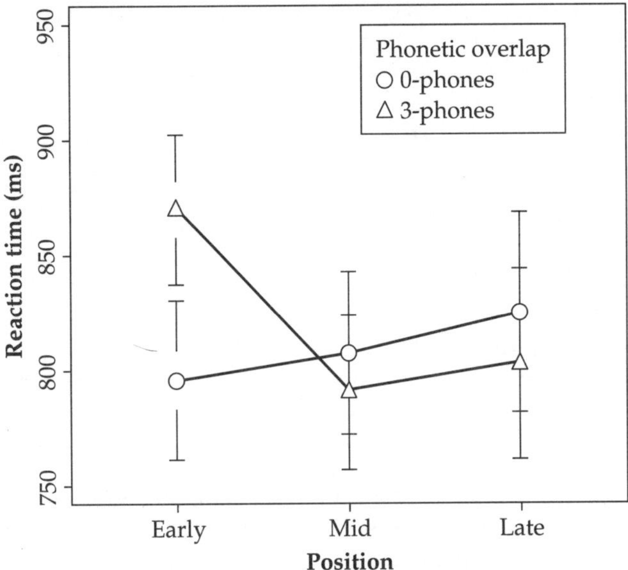

Figure 4.4 Phonological priming effect contrasting trials with 3 phones overlapping between the prime and target and with no overlap between prime and target. This comparison is made at three points during the experimental session (data from Pitt & Shoaf, 2002, experiment 2).

Table 4.7 Analysis of variance table for the repeated measures analysis of Pitt and Shoaf (2002) experiment 2. The R call to produce this table was: `anova(lm(rt~position*overlap*subj,data=ps3))`.

	Df	Sum Sq	Mean Sq	F value	Pr(>F)
position	2	111658	55829		
overlap	1	19758	19758		
subj	96	10187344	106118		
position:overlap	2	284424	142212		
position:subj	192	4985721	25967		
overlap:subj	96	1494378	15566		
position:overlap:subj	192	2697804	14051		
Residuals	0	0			

Table 4.8 Repeated measures ANOVA table for Pitt and Shoaf (2002) experiment 2. The R call to produce this table was:
`summary(aov(rt~position*overlap+Error(subj/(position*overlap)),data=ps3))`.

	Df	Sum Sq	Mean Sq	F value	Pr(>F)
position	2	111658	55829	2.15	0.12
position:subj	192	4985721	25967		
overlap	1	19758	19758	1.27	0.26
overlap:subj	96	1494378	15566		
position:overlap	2	284424	142212	10.12	<0.01
position:overlap:subj	192	2697804	14051		

use a different R call to compute the repeated measures statistics for us. It isn't hard to compute the *F*-values that we are interested in. The position main effect is $MS_p/MS_{p:s}$ = 55,829/25,967 = 2.15. The overlap main effect is $MS_o/MS_{o:s}$ = 19,758/15,566 = 1.27. And the position by overlap interaction is $MS_{p:o}/MS_{p:o:s}$ = 142,212/14,051 = 10.12. A call to `summary(aov())` with these data, and the error term `Error(subj/(position*overlap))` indicating that position and overlap are within-subject factors, produces the same *F*-values that I calculated above, but also gives their probabilities. In the earlier analysis we had a significant main effect for position as well as the significant interaction between position and overlap. With the larger set of data it becomes apparent that the interaction is the more robust of these two effects.

Naturally, we want to explore these findings further in a planned comparison or post-hoc test. However the *t*-tests that we used earlier assume the independence of the observations, and since we have repeated measures we can't use t-test to explore the factors in more detail. The usual strategy at this point in psycholinguists is to perform another repeated measures ANOVA on a subset of the data. For example, I looked at the effect of overlap for the early, mid, and late trials in three separate repeated measures ANOVAs and found a significant difference between the no-overlap and 3-phone overlap conditions in the early list position [$F(1,96) = 21$, $p < 0.01$], but no significant phonological priming effects at the middle [$F(1,96) = 1.3$, $p = 0.25$] or end [$F(1,96) = 1.16$, $p = 0.28$] of the experiment. These analyses suggest

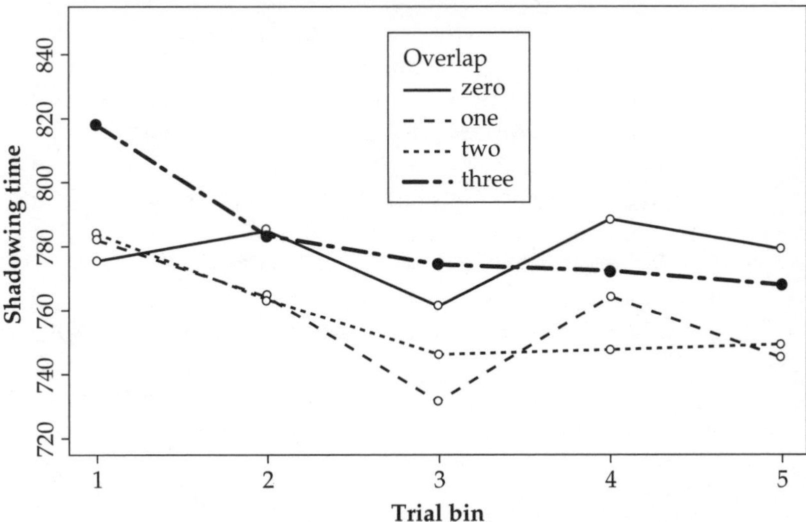

Figure 4.5 Response to phonological overlap between prime and target in Pitt and Shoaf (2002) experiment 2, as the experiment progressed from the first bin of 7 trials to the end.

that the first few trials involving a substantial amount of phonetic overlap between prime and target are in some sense surprising to the listener resulting in a delayed shadowing response.

I wanted to explore this a little further so I pulled trial-by-trial data out of Pitt and Shoaf's raw data. I binned these data taking the average reaction time for the first seven responses for each degree of phonological overlap between prime and target, and then for the next seven responses, and so on. This produced a somewhat smoothed representation of shadowing response times as the experiment progressed for prime/target pairs that overlapped by 0, 1, 2, and 3 phones. These data are shown in Figure 4.5, and seem to suggest that early in the experiment listeners were slowed by the 3-phone overlap, while later in the experiment they responded more quickly when there was an overlap of 1 or 2 phones. Interestingly though, neither of these effects looks like pure phonological priming (if such a thing exists) because the effects of overlap seem to change over the course of the experiment.

R note. Specifiying the Error term in the aov() command is a little tricky. For example, the specification Error(subj/position* overlap) is interpreted to mean that we want to test for a set of error terms – subj:position, overlap, and subj:position:overlap. This is not quite right. We want subj:position, subj:overlap, and subj:position:overlap and to get this set of error terms we need to specify the error term as Error(subj/(position*overlap)) – that position and overlap are both within-subject factors.

When the number of observations in each cell of the model is not equal, the printout from aov() includes a number of additional tests. The wanted *F*-values *are* printed and can be checked against the simple anova(lm()) printout, so I just ignore the extraneous tests given by aov().

```
> summary(aov(rt~position*overlap+Error(subj/(position*
overlap)),data=ps3))

Error: subj
          Df   Sum Sq Mean Sq F value Pr(>F)
Residuals 96 10187344  106118

Error: subj:position
           Df  Sum Sq Mean Sq F value Pr(>F)
position    2  111658   55829    2.15 0.1193
Residuals 192 4985721   25967

Error: subj:overlap
          Df  Sum Sq Mean Sq F value Pr(>F)
overlap    1   19758   19758  1.2692 0.2627
Residuals 96 1494378   15566

Error: subj:position:overlap
                  Df  Sum Sq Mean Sq F value    Pr(>F)
position:overlap   2  284424  142212  10.121 6.623e-05 ***
Residuals        192 2697804   14051
---
Signif. codes: 0 '***' 0.001 '**' 0.01 '*' 0.05 '.' 0.1 ' ' 1
```

The planned comparisons that I performed with this repeated measures ANOVA were done by taking a subset of data and then performing a one-way ANOVA on the subset, still using the subject:overlap mean square as the error term since we have repeated measures on the items being compared.

```
> subset(ps3,c(position=="early")) -> ps3.early
> summary(aov(rt~overlap+Error(subj/overlap),
data=ps3.early))

Error: subj
          Df   Sum Sq  Mean Sq  F value     Pr(>F)
Residuals 96  4133049    43053

Error: subj:overlap
          Df   Sum Sq  Mean Sq  F value     Pr(>F)
overlap    1   266252   266252    21.55  1.093e-05 ***
Residuals 96  1186098    12355
---
Signif. codes: 0 `***' 0.001 `**' 0.01 `*' 0.05 `.' 0.1 ` ' 1
```

Figure 4.4 was made using the `plotmeans()` function which is available in the "gplots" package of routines. This is not a standard part of the R package so you may need to download the package from CRAN using the "package installer." Once it is downloaded you use the `library()` function to make the functions in the package available in your R session. Here are the commands that I used for Figure 4.4:

```
> plotmeans(rt~position,data=ps3, subset=(overlap==
    "zero"), n.label=F, ylim=c(750,950), ylab="Reaction
    Time (ms)", xlab="", cex=2)
> plotmeans(rt~position,data=ps3, subset=(overlap==
    "three"), n.label=F, cex=2, pch=2, add=T)
> legend(2,950,title="Phonetic overlap",legend=c("zero
    phones","three phones"),pch=c(1,2))
```

4.3.2 *Repeated measures ANOVA with a between-subjects factor*

Here's another quick example of repeated measures ANOVA, this time with a between-subjects grouping variable. We're using a data set of reaction times in an AX phonetic discrimination task. Listeners hear two sounds and press either the "same" button if the two are identical or the "different" button if the two sounds are different in any way.

The raw data (correct responses only) were processed to give the median reaction time measurement for each listener for each pair of sounds presented. These are our estimates of how long it took each person to decide if the pair is the same or different, and we think that this is a good measure of how different the two sounds are. So each listener is measured on each of the pairs of sounds. This is our "within-subjects" repeated measurements variable because we have repeatedly measured reaction time for the same person, and we have an estimate of reaction time for each listener on each of three different pairs of sounds.

We also have one "between-subjects" variable because we have four groups of listeners – American English native speakers who never studied Spanish, have a beginner's knowledge of Spanish, or have an "intermediate" knowledge of Spanish, and then a group of Latin American Spanish native speakers.

When I analyzed this data in SPSS I set the data up so that there was one line for each listener. So subject 229, who is in the "beginning Spanish" group of listeners had a median RT for the same pair /d/-/d/ of 645 milliseconds, for the different pair /d/-/ɾ/ of 639, and so on.

```
group listener   d_d   d_r  d_th   r_r  r_th  th_th
begin      229 645.0 639.0 620.0 587.0 635.0 618.0
begin      230 631.0 635.5 595.0 607.0 603.0 728.0
begin      234 746.0 781.5 719.5 704.0 768.0 715.0
begin      235 800.5 708.5 668.0 708.0 663.0 719.5
begin      236 582.0 849.5 596.0 557.5 629.5 585.0
```

The SPSS "repeated measures" analysis produced using this data organization is very complete. Here's what I did to produce a similar analysis in R.

Note, this analysis style has the advantage that if you test several within-subjects factors the data file is easier to produce and manage.

1 Organize the data with a single column for the dependent measure – MedianRT – and a column also for each independent measure. I used the E-Prime utility program "Data Aid" to produce this data file. You can also use a spreadsheet program, just remember that

R wants to read files in raw .txt format. Here are the first few lines of the data file.

```
group  pair  listener  MedianRT
begin  d_d   229       645.0
begin  d_d   230       631.0
begin  d_d   234       746.0
begin  d_d   235       800.5
begin  d_d   236       582.0
begin  d_d   247       646.0
begin  d_d   250       954.0
begin  d_d   252       692.5
begin  d_d   253       1080.0
```

2 Read the data into R.

```
> spaneng <- read.delim("spanengRT.txt")
> spaneng$listener <- factor(spaneng$listener)
```

3 Take a subset of the data – just the "different" pairs. I could have done this in step (1) above, but it isn't too hard to do it in R either.

```
> speng.subset <- subset(spaneng, pair == "d_r" | pair ==
    "d_th" | pair == "r_th", select=c(group,pair,listener,
    MedianRT))
```

4 Now use the aov() function in R to perform the repeated measures analysis of variance. Notice in this command that we specify the data object "speng.subset" and a model to predict the MedianRT from which pair of sounds was being played and which group the listener belongs to. The key element of this analysis is that we are specifying that we want analyses for error terms that nest pair within the Subject factor. So the term "Error(Subject/pair)" is the key to making this a repeated measures analysis.

```
> summary(aov(MedianRT~pair*group+Error(listener/pair),
    data=speng.subset))

Error: listener
          Df   Sum Sq  Mean Sq  F value   Pr(>F)
group      3   461500   153833   3.3228  0.02623  *
Residuals 55  2546290    46296
---
Signif. codes: 0 `***' 0.001 `**' 0.01 `*' 0.05 `.' 0.1 ` ' 1
```

```
Error: listener:pair
             Df  Sum Sq Mean Sq  F value     Pr(>F)
pair          2  121582   60791  47.9356  1.069e-15  ***
pair:group    6   38001    6334   4.9942  0.0001467  ***
Residuals   110  139500    1268
---
Signif. codes: 0 `***' 0.001 `**' 0.01 `*' 0.05 `.' 0.1 ` ' 1
```

I'll leave as an exercise for the reader to explore the "pair by group" interaction further with planned comparisons and graphs. Here's one way to graph the results of this experiment:

```
> plotmeans(MedianRT~pair,data=speng.subset,subset=group==
   "nospan", n.label=F, ylim=c(600,950), ylab="Reaction Time
   (ms)", cex=2)
> plotmeans(MedianRT~pair,data=speng.subset,
   subset=group=="spannat", n.label=F, cex=2,add=T,pch=2,)
```

4.4 The "Language as Fixed Effect" Fallacy

The heading of this section is the title of a seminal paper by Herb Clark (1973). He pointed out that when we choose some words to ask people to say, or choose some sentences to ask people to rate, we are sampling from all of the possible words and sentences that could have been used in the experiment, just as we sample from a population of potential subjects. Do your results generalize to other similar words or sentences? In repeated measures analysis we treated subjects as a random effect by using the subjects by treatment interactions as the error variance estimates in ANOVA. Clark advocated doing this also with language materials, essentially suggesting that we do two separate analyses of each dataset. First, asking whether these effects seem to be generalizable to other people, and again asking if the results seem to be generalizable to other words or sentences.[1]

[1] Raaijmakers, Schrijnemakers, and Gremmen (1999) emphasize that it is important to report the minF′, which will be discussed later in this section, and not just the F1 and F2. They also point out that in many psycholinguistic studies the language items that are utilized are tested in counter-balanced designs or with matched item designs for which an items analysis is not needed at all. This is an important reference!

I will use an interesting data set donated by Barbara Luka (Psychology, Bard College) to illustrate the use of two *F*-values to test every effect – the subjects analysis and the items analysis. Following Clark's (1973) suggestion, we will combine *F*-values found in the subjects analysis and *F*-values from the items analysis to calculate the minF′ – our best estimate of the reliability of effects over people and sentences. Luka and Barsalou (2005) tested whether subjects' judgment of the grammaticality of a sentence would be influenced by mere exposure to the sentence, or even by mere exposure to a sentence that has a similar grammatical structure to the one they are judging. In their experiment 4, Luka and Barsalou asked participants to read a set of sentences out loud for a tape recording. Then after a short distractor task (math problems) they were asked to rate the grammaticality of a set of sentences on a scale from 1 "very ungrammatical" to 7 "perfectly grammatical." One half of the 48 sentences in the grammaticality set were related in some way to the sentences in the recording session – 12 were exactly the same, and 12 were structurally similar but with different words. Half of the test sentences were judged in a pretest to be highly grammatical and half were judged to be moderately grammatical.

(1) highly grammatical:

reading task	It was simple for the surgeon to hide the evidence.
identical	It was simple for the surgeon to hide the evidence.
structural	It is difficult for Kate to decipher your handwriting.

(2) moderately grammatical:

reading task	There dawned an unlucky day.
identical	There dawned an unlucky day.
structural	There erupted a horrible plague.

After the experiment was over Luka and Barsalou asked the participants whether they noticed the identical and structural repetition. Twenty-two of 24 said they noticed the identical repetitions and 18 of 24 said that they noticed the structural repetitions – saying things like "grammatical errors were alike in both sections" or "wording of the sentences was in the same pattern," but also "same type of words." So, just as with the Pitt and Shoaf (2002) phonological priming study, the participant's awareness of repetition and perhaps strategic response to the repetition may be a factor in this experiment.

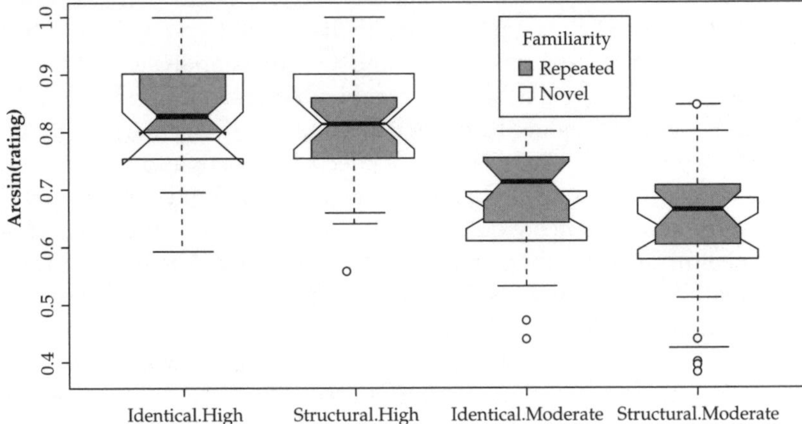

Figure 4.6 Results of Luka and Barsalou (2005) experiment 4. The two boxes on the left show results for the highly grammatical sentences, while the two boxes on the right are for the moderately grammatical sentences. Within these groupings the identical repetitions are on the left and the structural repetitions are on the right. Gray boxes plot the grammaticality rating when the sentence was repeated (identically or structurally) and white boxes plot the ratings when the same sentence was not primed during the reading portion of the experiment.

In a nutshell (see Figure 4.6), what Luka and Barsalou found is that repetition, either identical or structural, results in higher grammaticality judgments. This finding is rather interesting for a couple of different reasons, but before we get to that let's talk about how to test the result. The first step is that we conduct a repeated measures analysis of variance with repetitions over subjects. Luka and Barsalou did this by taking the average rating for each person in the experiment, for each combination of factors – familiarity, grammaticality, and type of repetition. This results in eight average rating values for each subject, corresponding to the eight boxes in Figure 4.6. Keep in mind here that we are averaging over different sentences, and acting as if the differences between the sentences don't matter. This is OK because later we will pay attention to the differences between the sentences.

The "subjects" analysis then is a repeated measures analysis of variance exactly as we have done in each of the examples in section 4.3. Using the raw rating data we get exactly the same *F*-values reported by Luka and Barsalou (2005). I decided to use the arcsine transform with these data because the rating scale has a hard upper limit and ratings for the "highly grammatical" sentences were smooshed up against that limit, making it difficult to measure differences between sentences. In this analyis, as in Luka and Barsalou's analysis, we have main effects for grammaticality [$F_1(1,25) = 221$, $p < 0.01$] and familiarity [$F_1(1,25) = 10.5$, $p < 0.01$]. Two effects came close to significant (this analysis is using $\alpha = 0.01$ as the critical value): repetition type [$F_1(1,25) = 5.6$, $p < 0.05$], and the three-way interaction between grammaticality, familiarity, and repetition type [$F_1(1,25) = 3.7$, $p = 0.06$]. Notice that in this report I am using the symbol F_1 in place of plain F. Following Clark (1973), this is the usual way that psycholinguists refer to the *F*-values obtained in a subjects analysis. The items analysis *F*-values are written with F_2 and in general we expect that if we are going to claim that we have found an effect in the experiment it must be significant in both the subject analysis and in the item analysis and the minF′ combination of *F*-values must also be significant.

The items analysis of these grammaticality rating data has repeated measures over just one factor. Sentences were reused in different lists of the materials so that each sentence was presented half the time as a novel sentence and half the time as a repeated sentence (either structural repetitition or identical repetition). Obviously Luka and Barsalou couldn't have used the same sentence in both the highly grammatical condition and in the moderately grammatical condition, so grammaticality was a between-items factor. In addition they treated the kind of repetition as a between-items factor as well. So the repeated measures analysis of variance uses the "items" main effect as the error term for the between-items effects, and the items by familiarity interaction as the error term for the familiarity main effect and all interactions involving familiarity.

This analysis, again using the arcsine transform to make the data distributions more normal, found the same two significant effects that we found in the subjects analysis. Highly grammatical sentences were judged to be more grammatical than the moderately grammatical sentences [$F_2(1,43) = 7\ 7$, $p < 0.01$]. This indicates that the participants in the experiment agreed with the participants in the pretest (whose judgments were used to determine the grammaticality category of each sentence). There was also a significant effect of familiarity [$F2(1,43) = 9.4$, $p < 0.01$]. New items had an average familiarity rating of 5.6 while repeated items (averaging over identical repetition and structural repetition) had a higher average rating of 5.8. This increased "grammaticality" for repeated sentences and sentence structures was found to be significant in both the subjects analysis and in the items analysis.

Now we combine the information from the subjects analysis and the items analysis to calculate the minF′ – the ultimate measure of whether the experimental variable had a reliable effect on responses, generalizing over both subjects and items. MinF′ is an estimate of the lower limit of the statistic F′ (F-prime) which cannot usually be directly calculated from psycholinguistic data. This statistic evaluates whether the experimental manipulations were reliable over subjects and items simulataneously. I would say at this point that the minF′ statistic is a high bar to pass. Because minF′ is a lower-limit estimate, telling us the lowest value F′ could have given the separate subjects and items estimates, it is a conservative statistic which requires strong effects in both subject and items analyses (which means lots of items). In experiments where the items are matched across conditions or counter-balanced across subjects, it may not necessary to use items analysis and the minF′ statistic. See Raaijmakers et al. (1999) for guidance.

To calculate minF′ divide the product of F_1 and F_2 by their sum:

$$minF' = \frac{F_1{*}F_2}{F_1 + F_2}$$

The degrees of freedom for the minF′ is also a function of the subjects and items analyses:

$$df = \frac{(F_1 + F_2)^2}{F_1^2 * n_2 + F_2^2 * n_1}$$

In this formula, n_1 is the degrees of freedom of the error term for F_1 and n_2 is the degrees of freedom of the error term for F_2.

Table 4.9 shows the results of the minF′ analysis of Luka and Barsalou's data. Both the grammaticality and familiarity main effects are significant in the minF′ analysis, just as they were in the separate subjects and items analyses, but the minF′ values make clear that the repetition type effect which was significant by subjects and somewhat marginally significant in the items analysis (p = 0.195) is not even close to being significant.

Before wrapping up this chapter I would like to say that I think that Luka and Barsalou's (2005) finding is very interesting for linguistics

Table 4.9 MinF′ values (and the error degrees of freedom) in the analysis of Luka and Barsalou's data. The *F*-values found in the subjects analysis are shown in the first column. The second column shows the *F*-values from the items analysis. *F*-values that are significant at $p < 0.05$ are underlined.

	F1	F2	minF′	df
grammaticality	221.0	77.0	57.10	65
familiarity	10.5	9.4	4.96	65
repetition type	5.6	1.7	1.32	63
fam*rep	1.4	3.5	1.00	45
gram*fam*rep	3.7	1.3	0.95	65

because it suggests that grammaticality is malleable – that "mere exposure" tends to increase the acceptability of a sentence structure. Additionally, it is interesting to me that it is structure that seems to be exposed in these sentences because there were no reliable differences between the identical repetitions and the structural repetitions and because the identical repetitions are also structural repetitions. The implication is that sharing the words in the repetition added nothing to the strength of the repetition effect. The picture of syntactic knowledge that seems to emerge from this experiment (and others like it in the literature) is that syntactic knowledge is about structures rather than exemplars, and yet that it emerges gradiently from exposure to exemplars.

R note. Many thanks to Barbara Luka for the data files. We have for this example two sets of data. One has the average rating given by each subject for each combination of factors in the experiment, so this means that there are eight data points for each of 26 subjects in this file. The commands to read the file and perform the "subjects" analysis are:

```
> LB1 <- read.delim("LukaBars05Exp4_subj.txt")
> LB1$SUBJ <- factor(LB1$SUBJ)
> summary(aov(2/pi*asin(sqrt((RATING/7)))~GRAMMATICALITY*
    FAMILIARITY* TYPE.TOKEN+Error(SUBJ/(GRAMMATICALITY*
    FAMILIARITY*TYPE.TOKEN)),data=LB1))
```

Note that I'm using the arcsine transform for this analysis. I felt that this was appropriate because the rating scale has a strict maximum value and there was a good deal of compression at the top of the range for the highly grammatical sentences. The arcsine transform expands the scale at the top so that rating differences near 7 will come out.

The items analysis uses a different data file which has the average rating value (averaged over subjects) for each test sentence. Different test sentences were used for the grammaticality and type.token experimental factors, so the only repeated factor was familiarity. That is, the same sentence was used (with different participants) as a novel or repeated sentence.

```
> LB2 <- read.delim("LukaBars05Exp4_items.txt")
> LB2$Item <- factor(LB2$Item)
> LB2 <- na.omit(LB2) # one sentence had to be omitted
> summary(aov(2/pi*asin(sqrt(RATING/7)) ~ GRAMMATICALITY *
    FAMILIARITY * REPETITION + Error(Item/FAMILIARITY),
    data=LB2))
```

Finally, for your appreciation and admiration, and so I'll have something to refer back to in similar cases, the lines below were used to create Figure 4.6. To keep the "boxplot" statements relatively clean I used `subset()` to select data for the plot statements.

```
> subset(LB1,FAMILIARITY=="New")->LB.New
> attach(LB.New)
> boxplot(2/pi*asin(sqrt(RATING/7))~ TYPE.TOKEN +
    GRAMMATICALITY, notch=T, ylab="Arcsin(rating)",
    boxwex=0.7)
> subset(LB1,FAMILIARITY=="Old")->LB.Old
> attach(LB.Old)
> boxplot(2/pi*asin(sqrt(RATING/7)) ~ TYPE.TOKEN +
    GRAMMATICALITY, notch=T, boxwex=0.5, col="lightgray",
    add=T)
> legend(2.7,0.99,legend=c("Repeated","Novel"),
    fill=c("gray","white"), title="Familiarity")
```

EXERCISES

1 In this chapter I said that the *F*-statistic is a ratio of two estimates of variance. What two estimates? I.e. what is the numerator in the *F*-statistic, and what is the denominator, and why is a ratio a meaningful way to present and test the strength of a hypothesized effect?

2 In Luka and Barsalou's (2005) experiment 4, the three-way interaction grammaticality by repetition type by familiarity was almost significant in the subjects analysis. The likely cause of the three-way interaction is visible in the data in Figure 4.6. What aspect of the results shown in Figure 4.6 would lead you to suspect that a three way interaction might be present?

3 Suppose that you analyze the results of an experiment using both subjects analysis and items analysis and find that F_1 is significant F_2 is not. What is going on?

4 The data file VCVdiscrim.txt is available on the book website. This "question" takes you step-by-step through a repeated measures ANOVA of this data. The interesting thing about this data set is that it has two within-subjects factors.

   (1) Use these commands to read this data into R and verify that it was read successfully.

   ```
   vcv <- read.delim("VCVdiscrim.txt")
   vcv$Subject <- factor(vcv$Subject)
   summary(vcv)
   ```

   (2) `vowel` and `pair2` are within-subjects factors. How many different listeners participated in this experiment, and how many repeated measures were taken of each listener? The `table()` command may help you answer these questions.

   ```
   table(vcv$Subject)
   table(vcv$vowel,vcv$pair2)
   ```

   (3) Now, do a univariate non-repeated measures analysis of variance. Be very patient, it is calculating a very large covariance matrix and a regression formula with several hundred coefficients. It didn't die, it is just working. With a long calculation like this it is helpful to save the result – I put it in a linear model object that I named `mylm`.

```
mylm <- lm(medianRT~L.lang*pair2*vowel*Subject,data=vcv)
```

To see the coefficients you can type: summary(mylm). But we are really most interested in the anova table: anova(mylm). Before you go on to step 4, fill in the following table (looking at the anova table for mylm). Keep in mind that L.lang is a between-subjects effect – I have two groups of listeners – and that both vowel and pair2 are within-subjects effects. What are the error terms for the following tests, and what is the *F*-ratio assuming those error terms?

	Name of error term	MS treatment	MS error	F
L.lang				
pair2				
vowel				
pair2:vowel				
L.lang:vowel				
L.lang:pair2				
L.lang:pair2:vowel				

(4) You can find the correct answers for this table by using the aov() command with the error term: Subject/(pair2*vowel). This calculates separate anova tables for the following error terms: Subject, pair2:Subject, vowel:Subject, and pair2:vowel:Subject. Then aov() matches these to the correct effects, just like you did in the table:

```
summary(aov(medianRT~L.lang*pair2*vowel+Error(Subject/
    (pair2*vowel)), data=vcv))
```

(5) One of the effects found in this analysis is the vowel main effect. It was also found that this effect was present for both groups of listeners (the vowel:L.lang interaction was not significant). Look at the table of reaction times, and the (hacky) graph produced by the following commands. What would it look like for there to be an interaction in these data? (hint: you can make up data and plot it using c() the way I made up the *x*-axis for the plot).

```
myv <- aggregate(vcv$medianRT,list(v=vcv$vowel,
    lang=L.lang),mean)
```

```
attach(myv)
plot(c(1,2,3),x[lang=="AE"],type="b",ylim=c(600,750),
   xlim=c(0.5,3.5))
lines(c(1,2,3),x[lang=="D"],type="b")
```

5 Try a repeated measures analysis of a different data set.

This example shows the analysis of an experiment with one within-subjects varianble and one between-subjects variable. We want to know whether these two factors interact with each other. Amanda Boomershine asked Spanish speakers to judge the dialect of other Spanish speakers. The question was: "Does this person speak local Spanish, or is he/she from another country?" The talkers and listeners were from Mexico and Puerto Rico. The data are in "dialectID.txt." The data set has four columns: "T.lang" is the dialect of the talker (Puerto Rican or Mexican), "L.lang" is the dialect of the listener (PR or M), "Listener" is the ID number of the listener, and "pcorrect" is the proportion of correct responses. We have two groups of listeners so the Listener variable is "nested" within the L.lang variable (subject #1 for example only appears in listener group M).

Boomershine took repeated measures of the talker dialect variable. That is, each listener provided judgements about both Puerto Rican and Mexican talkers. So T.Lang is a "within-subjects" variable because we have data from each listener for both levels. The L.lang variable is a "between-subjects" variable because for any one person we only have one level on that variable – each listener is either from Puerto Rico or Mexico. You should also apply the arcsine transform to the probability correct data.

```
2/pi*asin(sqrt(pcorrect)) # arcsine transform

dlect <- read.delim("dialectID.txt") # read the data
dlect$Listener <- factor(dlect$Listener) # treat listener as
nominal
```

5 Sociolinguistics

The main data that we study in sociolinguistics are counts of the number of realizations of sociolinguistic variables. For example, a phonological variable might span the different realizations of a vowel. In some words, like *pen*, I say [ɪ] so that *pen* rhymes with *pin*, while other speakers say [ɛ]. The data that go into a quantitative analysis of this phonological variable are the categorical judgments of the researcher – did the talker say [ɪ] or [ɛ]? Each word of interest gets scored for the different possible pronunciations of /ɛ/ and several factors that might influence the choice of variant are also noted. For example, my choice of [ɪ] in pen is probably influenced by my native dialect of English and the fact that this /ɛ/ occurs with a following /n/ in the syllable coda. Perhaps, also, the likelihood that I will say [ɪ] is influenced by my age, socioeconomic status, gender, current peer group, etc.

Other sociolinguistic variables have to do with other domains of language. For example, we can count how many times a person uses a particular verb inflection and try to predict this morphological usage as a function of syntactic environment, social group, etc. Or we could count how many times a person uses a particular syntactic construction, and try to model this aspect of language behavior by noting relevant linguistic and social aspects of the performance.

The key difference between these data and the data that we typically deal with in phonetics and psycholinguistics is that the critical variable – the dependent measure – is nominal. We aren't measuring a property like formant frequency or reaction time on a continuous scale, but instead are noting which of a limited number of possible categorical variants was produced by the speaker. So, in this chapter we turn to a couple of different analytical techniques to find patterns in these nominal response measures.

Of course, other areas of linguistics also deal with nominal data. In phonetics we sometimes count how many times a listener chooses one alternative or another in a listening task. In phonology we may be interested in how often a feature is used in the languages of the world, or how often a "free" variant pronunciation is used. In syntax, as we will see in Chapter 7, we analyze counts of the number of times particular constructions are used in different contexts. The methods discussed in this chapter on sociolinguistics are thus applicable in these and other subdisciplines of linguistics.

5.1 When the Data are Counts: Contingency Tables

We can compare the observed frequency of occurrence of an event with its theoretically expected frequency of occurrence using the χ^2 distribution. In some situations you can posit some expected frequency values on the basis of a theory. For example, you might expect the number of men and women in a statistics class to be about equal because there are about as many men as there are women in the world. So if the class has a total of 20 students the expected frequency of men is 10 and the expected frequency of women is 10.

In another type of case, if we assume that a set of observations comes from a normal distribution then we should find that most of the observations fall near the mean value and that a histogram of the data should have frequency counts that fit the normal curve defined by the data set's mean and standard deviation.

The difference between the observed counts and counts expected given a particular hypothesis, say that there should be an equal number of men and women in the class or that the data should follow a normal curve, can be measured on the χ^2 distribution. If the difference between observed and expected frequency is much greater than chance you might begin to wonder what is going on. Perhaps an explanation is called for.

To calculate χ^2 from observed and expected frequencies you sum over all of the cells in a contingency table the squared difference of the observed count (o = say 5 men in the class) minus the expected count

(e = 10 men) divided by the expected count. For the case in which we have 5 men and 15 women in a class of 20, and we expect 10 men and 10 women, the χ^2 value that tests the accuracy of our expectation is $\chi^2 = (5 - 10)^2/10 + (15 - 10)^2/10 = 2.5 + 2.5 = 5$.

$$\chi^2 = \sum_i \frac{(o_i - e_i)^2}{e_i} \quad \text{calculating } \chi^2 \text{ from observed and expected counts}$$

To determine the correctness of the assumption that we used in deriving the expected values, we compare the calculated value of χ^2 with a critical value of χ^2. If the calculated value of χ^2 is larger than the critical value then the assumption that gives us the expected values is false. Because the distribution is different for different degrees of freedom you will need to identify the degrees of freedom for your test. In the case of gender balance in a class, because we have two expected frequencies (one for the number of men and one for the number of women in a class) there is 1 degree of freedom. The probability of getting a χ^2 value of 5 when we have only 1 degree of freedom is only p = 0.025, so the assumption that men and women are equally likely to take statistics is probably not true (97 times in a 100 cases) when there are only 5 men in a class of 20. The remainder of this section explores how χ^2 can be used to analyze count data in contingency tables.

The way that the χ^2 test works is based in the definition of the χ^2 distribution as a sum of squared *z*-scores. In other words, the χ^2 distribution is just a particular way of looking at random variation. Because the *z*-scores are squared the χ^2 distribution is always positive, and because we expect a certain amount of randomness to be contributed by each *z*-score that is added to the sum, the χ^2 probability density distribution peaks at higher χ^2 values and becomes flatter as the number of *z*-scores increases (see figure 5.1).

$$\chi^2_{(n)} = \sum_i^n z_i^2 = \sum_i^n \frac{(y_i - \mu)^2}{\sigma^2} \quad \text{the definition of the } \chi^2 \text{ distribution}$$

Notice that the expression for how to calculate χ^2 from observed and expected frequencies has exactly the same form as the expression of χ^2 in terms of *z*-scores. This is why you can use the χ^2 distribution to measure how different the expected and observed frequencies are. We let e_i serve as our best estimate of σ^2 and use this to convert the

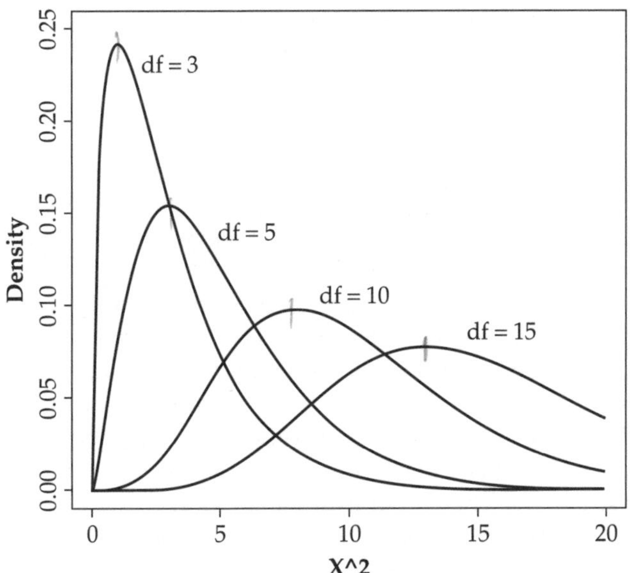

Figure 5.1 The χ^2 distribution at four different degrees of freedom. The peak of the probability density function is at a higher value for versions of the χ^2 distribution with higher degrees of freedom (e.g. the peak of the df = 15 distribution is near $\chi^2 = 13$ while the peak of the df = 10 distribution is near $\chi^2 = 8$).

differences between observed and expected frequencies into squared z-scores for evaluation with χ^2.

In Figure 5.1 you can see that the most highly probable value of χ^2 (the peak of the probability density function) is always just a little below the number of degrees of freedom of the statistic. χ^2 is different from the ratio statistics we discussed in Chapters 3 and 4. No matter what the degrees of freedom were, we expected the t and F statistics to be approximately equal to 1 if the null hypothesis were true and substantially larger than 1 if the null hypothesis were false. With χ^2 on the other hand, we expect the statistic to be almost equal to the degrees of freedom if the null hypothesis is true and substantially larger than the degrees of freedom if the null hypothesis should be rejected. This is because the expected value of z^2, on average over all y_i, is 1, and χ^2 is a sum of squared z-scores (this is because the average deviation from the mean in any data set is by definition a "standard" deviation).

5.1.1 *Frequency in a contingency table*

A contingency table is the count of events classified two ways – on two variables. For example, we might count the number of times that coda /l/ is "vocalized" in the speech of people of different ages. Robin Dodsworth did this in Worthington, Ohio and has kindly shared her data for this example. The pronunciation difference under examination here is between /l/ produced with the tongue tip against the alveolar ridge – usually also with the tongue body raised, a "dark" /l/ – versus a realization in which the tongue tip is not touching the roof of the mouth so that the /l/ sound would be transcribed as [w], or even a vowel off-glide like [ʊ]. The contingency table (see Table 5.1) has columns for each age level, and rows for the two realizations of /l/. If the rate of /l/ vocalization does not differ for people of different ages then we expect the proportion of /l/ vocalization to be the same for each age group. That is, our expectation for each age group is guided by the overall frequency of /l/ vocalization disregarding age.

This way of deriving expectations in a contingency table is exactly analogous to the way that I derived expected frequencies for the gender composition of statistics classes, however the expected values

Table 5.1 A two-way contingency table of the frequency of /l/ vocalization as a function of talker age. The expected table shows the expected values (the underlined numbers), which were calculated from the marginal proportions, assuming that age groups did not differ from each other.

		Teens	Twenties	Forties	Fifties	Total	Prop.
Observed	unvocalized	91	47	36	44	218	0.41
	vocalized	110	123	26	54	313	0.59
	total	201	170	62	98	531	
	proportion	0.38	0.32	0.12	0.18		1.00
Expected	unvocalized	83	70	25	40	218	0.41
	vocalized	118	100	37	58	313	0.59
	total	201	170	62	98	531	
	proportion	0.38	0.32	0.12	0.18		
$((o-e)^2)/e$	unvocalized	0.87	7.44	4.37	0.35		
	vocalized	0.61	5.18	3.04	0.24		
					$\chi^2 = 22.18$		

are taken from the overall observed proportion of vocalized and unvocalized utterances in the study rather than from population demographics (50% men).

So, in Table 5.1, the expected frequency of unvocalized /l/ for teens is 83 and this expectation comes from taking the total number of observations of /l/ produced by teens multiplied by the overall proportion of unvocalized /l/ (0.41 * 201 = 83). If you want you can get the same expected number of unvocalized /l/ for teens by taking the total number of unvocalized /l/ and multiplying that by the proportion of observations coming from teens (0.38 * 218 = 83). The expected number is calculated on the assumption that teens are just as likely to produce unvocalized /l/ as any of the other age groups. If, for example there was a tendency for teens to produce vocalized /l/ almost all of the time, then the expected value that we derive by assuming that teens are no different would be wrong. χ^2 tests the independence assumption inherent in these expected values by summing up how wrong the expected values are. As Table 5.1 shows, our expected values are pretty close to the observed values for teens and fifties, but people in their twenties and forties differed quite a lot from the expected frequencies (twenties showing less vocalization than expected and forties showing more). These deviations from the expected counts are enough to cause the overall χ^2 to total 22.1, which with 3 degrees of freedom is large enough to reject the null hypothesis that age doesn't matter for predicting /l/ vocalization. The degrees of freedom for this test is (number of age levels – 1) times (number of /l/ vocalization types – 1), which works out in this case as (4 – 1) * (2 – 1) = 3.

R note. I recoded Dodsworth's data a bit for this example. She had coded age with 1 for teens, 2 for twenties, and so on. To produce the contingency table, this would have to be converted into a factor anyway, so in the factor statement I added new, easy-to-read labels for the age groups. I did the same thing for Dodsworth's "/l/ vocalization" factor. She scored productions as 1 for "unvocalized," 3 for "vocalized," and 2 for "intermediate." There were only 11 productions scored as "intermediate" (out of 542 total observations), so I decided to exclude them from the dataset.

```
> rd <- read.delim("Robins_data.txt")
> rd$newage <- factor(rd$age,levels=c(1,2,4,5),
   labels=c("teens","twenties","forties","fifties"))
> rd$lvoc <- factor(rd$l,levels=c(1,3),
   labels=c("unvocalized","vocalized"),exclude=c(2))

   talker age l gender conscious  newage        lvoc
1      bh   5 3 female   connect fifties   vocalized
2      bh   5 1 female   connect fifties unvocalized
3      bh   5 3 female   connect fifties   vocalized
4      bh   5 3 female   connect fifties   vocalized
5      bh   5 3 female   connect fifties   vocalized
6      bh   5 3 female   connect fifties   vocalized
7      bh   5 1 female   connect fifties unvocalized
8      bh   5 1 female   connect fifties unvocalized
9      bh   5 3 female   connect fifties   vocalized
10     bh   5 2 female   connect fifties        <NA>
11     bh   5 1 female   connect fifties unvocalized
. . .
```

The frequency table that has counts for /l/ vocalization as a function of age is produced by `table()`, and the χ^2 test of the independence of `lvoc` and `newage` is given by `summary(table())`.

```
> attach(rd)
> table(lvoc,newage)
              teens twenties forties fifties
unvocalized      91       47      36      44
vocalized       110      123      26      54
> summary(table(lvoc,newage))
Number of cases in table: 531
Number of factors: 2
Test for independence of all factors:
Chisq = 22.118, df = 3, p-value = 6.166e-05
```

5.2 Working with Probabilities: The Binomial Distribution

It is often the case in analyzing the frequency of occurrence of a linguistic variable that we are dealing with binomial probabilities. That means that we classify each production as to whether a process applied or not – so we could code the data as 1 (process applied), 0 (process did not apply). There are number of ways of treating binomial probabilities in quantitative analysis. By way of introduction I will take an example from electoral politics, and then we will see how the techniques and concepts from this example extend to an analytic technique with regression analysis.

A warning: In this section and section 5.4 on logistic regression I will follow the standard practice in statistics and will use the symbol π to refer to the "population" probability which we are trying to estimate from a sample probability p. This is directly analogous to the use of Greek and Roman letter variables for variance (σ and s). However, most of us think of π as a geometric term for the number of radians in a circle, 3.14. Try to suppress this association and think of π from now on (in this book) as a probability.

5.2.1 *Bush or Kerry?*

Let's consider the closely contested state of Ohio two days before election day 2004 and use poll results as an example of how to test hypotheses about binomial data. Responses to a poll can be considered a "success" for Kerry when the respondent says he/she plans to vote for Kerry and a "failure" for Kerry for any other response. For instance, Cleveland, Ohio's largest newspaper, the *Plain Dealer*, asked 1,500 likely voters in Ohio who they planned to vote for and found that 720 said "Bush," 675 said "Kerry," and the rest were either undecided or had determined to vote for other candidates. These poll results can be given in a contingency table (see Table 5.2).

Table 5.2 Opinion poll results as "success" or "failure" of a particular candidate. The count of success and failure (in a sample of 1,500 voters) is shown in the left table. In the center table these are converted to observed probabilities, and the right table shows the model parameters that these probabilities estimate.

	Success	Failure	Success	Failure	Success	Failure
Kerry	675	825	0.45	0.55	π_k	$(1 - \pi_k)$
Bush	720	780	0.48	0.52	π_b	$(1 - \pi_b)$

The expected value of the probability of a "Kerry" response in the survey sample is π_k – the proportion in the sample who say they will vote for Kerry. The standard error of this estimate is given by,

$$\sigma(p) = \sqrt{\frac{\pi(1-\pi)}{N}}$$ expected value of the standard error of the parameter π

It may seem a little mysterious that you can calculate the standard error of a probability from the probability itself (if you want to see a derivation of this result see Hays, 1973). Figure 5.2 illustrates the standard error of a binomial variable for different sample sizes and proportions (p). You can imagine that if everybody said they would vote for Kerry (p = 1.0) then there would be no variation at all in the data set. Similarly if everyone planned to not vote for Kerry (p = 0.0) the standard error of the estimate would also be zero, and the situation where we have the greatest amount of variation is when the population is evenly split (p = 0.5). This is what we see in Figure 5.2. The

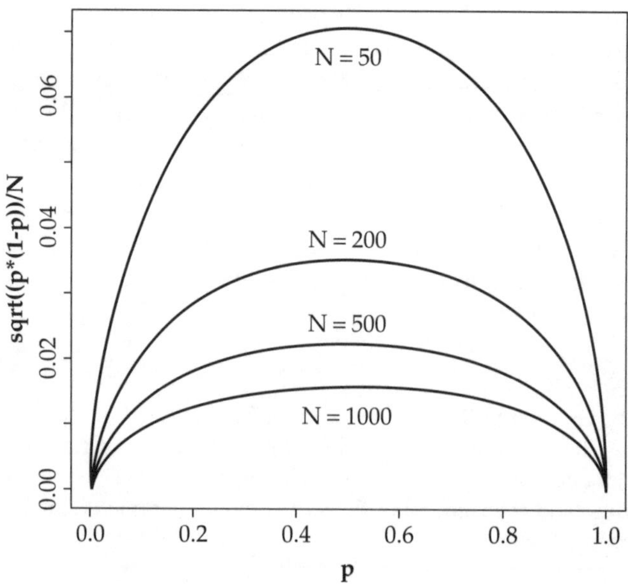

Figure 5.2 The standard error of p, for a samples of size 50, 200, 500, and 1,000. Standard error of a probability decreases near 0 and 1, and is also smaller as sample size increases.

figure also shows that larger samples have smaller standard error of the statistical estimate of π.

So, with a way of estimating the standard error of a proportion we can then test a hypothesis about the *Plain Dealer* poll. The hypothesis is that Bush and Kerry are tied in Ohio. That is: H_0: $\pi_k = \pi_b$. We'll test this null hypothesis by calculating a *z*-score from the difference between the two probabilities.

$$z = \frac{p_b - p_k}{s(p_b - p_k)}$$

The standard error used in this statistic is related to the method used to calculate standard error for a single probability.

$$s(p_b - p_k) = \sqrt{\frac{p_b(1 - p_b)}{n_b} + \frac{p_k(1 - p_k)}{n_k}}$$

Entering 0.48 for p_b, 0.45 for p_k, and 720 for n_b and 675 for n_k we get a standard error of 0.027 (this is the "plus or minus 2.7%" that is reported with poll results), and this gives a *z*-score of 1.123. This is not a very large *z*-score, in fact if we took 100 polls 13 of them would have a larger *z*-score even though Bush and Kerry are actually tied in Ohio. That is, this statistical test [$z = 1.123$, $p = 0.13$] does not lead me to reject the null hypothesis that $\pi_k = \pi_b$.

I conducted the same analysis for a number of different polls, and pooled results of them, from Ohio, Florida, and Pennsylvania. These results are shown in Table 5.3. The *z*-score for the sum of polls in Ohio is clearly not significant ($p = 0.39$), indicating that the poll results can't predict the winner in this state. The Florida sum of polls result shows Bush leading Kerry 48% to 47% and this difference is not significant ($p = 0.088$). The difference between Bush and Kerry in the Pennsylvania sum of polls is marginally reliable ($p < 0.03$).

What we saw on election night 2004 was an indication of the strengths and limitations of statistical inference. In all three states the candidate who was leading in the sum of polls ended up winning the state, though in two cases – Ohio and Florida – we couldn't have confidently predicted the outcome. However, we see the odd result that in Ohio more of the undecided or non-responsive people in the polls seem to have voted for Bush than for Kerry (about 65% vs. 35%). This discrepancy was even more pronounced in Florida (about 80% vs. 20%). The situation in Pennsylvania is more like we would expect given

Table 5.3 Poll results and signficance tests for three "battleground" states in the 2004 US presidential election.

		Counts		Proportions		H0: Bush=Kerry	
	Total	**Bush**	**Kerry**	**Bush**	**Kerry**	**error**	**z**
Ohio							
2004 results				0.51	0.49		
Sum of 7 polls	5279	2508	2487	0.475	0.471	0.014	0.28
Florida							
2004 results				0.52	0.47		
Sum of 10 polls	6332	3068	2958	0.48	0.47	0.013	1.35
Pennsylvania							
2004 results				0.49	0.51		
Sum of 9 polls	6880	3216	3377	0.467	0.49	0.012	−1.90

the nearly even split in the poll results – about 53% of the undecided or non-responsive voters ended up counting for Bush and 47% for Kerry. The discrepancy between the poll results and the election results indicates that there was either a bias toward Kerry in how the polls were taken, or a bias toward Bush in how the election was conducted.

R note. Instead of looking up the probability of *z*-scores like those in Table 5.3, you can use the `pnorm()` function in R.

```
> pnorm(0.28,lower.tail=F)     # ohio pooled polls
[1] 0.3897388
> pnorm(1.35,lower.tail=F)     # florida pooled polls
[1] 0.088508
> pnorm(-1.9)                  # pennsylvania pooled polls
[1] 0.02871656
```

One thing that I learned from this is why pollsters use samples of 600 people. If you look at the standard error values for the different polls, it is apparent that the polls with larger samples have lower standard error, but not substantially so. For instance, to go from standard error of 4.2% to 1.2% the sample size had to increase from 600 to 6,000. Probably, in most instances the extra effort and expense needed to interview 10 times as many people is not worth the extra accuracy.

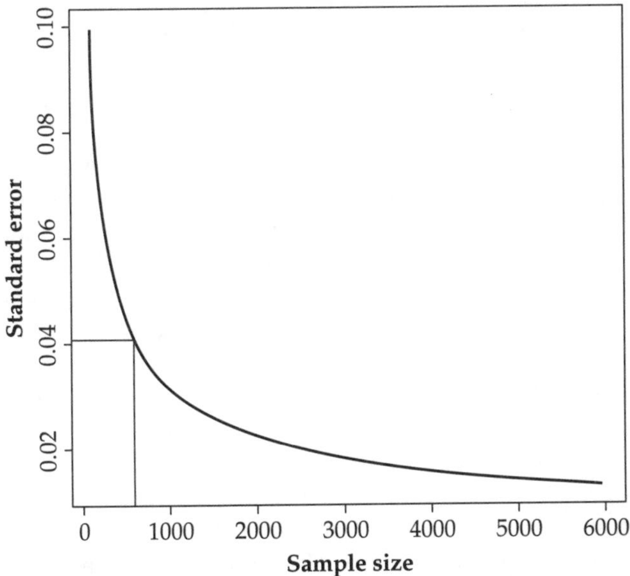

Figure 5.3 Standard error as a function of sample size for a two-alternative poll with $\pi_a = \pi_b = 0.5$.

The tradeoff between accuracy $[s(p_a - p_b)]$ and sample size in a two-alternative poll is shown in Figure 5.3. As you can see in the figure, the pollster's preferred sample size, 600, is just below the inflection point in this curve where increased sample size begins to result in sharply diminishing improved accuracy. I thought that that was an interesting thing to learn about binomial distributions and error in estimating a population proportion from a sample proportion.

5.3 An Aside about Maximum Likelihood Estimation

Maximum likelihood (ML) estimation of model parameters is a key building block of the main statistical analysis technique used in modeling sociolinguistic data – logistic regression. So before we dive into logistic regression we'll briefly touch on ML estimation.

It is perhaps intuitive to understand that the best possible estimate of a population parameter π – the probability of an event – is the observed probability that is found in the data. Indeed, the expected value of p (the observed probability) is π (the population probability). However, when you deal with multifactor models using logistic regression, direct estimation of model parameters from data is more complicated.

We saw in Chapter 4 that model parameters in analysis of variance and linear regression are estimated using the least squares (LS) criterion. The best model parameter is the one that produces the smallest sum of squared deviations from the observed data. This approach is very powerful because exact solutions are possible. For instance, the mean is the least squares estimate of central tendency and there is only one way to calculate the mean, with no guesswork. You calculate it and there you have it – the best-fitting (least squares) estimate of central tendency.

The main limitations of LS estimates are that we must have homogeneous variance across conditions (remember the equal variance test for t-test, section 3.1.2?) and it must be reasonable to assume that the data fall in a normal distribution. Neither of these assumptions is true of count data. We usually have different numbers of observations in each cell of a table and maybe even some empty cells, so the variance is not homogeneous. Additionally, dichotomous, "success/failure" responses do not fall on a normal distribution.

Maximum likelihood to the rescue. The idea with maximum likelihood estimation is that we determine a likelihood function for the parameter values being estimated and then find the peak in the likelihood function. For example, the likelihood function for estimating π from a binomial probability distribution with y successes and N total observations is:

$$\lambda = \binom{N}{y} \pi^{y}(1 - \pi)^{N-y} \quad \text{binomial probability density function}$$

In this function, the notation $\binom{N}{y}$ is the number of sets of size y from a list of N elements – the "choose" y from N. This can be calculated as the ratio of factorials $\binom{N}{y} = \frac{N!}{y!(N - y)!}$, where $N!$ is equal to 1 * 2 * . . . * N. You can use this binomial probability function in a number of ways, for example to rate the probability of finding 20 heads out of 30 tosses of a true ($\pi = 0.5$) coin (2.8% of samples).

R note. The binomial distribution is handled by a family of functions in R, just as the normal distribution, the t distribution, F, χ^2 and others. For example, to examine the coin toss example I used `dbinom()` to calcuate the probability of throwing 20 heads in 30 tosses of a fair coin. You can also calculate this directly utilizing the `choose()` function in the binomial probability formula.

```
> dbinom(20,30,.5)
[1] 0.0279816
> choose(30,20) * .5^20 * (1-.5)^(30-20)
[1] 0.0279816
```

Yet another way to get the same answer is to subtract the probability of getting 19 or fewer heads from the probability of getting 20 or fewer heads using the `pbinom()` function.

```
> pbinom(20,30,0.5)-pbinom(19,30,0.5)
[1] 0.0279816
```

In maximum likelihood estimation we know the values of our sample observations (the N and y) and we would like to find the most likely value of π – the one that produces the maximum value of λ. But, there is no direct way to calculate the maximum of the likelihood function, so instead the peak must be found using an iterative search. This is illustrated in Figure 5.4, where the likelihood function (from the binomial probability density function, above) is shown for a sample that has 5 successes in 50 trials. The horizontal axis shows different values of π while the vertical axis shows the resulting likelihood values λ. The aim of maximum likelihood estimation is to find the value of π that has the highest likelihood. The vertical line drawn at $\pi = 0.1$ is the peak of this likelihood function, the point that is chosen as the best estimate of the population parameter π. In this case, it is simply the probability of a success ($5/50 = 0.1$) in the sample. As we will see in the next section, this method can also be applied to find the model parameters of complicated regression models (of course I haven't actually said anything about the gradient ascent peak finding methods used in the search for the maximum likelihood, and I won't either).

A final note about maximum likelihood estimation. This method of finding the parameters of a model is not limited to logistic regression. You can also use ML estimation to find the coefficients of a regression

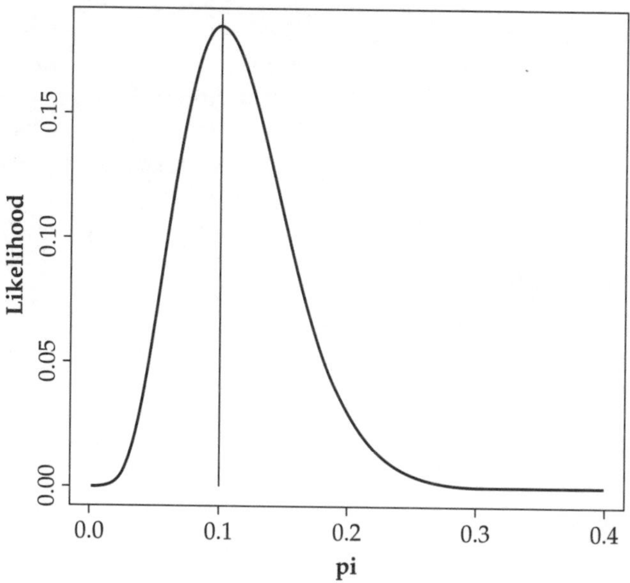

Figure 5.4 The likelihood function used to estimate π, for a sample of 50 trials in which 5 were "successes." The vertical axis is the likelihood of π [$\lambda(\pi)$], and the horizontal axis represents different values of φ that could be considered in the search for the π with the maximum $\lambda(\pi)$. The maximum likelihood estimate is 0.1 = 5/50.

equation or the effects of an analysis of variance. The only change is that the method of fitting the statistical model to the data is the maximum likelihood strategy rather than the least squares method. This parallelism is reflected in the R statistical language. The `lm()` function fits models using least squares estimation, while `glm()` uses maximum likelihood.

R note. Figure 5.4 is produced by this R command. Note that you could use `factorial()` in this plot statement to spell out the choose function, however the factorial function is undefined in R beyond 170, which is a huge number (7.257416e + 306)!

```
curve(choose(50,5)*x^5*(1-x)^(50-5),0,0.4,ylab=
      "likelihood", xlab="p i",main="Likelihood function for
      y=5, N=50")
```

5.4 Logistic Regression

Maximum likelihood is well suited to the type of data we usually have in sociolinguistics because it is a method that is nonparametric – it doesn't require equal variance in the cells of a model, and doesn't require that the data be normally distributed.

One other aspect of sociolinguistic data was emphasized in sections 5.1 and 5.2. The data are usually counts of "applications" of some process, so we are dealing with probabilities. You might recall from Chapter 1 that we used an "s"-shaped tranformation – the arcsine transform – to deal with the reduced variance of probabilities near 0 and 1. In logistic regression we use the logit function for the same purpose (see Cedergren & Sankoff 1974; Sankoff 1978, 1988 on the use of logistic regression in sociolinguistics). The logit function is preferable to arcsine because the resulting value has a sensible interpretation as the log value of the odds of application of the process.

$\pi(x)$ the proportion of "applications"

$\dfrac{\pi(x)}{1-\pi(x)}$ the odds of an application

$\log\left(\dfrac{\pi(x)}{1-\pi(x)}\right)$ the log odds of an application, the logit

The relationship between probability, odds, and logit is shown in Table 5.4. There we see that an event that occurs in 80% of the

Table 5.4 Comparison of probability, odds, and log odds for a range of probabilities.

Probability	Odds	Log odds
0.1	0.111	–2.197
0.2	0.25	–1.386
0.3	0.428	–0.847
0.4	0.667	–0.405
0.5	1.00	0.00
0.6	1.5	0.405
0.7	2.33	0.847
0.8	4.00	1.386
0.9	9.00	2.197

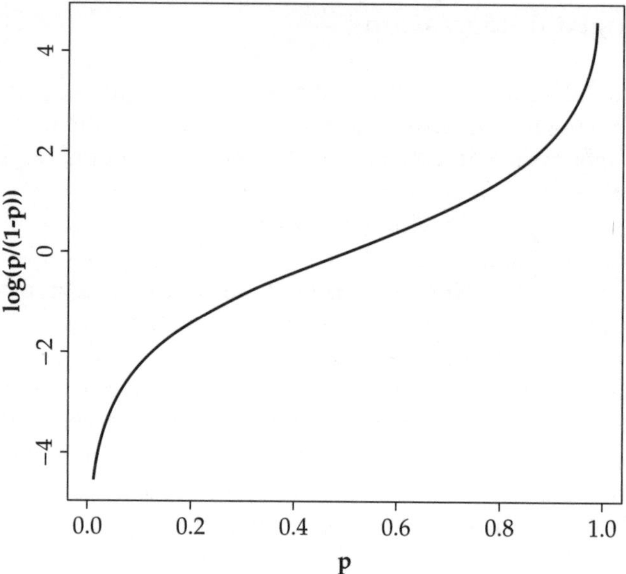

Figure 5.5 The logit transform $y = \log(p/(1-p))$. The inverse of this is $p = \exp(y)/(1 + \exp(y))$.

observed cases has an odds ratio of 4 to 1 (the event is 4 times more likely to occur than the non-event). The logit value of 1.386 is not intuitively meaningful if you don't normally deal in log odds (who does?), but it is easy to map logits into odds or probabilities, and the values are centered symmetrically around zero. The logit function is shown in Figure 5.5 as a function of probability. In interpreting the results of a logistic regression some analysts (particularly in medical research) refer directly to the odds or the log odds of an event, such as recovery from a disease. I find it more understandable to translate the coefficients that are found in logistic regression back into probabilities via the inverse logit function.

$$y = \log\left(\frac{\pi(x)}{1 - \pi(x)}\right)$$ the logit, or logistic, function

$$\pi(x) = \frac{e^y}{1 + e^y}.$$ the inverse logit (to calculate probabilities from logits)

5.5 An Example from the [ʃ]treets of Columbus

Now, let's turn to an example of a logistic regression analyis of some sociolinguistic data. These data are found in the file "DDRASSTR.txt" and were contributed by David Durian. Durian describes his study this way:

> Data from 120 Caucasian, native-English speaking Columbus, OH store clerks (40 store clerks working in a variety of stores at each of 3 Columbus malls [Easton, Polaris, and City Center]) were elicited via the Rapid Anonymous Survey technique. The entire set of store clerks were also stratified by the following social factors: age (15–30, 35–50, 55–70, 40 speakers in each age group); social class (working class – WC, lower middle class – LMC, and upper middle class – UMC, 40 speakers of each class); and gender (60 males/60 females).
>
> From each of the 120 speakers, two tokens of words containing word-initial "str" clusters were obtained. The first, in a less emphatic speech environment; the second in a more emphatic one. This leads to a total of 240 tokens (120 more emphatic; 120 less emphatic). The two variant realizations of "str" were rated impressionistically by the researcher as closer to [str] or [ʃtr].
>
> All of the data were elicited by the researcher asking for directions to a known street in the area of the mall that was misidentified as a "road." The speaker then corrected the researcher by saying "you mean X street," and the first "str" token was obtained. Following this first utterance, the researcher said, "excuse me, what did you say" and the speaker would more emphatically repeat the phrase "x street" producing the second "str" token. In the case of Polaris Mall no widely identified street is located within proximity to the mall (everything there is a Road, Parkway, Place, etc.), and so the researcher asked for directions to a part of the store that would yield the word "straight" in place of "street."
>
> Data were written down on a sheet of paper just after leaving eyesight of the informant. No audio recordings were made. The only judgment made on the sounds was the researcher's own impressionistic rating.

I edited Durian's description to simplify the description of how he assigned talkers to different class levels. After collecting the data from a number of different stores, in the initial design with 40 talkers from each of three presumed classes, he had students at Ohio State

Table 5.5 Number [ʃtr] and [str] productions as a function of emphasis.

	Emphasis	
	Less	**More**
ʃtr	43	14
str	77	106

University estimate the average class background of the shoppers in the stores. These judgments were used to estimate the clerks' class for the logistic analysis.

5.5.1 *On the relationship between χ^2 and G^2*

Logistic regression results in a statistic called G^2 which is the log-likelihood analog of χ^2. So, in this section we'll demonstrate the similarity between χ^2 and G^2 and talk about where this G^2 statistic comes from.

Table 5.5 shows the number of [ʃtr] and [str] productions in Durian's study as a function of whether the utterance was produced without emphasis or in a relatively more emphatic utterance. It looks as if people were much more likely to say [ʃtr] in the less emphatic case (35% versus 12%). The value of χ^2 for this table, found using the R statement `summary(table(str,emphatic))`, is 19.35, which is signficantly greater than chance for a χ^2 with one degree of freedom.

Now the logistic regression analysis of these same data is done using the general linear model – `glm()` – which fits model parameters using maximum likelihood estimation instead of least squares. Results of the glm model fit can be printed as an analysis of deviance table which is analogous to the analysis of variance table. This analysis of deviance table for the [ʃtr] by emphasis data is shown in Table 5.6. The G^2 value (labeled "Deviance") is 20.08 – almost the same as the χ^2 value.

Although, in the paragraphs to follow we will discuss how G^2 is derived from likelihood ratios in model fitting, it may be interesting to some readers to note that like χ^2, G^2 can be calculated directly from the observed and expected frequencies of a contengency table. Using the same counts of observed and expected frequency that are used in calculating χ^2,

Table 5.6 Analysis of deviance table for a logistic regression analysis of the data shown in Table 5.5.

	Df	Deviance	Resid. Df	Resid. Dev	P(>|Chi|)
NULL			239	263.13	
emphatic	1	20.08	238	243.04	7.416e-06

$$\chi^2 = \sum_i \frac{(o_i - e_i)^2}{e_i},$$

G^2 is calculated from the natural log of the ratio of observed and expected frequency. One of the exercises at the end of the chapter has you derive 19.35 as the χ^2 and 20.08 as the G^2 of the data in Table 5.5.

$$G^2 = -2\sum_i o_i \log\left(\frac{o_i}{e_i}\right),$$

R note. The command that produced the analysis of deviance table shown in Table 5.6 was:

```
> dd<-read.delim("DDRASSTR.txt")
> attach(dd)
> anova(glm(str~emphatic,family=binomial,data=dd),
    test="Chisq")
```

Parts of this command are familiar from previous chapters. For example, we specify a model `str~emphatic` such that the response variable, whether the person said [str] or [ʃtr], is a function of whether the utterance was emphatic or not. This model is evaluated by the `glm()` function much as we used the `lm()` function to produce analysis of variance tables in Chapter 4. Because the response measure is binomial rather than a measurement on a continuous scale, we specify that the model should be evaluated with `family=binomial`. This results in the use of the logistic scores. Finally, `anova()` requests that the results be printed as an analysis of deviance table and `test="Chisq"` specifies that the deviance score should be evaluated on the χ^2 distribution.

In logistic regression, since we are using maximum likelihood parameter estimation to find the best-fitting model of the data, the measure that is used to test the degree of fit of a model is the likelihood ratio. The idea here is to compare the maximum likelihood found in a model that includes a possible explanatory factor (like emphasis) with the maximum likelihood of a model that does not include that explanatory factor. In the null model, which includes no explanatory factors at all, the only basis for making a prediction is the average probability of [ʃtr] productions. This serves as a baseline and then we add a possible explanatory factor and measure how much the likelihood of the model improves.

To compare models with and without a factor we take the likelihood ratio. The idea here is analogous to the use of ratio measures in all of the other statistical hypothesis tests that we've discussed so far (*t*-test, *F*-test, *z*-score). If the ratio is close to unity (1) then the improved fit offered by the added factor is insubstantial and considered a non-significant predictor of the criterion variable.

Likelihood ratios fall on a different distribution than variance ratios, so we use a different statistic called G^2 to test their significance. G^2 has the same distribution as χ^2, so in looking up significance of G^2 you use the χ^2 tables, but because it is calculated a different way we give it a different name. G^2 is called Deviance in Table 5.6 and can be calculated from the sum of deviance scores $(y_i - \hat{y}_i)$ when the data are normally distributed and the true σ is known.

$$G^2 = -2\log\left(\frac{l_m}{l_{m-1}}\right), \quad \text{comparing the likelihoods of two models}$$

The likelihood ratio in this formula compares two models, m and $m - 1$, where m has one additional predictive factor that was not included in $m - 1$. This value in table 5.6 was 20.08. In practice it is convenient to calculate G^2 from two other G^2 (deviance) scores. The highest possible likelihood value can be obtained when there is a parameter for every observation in the data set. This one-parameter-per-data-value model is called the saturated model. Any other model can be compared to the saturated model with a G^2 value to measure the improvement in fit. This gives a "residual Deviance" that indicates how much better the saturated model predicts the data compared to a smaller (perhaps more explanatory) model.

$$G^2(m) = -2\log\left(\frac{l_m}{l_s}\right) = -2[\log(l_m) - \log(l_s)]$$
$$= -2[L_m - L_s] \quad \text{deviance of model } m$$

Note that in this statement we take advantage of the fact that the log of a ratio is equal to the difference of the log values. So to calculate the log of the ratio we can take the difference of the log-likelihoods. Now to calculate G^2 comparing model m and model $m - 1$ we can simply take the difference between deviance scores.

$$G^2(m|m-1) = -2[L_m - L_{m-1}] = -2[L_m - L_s] - [-2[L_{m-1} - L_s]]$$
$$= G^2(m) - G^2(m-1)$$

This is distributed on the χ^2 distribution with degrees of freedom equal to the difference between the residual degrees of freedom for the two models (the number of coefficients added to the model in going from $m - 1$ to m).

This has been a fairly long explanation of the central observation of this section. The G^2 that we get in logistic regression analysis of deviance is simply a different way to measure the same thing that we measured with χ^2. In the case of our example from the [ʃ]treets of Columbus, Ohio the question is: "Does emphasis play a role in the production of [str]"? With a Pearson's χ^2 analysis of the tabulated data we found a significant χ^2 value of 19.35 (with one degree of freedom). With logistic regression we found a significant G^2 value of 20.08 (again with one degree of freedom). This is supposed to illustrate that these two analyses are two ways of testing the same hypothesis.

Logistic regression has several advantages, some of which we will explore in the remaining sections of this chapter.

5.5.2 *More than one predictor*

One of the main advantages of logistic regression over Pearson's χ^2 is that we can fit complicated models to the data using logistic regression. As an example of this we will consider a set of four predictor variables and their interactions in the Durian [ʃtr] data. Recall that in addition to recording productions in emphatic and non-emphatic context, he collected data from an equal number of men and women, from people in three different age ranges, and classified his talkers according to the economic/social class of their customers. With logistic regression, as with analysis of variance, we can test all of these factors at once.

I want to emphasize that this analysis is possible not only because logistic regression is a great analysis tool, but also because Durian collected enough data to provide a relatively balanced model with about 10 observations in each cell of the model. This involved collecting data from 120 people. Less than this and he would have had to give up an experimental variable, like age or class, for lack of statistical power to examine the interactions among the factors. It is often necessary in sociolinguistics to study many fewer people because ethnographically careful data collection requires a substantial investment of the investigator's time for each subject in a research study. The tradeoff that we have to keep in mind in these cases is that there may not be enough data to permit investigation of more than one or two research variables, and particularly not the interaction of variables. This is too bad because interactions are often much more informative than main effects.

The interaction that we will be exploring in the [ʃtr] data is between age and gender. The conclusion is that young women are much more likely to use [ʃtr] than either young men or older women, i.e. that young women are leading a sound change in Columbus, Ohio. We'll look at two strategies for approaching this analysis.

The first analysis is exactly like the one shown above in Table 5.6, except here we specified a full model which includes 15 predictive factors – four main effects (age, gender, emphasis, and class) plus all of the possible interactions of these effects. As the bold print in Table 5.7 indicates, all four of the main effects were found to have a significant effect on the frequency of [ʃtr] production, while only one interaction seems to matter. That interaction is between age and gender.

Notice in Table 5.7 the statement at the top that the terms were added sequentially. What this means is that unlike analysis of variance, in logistic regression the order in which the factors are mentioned in our model statement (when invoking `glm()`) has an impact on the statistical test of the factors. In particular, if two predictive factors T1 and T2 are highly correlated with each other, if we enter T1 first then T2 will probably not show up as significant, because to test the effect of T2 the regression tests whether adding T2 to a model that already includes T1 is an improvement over the model with T1. When T2 is correlated with T1 then it provides very little improvement over a model that includes T1, and the nature of the model-fitting procedure never tests T2 alone without T1 already in the model. The situation is reversed if T2 is mentioned first in the list of predictor variables.

Table 5.7 Analysis of deviance table for a full model of the [ʃtr] data. Statistically reliable main effects and interactions are printed in bold face.

Model: binomial, link: logit
Response: str
Terms added sequentially (first to last)

		Df	Deviance	Resid. Df	Resid. Dev	P(>|Chi|)
	NULL			239	263.127	
Main effects	**age**	2	17.371	237	245.756	1.690e-04
	gender	1	9.019	236	236.737	0.003
	emphatic	1	22.537	235	214.200	2.062e-06
	class	2	21.481	233	192.719	2.165e-05
2-way	**age:gender**	2	8.187	231	184.532	0.017
	age:emphatic	2	0.151	229	184.381	0.927
	age:class	4	7.656	225	176.725	0.105
	gender:emphatic	1	1.463	224	175.262	0.226
	gender:class	2	3.542	222	171.719	0.170
	emphatic:class	2	1.528	220	170.191	0.466
3-way	age:gender:emphatic	2	4.960	218	165.231	0.084
	age:gender:class	4	5.356	214	159.876	0.253
	age:emphatic:class	4	3.333	210	156.543	0.504
	gender:emphatic:class	2	0.001	208	156.542	1.000
4-way	age:gender:emphatic:class	4	0.001	204	156.541	1.000

Notice also that interactions are always added into the analysis after the main effects or smaller interactions (in both the full model and in the stepwise procedure below). This is entirely appropriate because we want to test if there is any variance to account for by the interaction after removing variance due to the higher-level effects.

But to determine whether it would be better to use T1 or T2 to predict our data we might want to use a stepwise procedure that will test them independently in order to determine their best order in the model statement. We saw stepwise regression procedures earlier in Chapter 3 and here will use the `step()` function with logistic regression just as we did with linear regression.

As Table 5.8 shows, the stepwise procedure selected the main effects in a different order than I had entered them for the full model analysis in Table 5.7, but the results are unchanged – all four main effects, as well as the age by gender interaction, are selected as significant.

Table 5.8 Analysis of deviance table for the stepwise analysis of the [ʃtr] data.

	Df	Deviance	Resid. Df	Resid. Dev	P(>|Chi|)
NULL			239	263.127	
emphatic	1	20.083	238	243.044	7.416e-06
class	2	23.583	236	219.462	7.570e-06
age	2	16.153	234	203.308	3.107e-04
gender	1	10.589	233	192.719	0.001
age:gender	2	8.187	231	184.532	0.017

We've seen the effect of emphasis – namely that the rate of [ʃtr] is 35% in less emphatic context and drops to 12% in more careful speech. Class had a similarly dramatic influence on [ʃtr] rates with 37% for working class, 27% for lower middle class and only 8% for upper working class averaged across levels of all other factors. By the way, averaging across all other factors is justified by the lack of any interactions with

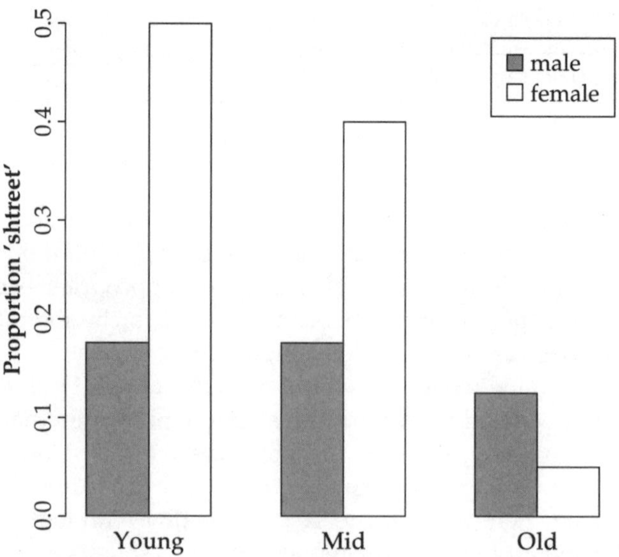

Figure 5.6 The age by gender interaction in Durian's [ʃtr] study. Data for male talkers is shaded gray, while the bars showing data for female talkers are white.

other factors in the logistic regression. Younger speakers had a greater proportion of [ʃtr] than did older speakers (34% versus 9%). Similarly, women were more likely to use [ʃtr] than were men (32% versus 16%). However, the age by gender interaction indicates that it is misleading to average over gender when we evaluate the age effect, or to average over age when we evaluate the gender effect. Figure 5.6, which shows the age by gender interaction, illustrates why this is so. Men had a relatively constant rate of [ʃtr] production regardless of age, while the young and middle age women had much higher rates of [ʃtr] than did the older women. Thus, the age effect is confined primarily to women and the gender effect is confined primarily to the young and mid aged speakers.

R note. The first analysis was called the "full" analysis, because I included all four factors and all of their their interactions. The order in which the factors are listed in the model statement – here with age first and class last – matters in the statistical test.

```
anova(glm(str~age*gender*emphatic*class, family=binomial,
    data=dd), test = "Chisq")
```

The stepwise logistic regression was performed with this statement:

```
dd.glm <- step(glm(str~1, family=binomial, data=dd),
    str ~ age * gender * class * emphatic)
```

Table 5.9 can then be produded by `anova(dd.glm,test="Chisq")`. The stepwise procedure gives you a blow-by-blow printout as it builds up the model from the null model to the model that contains only those factors that are determined to be statistically reliable.

Figure 5.6 was produced with the `barplot()` command, which requires that the input be a matrix. I constructed the matrix from a vector of the proportion [ʃtr] responses.

```
v <- c(7,7,5,20,16,2)/40
m <- matrix(v,nrow=2,byrow=T)
barplot(m,beside=T,names.arg=c("young","mid","old"),
    legend=c("male","female"),col=c("gray","white"),
    ylab="Proportion 'shtreet'")
```

5.6 Logistic Regression as Regression: An Ordinal Effect – Age

Just briefly here it makes sense to consider how an ordinal effect can be treated in a regression model – this applies both to the least squares models that we discussed in previous chapters and to the maximum likelihood models that we are considering in this chapter. For instance, in Dodsworth's /l/ vocalization data set (section 5.1) we have a factor "age" that takes one of four levels – teens, twenties, forties, or fifties. The levels of this factor are obviously ordered from youngest to oldest, so it would make sense to treat age as an ordinal variable. This is done by using "polynomial" coding to convert the levels of the age factor into a numeric code. The three variables are used to encode ordered trends as age relates to /l/ vocalization. For example, if /l/ vocalization occurs more frequently in the speech of older talkers than in younger talkers, we would expect the linear encoding of age to be significant, meaning that as age increases /l/ vocalization increases just as the linear coefficient values increase linearly from –0.67 to 0.67. The encoding scheme for age from Table 5.9 is shown also in Figure 5.7.

Just as with other coding schemes (treatment coding and effects coding) there are three variables in the regression formula for this four-level factor – one variable fewer than the number of levels. However in this case the first variable encodes a linear increase over the four levels, the second factor encodes the possibility of a dip or bulge in the middle of the age range, while the third factor encodes the more complicated possibility that /l/ vocalization "zigzags" among the age levels.

Now, when we conduct the logistic regression with age as an ordinal factor, the regression coefficient (Table 5.10) for the cubic ordered pattern `age.C` is larger than either the linear or the quadratic

Table 5.9 Polynomical coding of an ordinal factor.

	Linear	**Quadratic**	**Cubic**
Teens	–0.67	0.5	–0.22
Twenties	–0.22	–0.5	0.67
Forties	0.22	–0.5	–0.67
Fifties	0.67	0.5	0.22

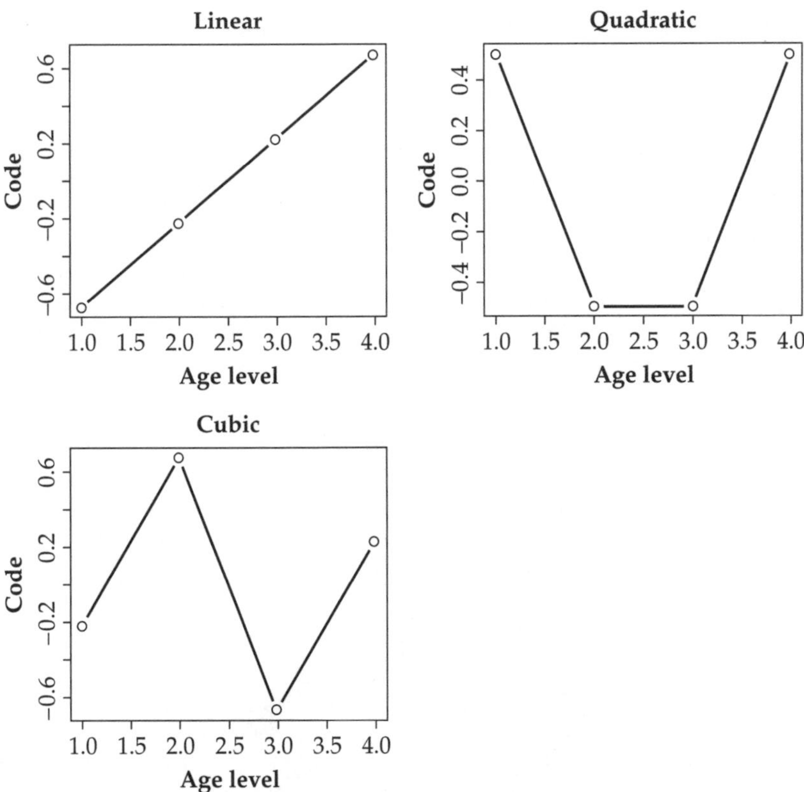

Figure 5.7 The polynomial encoding scheme for the different levels of "age" – "teens" (1.0 on the x-axis), "twenties" (2.0 on the x-axis), etc. The linear, quadratic, and cubic encoding schemes are shown.

coefficients, and the cubic coefficient is also reliably different from zero. This means that the pattern of /l/ vocalization as a function of the age of the talker was more like the "zigzag" pattern shown by the cubic encoding scheme in Figure 5.7. That this is in fact the pattern of of /l/ vocalization is shown in the graph of proportion of /l/ vocalization in Figure 5.8.

So, it is possible, by treating an ordinal factor as ordinal, to determine whether the relationship between that factor and the predicted variable is basically linear, or if there are quadratic, or cubic powers (or higher powers, if more levels are considered). The overall independence of /l/ vocalization from age is tested in exactly the same way whether we treat age as ordinal or as nominal, and the success of the

Table 5.10 Regression coefficients from a logistic regression analysis of /l/ vocalization. This analysis focused on the ordinal effect of age.

	Coefficients:			
	Estimate	**Std. Error**	**z value**	**Pr (>|z|)**
(Intercept)	0.25776	0.09905	2.602	0.00926**
age.L	−0.27771	0.17994	−1.543	0.12275
age.Q	−0.12110	0.19810	−0.611	0.54099
age.C	−0.86705	0.21473	4.038	5.39e-05***

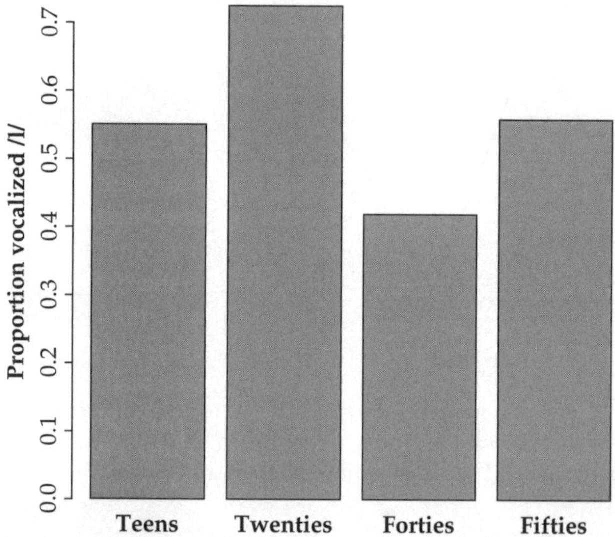

Figure 5.8 Proportion of /l/ vocalization for each of four different age groups. The pattern here is most like the "cubic" ordinal effect.

regression model does not depend on this – effects coding of age, and ordinal coding of age captures exactly the same amount of variation. However, being able to specify that a factor is ordinal lets us determine the type of trend that relates this ordered factor to the response variable. I guess in most situations you would hope for something pretty simple like a linear or quadratic trend. This cubic trend requires a special kind of theory to explain it.

R note. I mentioned earlier that I recoded Dodsworth's data a little for this chapter. To encode the fact that age is an ordinal variable I added "`ordered = T`" to the `factor()` statement that I had earlier used to recode "age" into "newage." Additionally, you can use `ordered()` to indicate that an existing factor should be treated as an ordered factor – this using the `levels` option to list the factor levels in order.

```
rd$newage <- factor(rd$age,levels=c(1,2,4,5), labels=
    c("teens", "twenties", "forties", "fifties"), ordered = T)
rd$newage <- ordered(rd$newage, levels = c("teens",
    "twenties", "forties", "fifties"))
```

Table 5.9 is the output from `contrasts(rd$newage)`, and table 5.8 was produced by the following command:

```
> summary(glm(lvoc ~ newage, data=rd, family=binomial))
```

For example, when we consider whether age influences /l/ vocalization the analysis of deviance table from the logistic regression analysis shows that the null model has a deviance, or G^2, value of 719.03. This is $G^2(m-1)$. When we add age as a predictor variable the deviance of this new model m is 696.47. This is $G^2(m)$. The difference between these two gives the G^2 value that we use in testing the hypothesis that age influences /l/ vocalization. This difference value $G^2(m|m-1)$ is 22.56, which on the χ^2 distribution with 3 degrees of freedom is a large enough value that is unlikely to have occured by chance. We conclude that age is an important predictor of /l/ vocalization. One thing to recall is that the χ^2 value testing the independence of /l/ vocalization and age was also 22. In other words these are two ways of calculating the same thing.

```
Analysis of Deviance Table
        Df  Deviance  Resid. Df  Resid. Dev
NULL                        530      719.03
newage   3     22.56        527      696.47
```

This illustrates the similarity between G^2 and χ^2 in the case where a single factor is being tested. Now if you think about it a bit you may realize that the order in which you add factors to a model will have an impact on the G^2 value that you find for each factor in the model. This is because G^2 for a particular factor is not being tested against an overall residual error variance but against the likelihood of a model that differs only by not having the factor in the model.

Consider, for example, a two-factor model that has age and conscious as factors for /l/ vocalization. When we add age first the deviance is as we found in the one-factor model, but when we add age second the G^2 value drops to 13.68. This is still significant but highlights the importance of the order in which the factors are added to a model.

```
Analysis of Deviance Table
          Df  Deviance  Resid. Df  Resid. Dev
NULL                          530      719.03
newage     3     22.56        527      696.47
conscious  3      9.41        524      687.06

Analysis of Deviance Table
          Df  Deviance  Resid. Df  Resid. Dev
NULL                          530      719.03
conscious  3     18.29        527      700.74
newage     3     13.68        524      687.06
```

There are a couple of ways that you could choose to order factors in a model. Cohen and Cohen (1983) recommend adding prior factors first. That would mean putting factors that describe unchanging aspects of the situation before adding factors that describe aspects that might change from observation to observation. So factors that describe people come first and factors that describe the words they say come last. However, in this case both age and social consciousness describe the people under study.

A second approach is to add factors according to their "importance," in a stepwise model selection procedure. We've seen this before in Chapter 3.

5.7 Varbrul/R Comparison

Varbrul is an implementation of logistic regression that is used by many sociolinguists (Cedergren & Sankoff, 1974; Sankoff, 1978, 1988). This implementation of logistic regression has been very important in the history of sociolinguistics because it conveniently made logistic regression available to researchers before the standard statistical packages included logistic regression. At this point Varbrul is a bit of a "legacy" program because most major statistical packages now do provide logistic regression. There are several reasons to use a general purpose software package rather than a specialized implementation like Varbrul. For instance, data handling, graphics, and model specification are additionally supplied in the general purpose package, as are other data analysis techniques (such as repeated measures logistic regression, which will be discussed in Chapter 7).

One hurdle, though, in using a general purpose statistics package is that the analytic procedures (such as stepwise regression) are quite flexible, presenting a wide range of possible analysis strategies. This can be confusing at times. Unfortunately I will not be able to explore the range of analysis strategies that one might employ using the R `glm()` function. We have seen that `step()` implements a stepwise regression strategy that is familiar to Varbrul users. We will also see a training/testing strategy in Chapter 7, which should be seriously considered for sociolinguistic data analysis.

Another hurdle we face with a general purpose software package is that one doesn't know which of the sometimes many values reported in summary and print statements should be used. In this section we will compare a Varbrul analysis of the Durian str/ʃtr data to a logistic regression in R. My aim here is to show the interested reader how to compute the familiar Varbrul results table.

David Durian provided a Varbrul analysis of his data which is shown here as Table 5.11.

R note. In conducting the analyses described in this section I used a couple of helpful functions that are described in more detail in this note.

We start the R analysis with the R commands to read in the data and produce a logistic regression analysis of these data.

```
> dd<-read.delim("DDRASSTR.txt")
> dd.glm <- glm(str~emphatic+class,data=dd,family=binomial)
```

In preliminary analyses I noticed that because of the order of the levels "str" and "shtr" in the description of the data, my analyses were treating "str" as a "success" or an "application" of the

Table 5.11 Results from a Varbrul analysis of the Durian str/ʃtr data.

Log Likelibood =86.816
Significance .001
Input 0.102
Chi-square Cell .7579

Group	Factor	Weight	App/Total	Input & Weight
1: Gender	M	0.334	0.016	0.05
	W	0.666	0.032	0.18
2: Environment	Less Emphatic	0.731	0.36	0.24
	More Emphatic	0.269	0.12	0.04
3: Age	15-55*	0.663	0.31	0.18
	55-70	0.206	0.09	0.03
4: Region	Polaris/Enston*	0.562	0.27	0.13
	City Center	0.376	0.16	0.06
5: Social Class	MWC-LWC	0.863	0.47	0.42
	LWC-MWC	0.711	0.26	0.22
	UWC-LMC	0.740	0.367	0.24
	LMC-MMC	0.584	0.22	0.14
	UMC-UC	0.061	0.02	0.01

process. I wanted to have the opposite be true, that "shtr" be the focus of the investigation. So I used `relevel()` to stipulate that "str" is the default value of response.

```
> dd$response <- relevel(dd$response,"str")
```

I also found, in presenting the results in this section, that it was useful to be able to know how the different factor coding schemes work. For this, the `contrasts()` is invaluable. The output from `contrasts()` shows the mapping between nominal variables, listed in rows, and the numerical codes used in the regression. For example, the columns below correspond to "classUMC" and "classWC" in the regression formula.

```
> contrasts(class)
      UMC  WC
LMC     0   0
UMC     1   0
WC      0   1
```

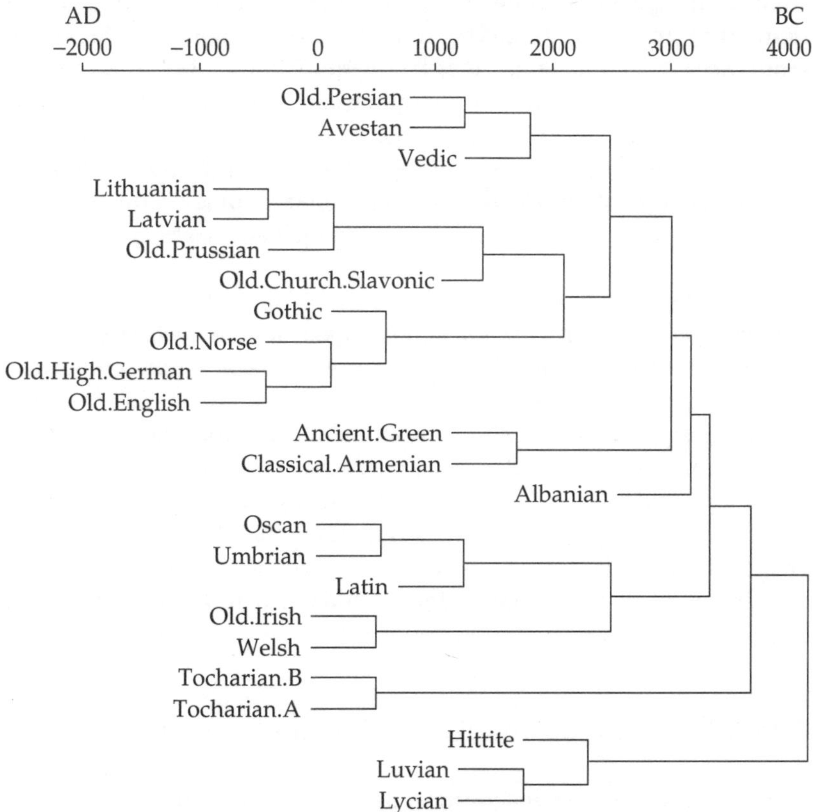

Figure 6.1 A phylogenetic tree of Indo-European proposed by Nakhleh, Ringe, and Warnow (2005).

6.1 Cladistics: Where Linguistics and Evolutionary Biology Meet

The aims of historical linguistics are to trace the history of languages and offer explanations of language change. Central to this research is the observation that languages can be grouped into families on the basis of their shared history – so that two distinct languages in the present (e.g. French and Italian) can be grouped together in a family tree because they are both descendants of Latin, and thus "genetically" related, arising from the same source.

This conception of language history assumes (1) that it is possible to identify groups of languages that are related by descent to a common ancestor language, (2) that languages change over time, and (3) that a language will split into daughter languages when the speakers of the language split into different geographically or culturally separated communities. Analogs of these three assumptions also underlie the construction of family trees in evolutionary biology. Consequently, historical linguists and evolutionary biologists have been exploring methods of quantitative analysis that they call "cladistics" (Gk. κλαδοσ – "branch").

From the point of view of general quantitative methods in data analysis, cladistics is interesting because in these studies biologists and linguists have, to some extent, made simultaneous independent discoveries, arriving at data analysis techniques that have also been explored in other areas of science (and are available in R). However, the unique set of constraints on biological and linguistic evolution has resulted in unique analysis strategies. Thus, we will see in this chapter that special purpose software is being used for state-of-the-art cladistic analysis and although the functionality of this software could in principle be replicated in R, so far it hasn't been.

6.2 Clustering on the Basis of Shared Vocabulary

One quantitative approach to judging historical relatedness was reported by Dyen, Kruskal, and Black (1992). They took the number of shared cognates in a list of 200 cross-linguistically common words (Swadesh 1952) as a measure of overall similarity among 84 Indo-European languages and then used a cluster analysis to produce a phylogenetic tree of Indo-European. For example, a portion of the Dyen et al. data set is shown in Table 6.1. There are four cognate sets for words meaning "animal" among the 19 languages listed here – I numbered them 1 through 4. The English word *animal* is listed as "B" for borrowed because this word did not come into modern English by descent from Old English, instead it was borrowed from French after the Norman invasion of England.

With this list of words we can calculate the similarity of Spanish, Portuguese, French, and Italian as 100% because all five of the words are cognates with each other in these languages. The Romance languages share no cognates (in this set of only five words) with Hindi, one with class seems to be more sensible or valuable in analyzing the data (if such a determination can be made).

```
dd.glm.class <- glm(str~age*gender*class*emphatic,
    family=binomial, data=dd)
dd.glm.bank <- glm(str~age*gender*bank*emphatic,
    family=binomial, data=dd)
```

6 Historical Linguistics

Though there are many opportunities to use quantitative methods in historical linguistics, this chapter will focus on how historical linguists take linguistic data and produce tree diagrams showing the historical "family" relationships among languages. For example, Figure 6.1 shows a phylogenetic tree of Indo-European languages (after figure 6 of Nakhleh, Ringe, & Warnow, 2005). This tree embodies many assertions about the history of these languages. For example, the lines connecting Old Persian and Avestan assert that these two languages share a common ancestor language and that earlier proto-Persian/Avestan split in about 1200 BC. As another example, consider the top of the tree. Here the assertion is that proto Indo-European, the hypothesized common ancestor of all of these languages, split in 4000 BC in two languages – one that would eventually develop into Hittite, Luvian and Lycian, and another ancient language that was the progenitor of Latin, Vedic, Greek and all of the other Indo-European languages in this sample. The existence of historical proto-languages is thus asserted by the presence of lines connecting languages or groups of languages to each other, and the relative height of the connections between branches shows how tightly the languages bind to each other and perhaps the historical depth of their connection (though placing dates on proto-languages is generally not possible without external historical documentation).

```
Coefficients:
               Estimate Std.  Error   z value  Pr(>|z|)
(Intercept)     -2.3724 0.3682  -6.443  1.17e-10    ***
gender1         -0.6937 0.2017  -3.439  0.000585    ***
emphatic1        1.0044 0.2110   4.760  1.94e-06    ***
age1             1.0168 0.2656   3.829  0.000129    ***
Mall1           -0.3778 0.2426  -1.557  0.119370
bank1            0.7714 0.4397   1.754  0.079353
bank2            0.0633 0.3584   0.177  0.859800
bank3            0.6262 0.4830   1.296  0.194813
bank4           -3.0241 0.8539  -3.542  0.000398    ***
```

Now to calculate the weights we can take the inverse logits of the logistic regression coefficients. For example, the weights for gender in the Varbrul analysis were 0.33 for men and 0.66 for women. We see from the R analysis that the contrast for gender `contrasts(dd$gender)` has men coded as 1 and women coded as –1. So, taking the inverse logit of the gender coefficient times the gender codes gives the same values that are in the Varbrul output.

```
inv.logit(-.6937 * 1) = 0.3332105    # for men
inv.logit(-.6937 * -1) = 0.6667895   # for women
```

Similarly, the Varbrul weights for more and less emphatic productions are given by noting (from `contrasts(dd$emphatic)`) that less emphatic was coded with 1 and more emphatic was coded with –1. The inverse logit of the coefficient gives the Varbrul weights.

```
inv.logit(1.004 * 1) = 0.7318443    # less emphatic
inv.logit(1.004 * -1) = 0.2681557   # more emphatic
```

The App/Total column in the Varbrul output is the actual probability of "shtr" in the dataset. In R we compute this from the contingency table. For example, the proportion of utterances with "shtr" in speech produced by men was 19 out of 120 total observations, for a proportion of 0.158. This is the value shown in the App/Total for men in the Varbrul printout.

```
> table(dd$str,dd$gender)
        m   w
str   101  82
shtr   19  38
```

Finally, the Input & Weight column is the predicted proportion of "shtr" given by the model parameters. In this case we find the same degree of mismatch between predicted and actual that was found in Varbrul. The predicted proportion of "shtr" productions is the inverse logit of the intercept plus the factor coefficient.

```
inv.logit(-2.3724 - 0.6937) = 0.04452746  # for men
inv.logit(-2.3724 + 0.6937) = 0.1572677   # for women
```

The logistic regression model is predicting that men will produce "shtr" 4% of the time, when actually they say "shtr" in almost 16% of their utterances.

EXERCISES

1 Calculate χ^2 to test the hypothesis that one of your classes has an equal number of men and women.
2 In section 5.5.1, I said that the χ^2 for the data in Table 5.5 (testing whether emphasis influences [ʃtr] production) was 19.35. Table 5.6 also shows that the G^2 value from a logistic regression of these data is 20.08. Compute these two numbers using the formulas in section 5.5.1.
3 Using "Robins_data.txt" produce a contingency table of the variables lvoc (which you will have to create as in the R-note above) and gender. Show how to calculate the χ^2 to test whether /l/ vocalization depends on the gender of the talker – this means that you produce a table like Table 5.1. Then check your answer with `summary(table(lvoc,gender))`.
4 Two variables in the DDRASSTR.txt data set code economic class. One is called "class" and has three levels (working class, lower middle class, and upper middle class). The other is called "bank" and has five levels (middle and upper working class, and three levels of middle class). Compare logistic regression models that include one or the other of these economic class variables evaluating their overall significance and the significance of their interactions with other predictor variables. Also examine the model coefficients that correspond to different levels of these factors. Last, but not least, look at the data! Examine the actual probability of "shtr" as a function of economic class and other variables. Your goal in all of this activity is to decide which of the two methods of encoding economic

Similarly, when the coding scheme is `contr.sum`, `contrasts()` shows how the three levels of "class" will be coded. The first column shows the coding scheme for the class1 variable in the regression formula, and the second column shows the coding for the class2 variable.

```
> contrasts(class)
     [,1] [,2]
LMC     1    0
UMC     0    1
WC     -1   -1
```

There are two different ways to specify that you want "sum" coding instead of "treatment" coding. One is to add a list of contrasts to the `glm` command. In the list you name the contrast coding scheme for each variable.

```
> dd.glm <- glm(str~emphatic+class, data=dd,
    family=binomial, contrasts=list(emphatic="contr.sum",
    class="contr.sum"))
```

An alternative method is to change the global options used in R. There are two default contrasts specifications in R. The first indicates how nominal variables will be treated and the second indicates how ordinal variables will be treated. So, using `options()` we can specify that we want all nominal variables to be coded using the "contr.sum" coding scheme.

```
> options(contrasts = c("contr.sum","contr.poly"))
```

Finally, to find the inverse of the logit function (to translate from coefficients in the logistic model to predicted probabilities) you can use the `inv.logit()` function. Naturally enough there is also a `logit()` function to calculate the log odds of a probability.

```
> library(gtools) # this library has the inv.logit() and
    logit() functions
> inv.logit(0.1889)
[1] 0.54708
```

Two factors here were compressed into two levels from three. Here's how I did that in R.

```
> summary(dd$age)
mid  old  young
 80   80     80
> levels(dd$age) <- c("15-55","55-70","15-55")

> summary(dd$Mall)
CityCenter  Easton  Polaris
        79      80       81
> levels(dd$Mall) <- c("CityCenter","EastonPolaris",
"EastonPolaris")
```

The logistic regression is then:

```
> dd.glm <- glm(str~gender+emphatic+age+Mall+bank,
family=binomial, data=dd)
> anova(dd.glm,test="Chisq")
Analysis of Deviance Table

Model: binomial, link: logit

Response: str

Terms added sequentially (first to last)

         Df  Deviance  Resid. Df  Resid. Dev  P(>|Chi|)
NULL                         239     263.127
gender    1     8.432        238     254.695      0.004
emphatic  1    20.837        237     233.858  5.001e-06
age       1    19.102        236     214.755  1.239e-05
Mall      1     5.171        235     209.584      0.023
bank      4    38.469        231     171.115  8.965e-08
```

Recall that Deviance is –2[L] where L is the log-likelihood of the current model versus the saturated model. So, the log-likelihood of the final model in the list (the one that has all of the terms added is:

```
> 171.115/-2
[1] -85.5575
```

This corresponds to the Varbrul overall log-likelihood which is reported as −86.8 for this analysis (the R results are close but not exactly identical to the Varbrul output – perhaps a difference in the search algorithm being used or in the details of the data?).

From the table of coefficients (`summary(dd.glm)`) we can calculate the Varbrul weights.

R note. DKB's percent cognates data set is in "IE-perc84.txt." To produce the cluster analysis presented in this section I used the following R commands.

Read it as a matrix.

```
> m <- read.table("IE-perc84.txt")
```

This is a matrix of similarity measures, and the `hclust()` algorithm wants to have distance measures. Also I wanted to present the data in percentages, while the DKB table is in 1/10 of a percent, so I converted the values by applying a function to the table that subtracts the percent cognates values in the table from 1,000 and divides by 10. The `c(1,2)` says to apply this to both the rows and columns of the table. `as.dist()` converts the matrix into a distance matrix object which is expected by `hclust()`.

```
> subtr <- function(x) c((1000-x)/10)
> d <- as.dist(apply(m[1:84],c(1,2),subtr))
```

Now for a pretty printout we add names to the distance matrix. This was stored as column 85 of the input matrix in IE-perc84.txt.

```
> names(d) <- m$V85
```

Finally, we use average linkage in the clustering algorithm and plot the resulting object, which because it is a cluster object plots as a hierarchical tree.

```
> clus <- hclust(d,"ave")
> plot(clus)
```

6.3 Cladistic Analysis: Combining Character-Based Subtrees

An important alternative to cluster analysis for the determination of historical family trees comes to linguistics from evolutionary biology. Biologists have worked out a set of methods to reconstruct family trees of species on the basis of shared inherited traits and this "cladistic" analysis is now also being used in historical linguistics. In this section I will explain the cladistic approach and the assumptions that it involves, and then give a specific example using a portion of the Dyen et al. (1992) data set. The main points of this section are that cladistics is not hard to understand and the software is easy to download and use.

> **R note**. That's right, here finally we have found something that isn't implemented yet in R. However, the "ape" library does have some utility functions that are evidently useful to evolutionary biologists, and I guess this is a good time to mention that there are hundreds of contributed packages that contain libraries of useful R functions. Well, some are more useful than others and the R development team includes the most useful and bug-free in the standard distribution of R. The fact that some evolutionary biologists have been adding functions to a specialized phylogenetic analysis package suggests that in the not too distant future you will be able to peform cladistic analysis in R.

Let's say that when languages share a cognate word they share a heritable "character." In biology, characters may be things like "has legs" or "is warm blooded." In linguistics we may consider characters that are based on the lexicon such as "the word for 'animal' decends from a proto form [dyr]," but may also include things like "has the RUKI rule", or "underwent Grimm's law." I won't say much about how one determines the characters that go into the cladistic method, except to say that, as with all quantitative methods, the data that go into the analysis determine its success. Phylogenetic trees produced by computer programs can be just as wrong as trees produced by hand; it depends on the quality of the data. I'll be illustrating this principle further in this section, when I show you "family trees" of Indo-European that are obviously wrong. One key thing to avoid in constructing a data set for cladistic analysis is to avoid using language "characters" that could easily develop independently in different languages. For example, basic clausal word order is probably not a good character to use in grouping languages because SOV languages have developed into SVO independently in different language families. Cognate words are good because analysis of sound change can identify words that are similar in two languages because of common descent, clearly indicating a historical genetic relation between the languages.

Table 6.5 Collapsing Table 6.4 by one row and one column (using single linkage).

	Irish A	Irish B	Cluster 2	Cluster 1
Irish A				
Irish B	82.6			
Cluster 2	*34.4*	**36.0**		
Cluster 1	*31.9*	**33.5**	64.1	

In Table 6.4, the most similar items are Breton List and Cluster 1, so we add Breton List to Cluster 1 and collapse their rows keeping the bold-face highest similarities and deleting the italicized lowest similarities. The result is in Table 6.5. Irish A and B will be joined together into a third cluster because they have the highest similarity, and then Cluster 1 and Cluster 2 will be joined on the basis of the 64% cognation between Welsh N and Breton List, and finally Cluster 3 (the Irish varieties) will be joined to the Breton/Welsh varieties on the basis of the 36% cognatives between Irish B and Welsh C.

The two other most commonly used hierarchical clustering methods are almost identical to this one, except that in "complete linkage" we keep the italicized similarities instead of the bold-faced ones, and in "average linkage" we keep the average of the italicized and bold-face similarities. The two extreme methods (single linkage and complete linkage) ignore either the lower or higher similarities and tend to be a little less stable than average linkage, so in the analyses presented below I used average linkage. Dyen et al. also indicated that, in their method of clustering, average linkage was used. For more details about cluster analysis, measures of similarity, and very helpful practical suggestions, see Aldendorfer and Blashfield (1984).

As seen in Figure 6.3, cluster analysis of the DKB cognates data produces a family tree that is very sensible from a historical perspective. All of the major subfamilies of Indo-European are found (when representatives were available in the data set) and the further subgroupings are interesting and possibly correct. Nakhleh, Warnow et al. (2005), however, compared single linkage clustering with the cladistic methods that I will discuss in the next section and concluded single linkage was "clearly inferior."

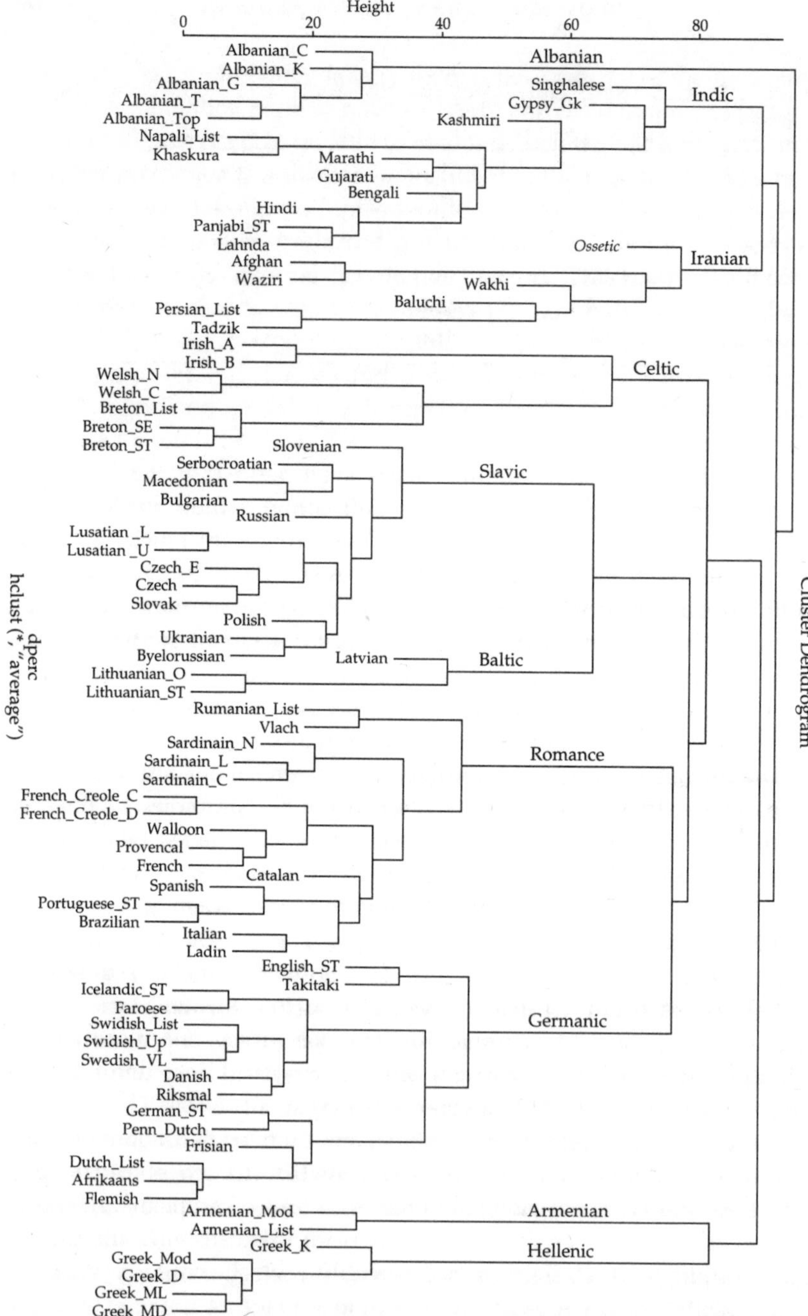

Figure 6.3 The full cluster solution for the DKB percent cognates data, plotted as a "dendrogram."

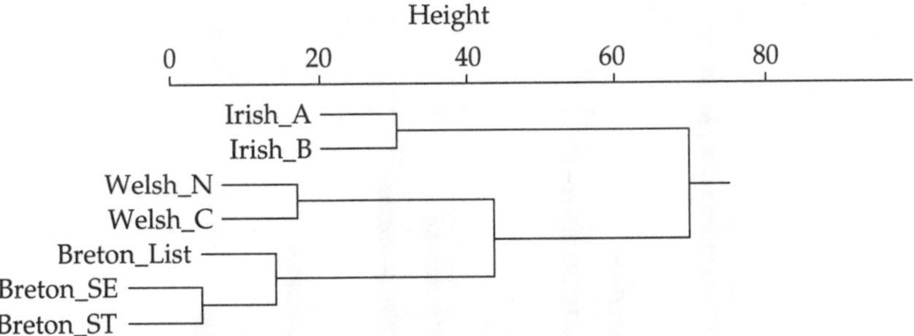

Figure 6.2 Results of hierarchical clustering of the data in Table 6.2. Height, measured at nodes where clusters join each other, is 100 minus the percentage of cognates, so that the data reflect distance rather than similarity, and the linkage was done by averaging.

was calcuated in terms of the percent cognates in their 200 words. This set of similarity measures provides a nice way to demonstrate three key methods of clustering languages into a family tree. The tree given by hierarchical clustering using the "average linkage" model is shown in Figure 6.2.

Perhaps the simplest hierarchical clustering algorithm is called single linkage. The idea is to join items into clusters on the basis of the similarity of a to-be-added item and the most similar member of the cluster. There are three steps:

Single linkage
1 Find two most similar items.
2 Link them into a cluster and collapse the rows and columns for the two items. If one is in an existing cluster add the new item into that cluster.
3 Repeat steps (1) and (2) until all items belong to a cluster.

So, for example, in Table 6.2 Breton SE and Breton ST are the most similar two languages because they have the highest percentage of cognates (94.9%). So we join them into a cluster and measure the similarity of that cluster with the remaining languages in terms of the highest similarity between either Breton SE and Breton ST. This means that we can keep the percent cognate values shown in bold face in Table 6.2 and remove the values shown in italics. Now we have

Table 6.3 Collapsing Table 6.2 by one row and one column (using single linkage).

	Irish A	Irish B	Welsh N	Welsh C	Breton List	Cluster 1
Irish A						
Irish B	82.6					
Welsh N	**34.4**	*35.5*				
Welsh C	*34.2*	**36.0**	93.9			
Breton List	31.1	33.5	**63.9**	*61.5*		
Cluster 1	31.9	32.8	**64.1**	*61.7*	92.9	

reduced the size of the similarity matrix by one row and one column (Table 6.3). This single linkage method looks for only one good match between a member of the cluster and the other items to be clustered. It could have happened that Breton SE is very similar to Breton List, while Breton ST is not similar to Breton List at all. In single linkage we ignore the mismatch between Breton ST and Breton List and base our decision about whether or not to add Breton List to Cluster 1 on the basis of the similarity of Breton SE and Breton List. As we will see, other clustering methods do not ignore mismatches. Now, we return to step (1) and search for the two most similar items in the matrix. This time Welsh N and Welsh C are most similar, and following the single linkage rule for collapsing rows and columns we keep the bold face items and delete the italicized similarity measures. This gives us Table 6.4.

Table 6.4 Collapsing Table 6.3 by one row and one column (using single linkage).

	Irish A	Irish B	Cluster 2	Breton List	Cluster 1
Irish A					
Irish B	82.6				
Cluster 2	34.4	36.0			
Breton List	*31.1*	**33.5**	*63.9*		
Cluster 1	**31.9**	*32.8*	**64.1**	92.9	

Table 6.1 Patterns of cognation among some of the languages in the Dyen et al. data set for 5 of the 200 meanings listed in that set.

	"animal"		"bark (of a tree)"		"bird"		"black"		"to breathe"	
Dutch	dier	1	schors	3	vogel	4	zwart	1	ademen	2
Danish	dyr	1	bark	1	fugl	4	sort	1	aande	5
Swedish	djur	1	bark	1	fagel	4	svart	1	andas	5
German	tier	1	rinde	2	vogel	4	schwarz	1	atmen	2
English	animal	B	bark	1	bird	B	black	6	to breathe	B
Slovenian	zver	2	kora	3	ptica	5	crn	3	dihati	1
Russian	zver	2	kora	3	ptica	5	cernyj	3	dysat	1
Polish	zwierze	2	kora	3	ptak	5	czarny	3	oddychac	1
Czech	zvire	2	kura	3	ptak	5	cerny	3	dychati	1
Greek Mod	zoo	2	fludha	6	pouli	1	mauros	7	anapneo	3
Kashmiri	janawar	3	del	B	pankhi	3	kala	2	shah hyonu	4
Gujarati	jenawer	3	chal	4	penkhi	3	kalu	2	swaslewo	4
Marathi	jenaver	3	sal	4	peksi	3	kala	2	svas ghene	4
Hindi	janver	3	chal	4	peksi	3	kala	2	sas lena	4
Waziri	dzanawar	3	patikai	5	marghai	6	tor	5	saya	4
Portuguese	animal	4	cortica	3	ave	2	negro	4	respirar	6
Spanish	animal	4	corteza	3	ave	2	negro	4	respirar	6
Italian	animale	4	scorza	3	uccello	2	nero	4	respirare	6
French	animal	4	ecorce	3	oiseau	2	noir	4	respirer	6

Russian, and none with German. Dyen et al. (1992) counted the number of cognate words between languages in this way to estimate the phylogenetic relatedness of the 84 Indo-European languages. That is to say, they collected a list of 200 words from each of 84 languages and for each word judged the cognate sets as I have illustrated for a small subset of only five words in Table 6.1.

I will now use a small portion of the Dyen et al. (DKB) database to illustrate how one goes about cluster analysis. We'll do this by hand for this small example and then see how to perform cluster analysis in R.

Before turning to this example, though, I want to make a pitch for using general purpose statistical software rather than discipline-specific software. Hierarchical clustering is a well-known procedure in statistics, though in evolutionary biology different names are given to the same procedures. For example, I think that the "single linkage" method described in this section is the same as the method called Unweighted Pair Group Method of Arithmetic averages (UPGMA) in the evolutionary biology literature, while the "average linkage" method is the method called by the biologists the Weighted Pair Group Method of Arithmetic averages (WPGMA). My preference is to use the more generally accepted terms (as with "logistic regression" instead of "Varbrul" in Chapter 5) so that our research is more closely tied with the state of the art in statistics and other sciences, and so that statistics manuals won't seem so disconnected from what we do in linguistic research. For example, identifying UPGMA and WPGMA with the single linkage and average linkage methods of hierarchical clustering opens the way to using general purpose statistical software like R in historical linguistics. This has many advantages including that (1) data entry and management are much easier and more convenient, (2) the general purpose software is less brittle with a wider base of users working out the kinks, (3) linguists use the same tools as other scientists, enhancing interdisciplinary possibilities, and (4) alternative data analysis methods may be suggested. On this last point I'm thinking, for example, of Ward's method of clustering, or the complete linkage approach. These clustering methods share features of single and average linkage and have not yet found their way into the biologist's toolbox (perhaps for good reason, perhaps not).

Now back to the example of cluster analysis. Table 6.2 shows a small portion of the DKB Celtic speech varieties "relatedness" matrix which

Table 6.2 Percent cognate words among seven Celtic speech varieties (Dyen et al. 1992).

	Irish A	**Irish B**	**Welsh N**	**Welsh C**	**Breton List**	**Breton SE**	**Breton ST**
Irish A							
Irish B	82.6						
Welsh N	34.4	35.5					
Welsh C	34.2	36.0	93.9				
Breton List	31.1	33.5	63.9	61.5			
Breton SE	*30.9*	*32.1*	*62.9*	*61.0*	*88.8*		
Breton ST	**31.9**	**32.8**	**64.1**	**61.7**	**92.9**	94.9	

Phylip note. In this section I used programs in the Phylogeny Inference Package (Phylip) by Joseph Felsenstein (see http://evolution.gs.washington.edu/phylip.html to download it). I stored the data set that was shown in Table 6.5 in a file called "dyen_subset_coded.txt" and used that as input to the `pars` program. `pars` uses the Wagner parsimony method to find maximum parsimony phylogenetic trees. I used the "J" option to randomize the input order of the data differently for different runs so that a range of possible trees would be generated. The program saves all of the trees (up to 100 by default) that are tied for best. The output of `pars` is then fed into the program `consense` to compute one tree that captures most of the structure that is shared by the trees found by `pars`. Finally, the `retree` program is used to add a root to the consensus tree and to adjust the orientation of the leaves of the tree so that it looks good. Finally, not shown here, there is a program to draw a nice picture using the tree file created by `retree`.

In general, you must interact with these programs in a rather clunky text interface. The problem with this is not that it is a text interface, but that you can't save a set of commands for later reference or reuse. You basically have to remember what you did and go through the entire procedure again next time. Also, all input files, such as dyen_subset_coded.txt, must be copied into the phylip folder and output files are automatically written in that folder. Here are what the interfaces of each of these programs look like.

------------------- Interacting with the `pars` program ------------------

```
Pars: can't find input file "infile"
Please enter a new file name> dyen_subset_coded.txt

Pars: the file "outfile" that you wanted to
  use as output file already exists.
  Do you want to Replace it, Append to it,
  write to a new File, or Quit?
  (please type R, A, F, or Q)
r

Discrete character parsimony algorithm, version 3.65
```

```
Setting for this run:
U                 Search for best tree?  Yes
S                        Search option?  More thorough search
V              Number of trees to save?  100
J   Randomize input order of species?  No. Use input order
O                       Outgroup root?  No, use as outgroup species 1
T             Use Threshold parsimony?  No, use ordinary parsimony
W                     Sites weighted?  No
M          Analyze multiple data sets?  No
I           Input species interleaved?  Yes
0  Terminal type (IBM PC, ANSI, none)?  (none)
1    Print out the data at start of run  No
2  Print indications of progress of run  Yes
3                        Print out tree  Yes
4          Print out steps in each site  No
5  Print character at all nodes of tree  No
6        Write out trees onto tree file?  Yes
Y to accept these or type the letter for one to change
```

--------------- Interacting with the **consense** program -------------

```
Consense: can't find input tree file "intree"
Please enter a new file name> parstree
Consense: the file "outfile" that you wanted to use as output
  file already exists.
  Do you want to Replace it, Append to it,
  write to a new File, or Quit?
  (please type R, A, F, or Q)
f
Please enter a new file name> consenseout.txt
Consensus tree program, version 3.65
Settings for this run:
C  Consensus type (MRe, strict, MR, Ml):  Majority rule (extended)
O                        Outgroup root:  No, outgroup species 1
R          Trees to be treated as Rooted:  No
T    Terminal type (IBM PC, ANSI, none):  (none)
1            Print out the sets of species:  Yes
2  Print indications of progress of run:  Yes
3                          Print out tree:  Yes
4         Write out trees onto tree file:  Yes
Are these settings correct? (type Y or the letter for one to
change)
```

The data that we'll analyze is again drawn from Dyen et al.'s Indo-European cognates data. Table 6.6 shows the cognates data that were used as input to the analysis. You may recognize the first six columns of data as coming from Table 6.1. That is, the column that reads 1,1,1,1,B,2,2, etc. codes the cognates among words for "animal". The second column (beginning 3,1,1,2,1, etc.) codes the cognates among words for "bark (of a tree)", and so on. Table 6.1 has only five words in it and for this analysis I added nine more words so it would be a little less of a toy problem. The format of the first column – the list of names – is very strict. There must be exactly ten characters in this column. The first line is also needed by the Phylip software. This line specifies that there are 19 rows and 14 columns of data (not counting the names).

To construct a phylogenetic tree that shows the linguistic family tree (Figures 6.7 and 6.8) I used a sequence of three programs in the Phylip

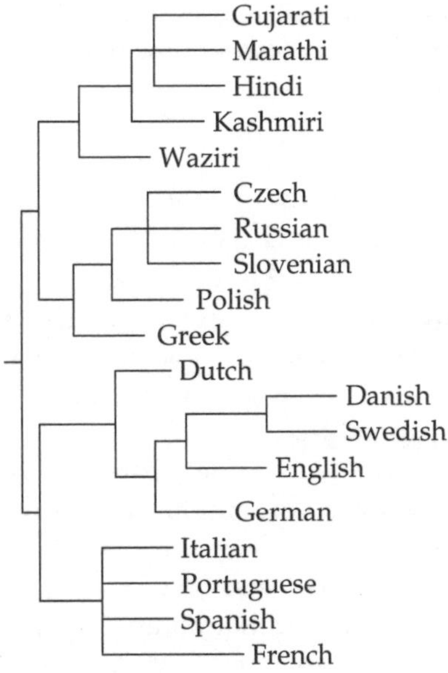

Figure 6.7 The consensus tree produced by maximum parsimony cladistic analysis of the data in Table 6.6. The tree is rooted from its midpoint, with about as many languages on either branch from the root. Line length indicates the number of characters that distinguish the cluster or language linked by the line.

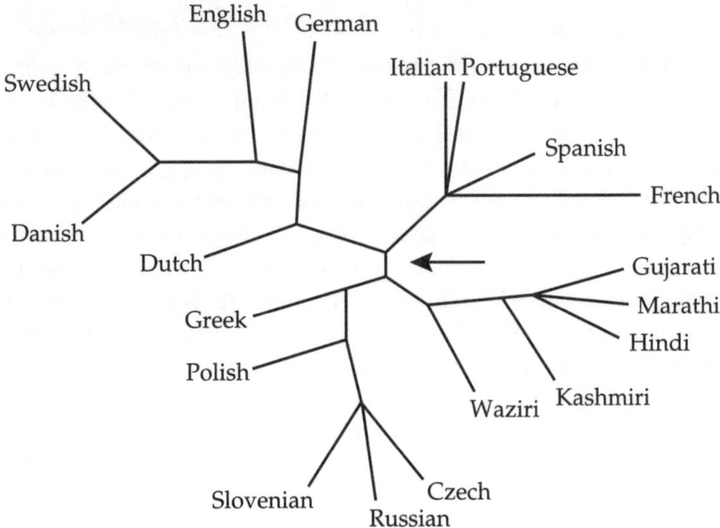

Figure 6.8 The same tree as in Figure 6.7, but with no root assigned. The arrow marks the link that was chosen for the root in Figure 6.7.

package (these are discussed in more detail in the "Phylip note" below). As we saw above, it is usually the case that there is no one best tree to account for all of the data whether we use the maximum compatibility method or the maximum parsimony method, so the usual method in cladistic analysis is to produce a number of equally good trees and then construct a consensus tree that retains clusters that are in most of the "good" trees.

In order to explore the (very large) space of possible good trees for this data set I had the program randomize the order in which the languages would be considered differently for each new tree, and to keep as many as 100 different trees that tied for best. Then I used a majority rule method to select a tree that retains groupings that are present in most of the candidate trees. Interestingly, this process results in the tree shown in Figure 6.8, with no root node. Selection of a root node is actually sort of arbitrary. You can imagine picking the tree in Figure 6.8 up by any node, which then becomes the root. For Figure 6.7 I used a third program to "retree" the tree assigning a root node using the midpoint method.

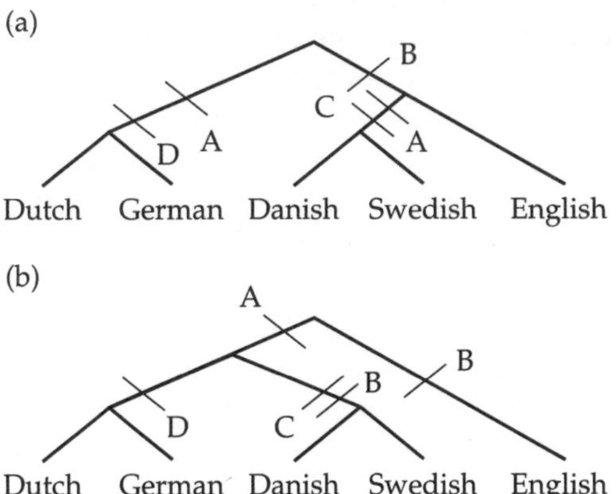

Figure 6.6 Two possible trees of Germanic languages showing character-state changes for calculation of the maximum parsimony goodness criterion.

2005). Interestingly, though, in evolutionary biology a different method – the maximum parsimony criterion – is the most common method of measuring the goodness of a phylogenetic tree, and most software packages are designed to optimize parsimony rather than compatibility. In practice, the maximum parsimony method (see below) is used to generate a set of candidate trees which can then be evaluated by the maximum compatibility method.

Figure 6.6 illustrates how maximum parsimony is calcuated for the two candidate trees of Germanic that we saw in Figure 6.5. The trees have now been labeled with letters that correspond to the characters (that is, the subtrees) shown in Figure 6.4. For example, both trees have a hatch mark labeled D on the branch that leads to Dutch and German. This signifies that Dutch and German "developed" character D – a cognate word for 'to breathe' that is different from the word 'to breathe' in the other languages. This concept of developing a character, or sharing a character state change, is obviously relevant for physical characters like "has legs" but can also be applied to linguistic characters as well (perhaps more naturally for sound changes like "underwent the RUKI rule"). So, each labeled hatch mark on the tree corresponds to the development of a character. Notice that in Figure 6.6(a) character A appears on the tree in two places – on the branch leading to Dutch and German, and on the branch leading to Danish and Swedish. The most parsimonious tree will have each character listed in only one place, so we can measure the parsimony of the tree by simply counting the number of hatch marks on it.

Tree 6.6(b) is more parsimonious than tree 6.6(a) with respect to character A, but now character B has to be marked at two places on the tree. The net result is that the two trees are equally parsimonious, just as they are equally compatible with the set of subtrees defined by the character set.

Now, to conclude this section I'd like to walk you through an analysis using a parsimony-criterion optimization method for finding phylogenetic trees. The analysis is carried out using the software package Phylip which was developed by Joseph Felsenstein. This package is one of the two most frequently cited in the evolutionary biology literature and unlike the other "Paup" is available for a free download (see http://evolution.gs.washington.edu/phylip.html).

Table 6.6 A subset of the Dyen et al. (1992) Indo-European cognates data. This data is formatted for input to the Phylip "pars" program.

19 14														
Dutch	1	3	4	1	2	3	3	2	1	2	3	1	1	2
Danish	1	1	4	1	5	3	3	2	1	4	3	1	1	2
Swedish	1	1	4	1	5	3	3	2	1	4	3	1	1	2
German	1	2	4	1	2	3	3	2	1	2	3	1	1	2
English	B	1	B	6	B	3	3	B	1	2	3	1	1	2
Slovenian	2	3	5	3	1	2	3	2	1	3	1	2	4	3
Russian	2	3	5	3	1	2	3	2	2	3	1	2	4	3
Polish	2	3	5	3	1	2	3	2	1	3	2	2	4	3
Czech	2	3	5	3	1	2	3	2	1	3	1	2	4	3
Greek	2	6	1	7	3	1	3	2	1	5	3	2	7	6
Kashmiri	3	B	3	2	4	2	2	B	1	B	3	2	5	4
Gujarati	3	4	3	2	4	2	2	1	1	3	B	B	5	B
Marathi	3	4	3	2	4	2	2	1	B	3	3	2	6	4
Hindi	3	4	3	2	4	2	2	1	1	3	3	2	5	4
Waziri	3	5	6	5	4	4	1	2	3	6	4	2	2	5
Portuguese	4	3	2	4	6	2	3	2	1	1	3	2	3	1
Spanish	4	3	2	4	6	2	3	2	1	1	3	2	3	1
Italian	4	3	2	4	6	2	3	2	1	1	3	2	3	1
French	4	3	2	4	6	2	3	2	1	1	3	2	3	1

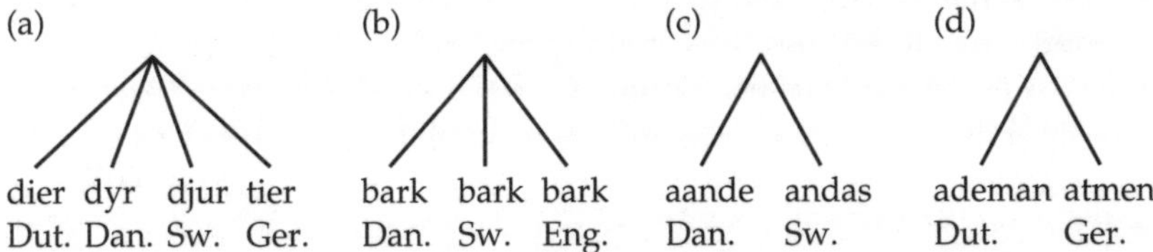

Figure 6.4 Germanic language groupings suggested by cognates for the words "animal", "bark (of a tree)", and "to breathe" in Table 6.1. (Dut. = Dutch, Dan. = Danish, Sw. = Swedish, Ger. = German, Eng. = English).

Figure 6.4 shows groups of Germanic languages that we can identify on the basis of the words for "animal", "bark (of tree)", and "to breathe" from Table 6.1. We can consider these groupings to be subtrees of a single larger tree and consider ways to join the trees with each other. For example, if we start with the largest group (a) and look at the two groups that are embedded in it, namely trees (c) and (d), we come up with the tree shown in Figure 6.5(a). There is a node that encompases Dutch and German (group d), a node that encompases Danish and Swedish (group c) and a node that encompases all four languages (group a). Unfortunately, though, there is no node that groups together Danish, Swedish, and English as is suggested by the word for "bark" (group b). The tree in Figure 6.5(b) shows a configuration that does have a node for group (b). However, note now that group (a) is not represented.

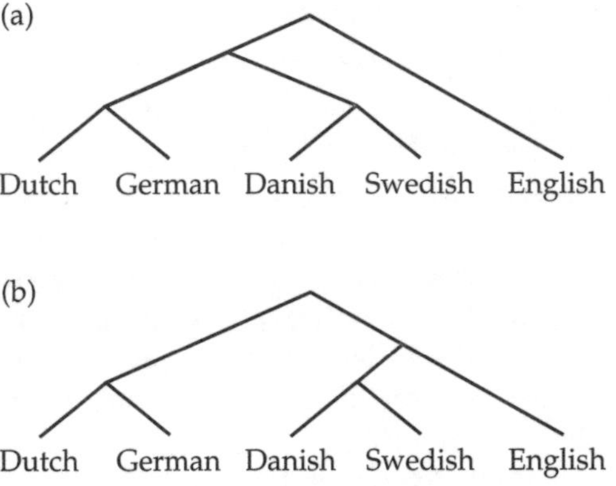

Figure 6.5 Two phylogenetic trees that are suggested by the groupings in figure 6.4.

This short illustration gives a flavor of the subtree combining method and illustrates the main problem in cladistics. Real data almost never define a single best-fitting tree, thus the method must choose from among many possible trees. Well, actually the method must be smart enough to generate lots of different trees that are all fairly consistent with the set of characters, and then measure how well the trees fit the data, and from a set of equally good trees choose a consensus tree that best represents the set of equally good trees.

Generating lots of different trees involves repeating the process of generating a tree from a number of different starting points (note how I suggested we start from group (a) or group (b) above), and adds nodes to the tree in different random orders. The options are fairly limited in the simple example in Figures 6.4 and 6.5, but you can probably imagine how complicated the picture can become as we add hundreds of characters and dramatically increase the number of languages in the set as we would in a real research question.

When it comes to measuring how well a tree fits the data, one of the most successful solutions is a maximum compatibility criterion that measures the success of a tree in term of the number of subtrees that are compatible with the overall tree. For example, both of the trees in Figure 6.5 are compatible with three of the four subtrees in Figure 6.4. The tree in Figure 6.5(a) is incompatible with 6.4(b) and the tree in Figure 6.5(b) is incompatible with 6.4(a). This means that they are equally compatible with the subtrees suggested by the characters we derived from the words for "animal", "bark", and "to breathe". To decide between these two options we need data from more words, or we need to put different weights on some of the characters so that some kinds of incompatibility are more costly than others. For example, if I were to decide that the weight of a character should be proportional to the number of languages that share that character (warning, I have no good reason for supposing this), then tree 6.5(a) wins because character 6.4(a) is shared by four languages and 6.4(b) is shared by only three. In a more realistic example of character weighting, Nakhleh et al. (2005) gave larger weights to phonological or morphological characters (like Grimm's law and the RUKI rule) than they did to lexical cognates. This is a way of allowing for the possibility that some of the cognate decisions may have been wrong.

To me the maximum compatibility measure is a pretty intuitive measure of how well a tree accounts for character data. It also seems to be the measure of choice in recent linguistic research (Nakhleh et al.

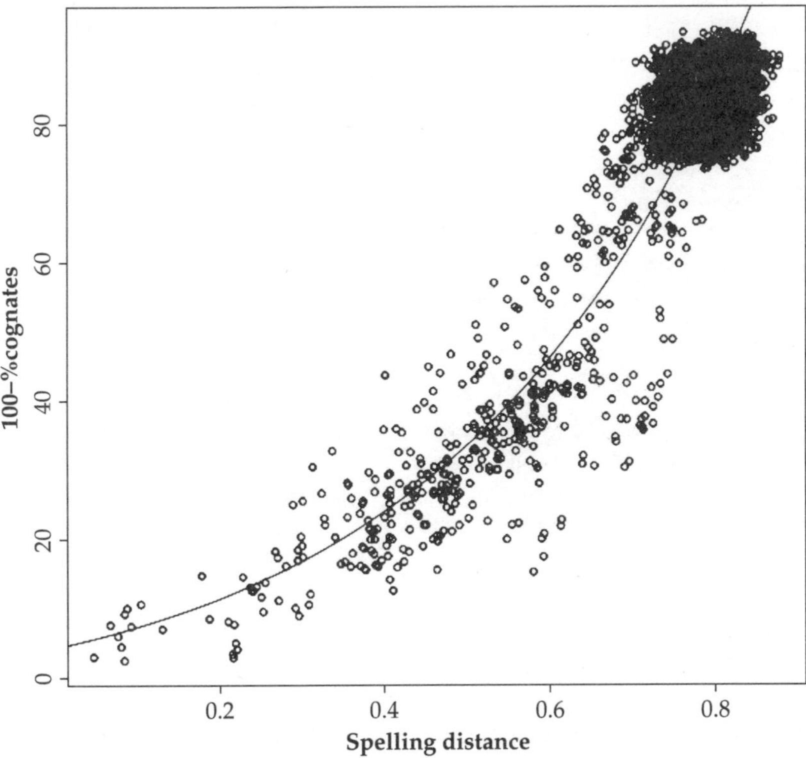

Figure 6.10 Spelling distance is correlated with genetic distance. Each dot in this graph is a language comparison representing the overall distance on the 200-word Swadesh (1952) list. Most languages in the data set share fewer than 25% cognate words (the clump of dots in the upper right of the graph). The regression line is for the formula: log(cognate_distance + 5) = 2.2299 + 2.83923 * spelling_distance.

(percent non-cognates) and found by trial and error that adding 5% (i.e. increasing the cognates distance slightly) and then taking the log produced a slightly better fit to the data.

```
> summary(lm(log(vcog2+5)~vspell2))
Call: lm(formula = log(vcog2 + 5) ~ vspell2)
Residuals:
Min        1Q         Median   3Q        Max
-0.86603  -0.06250  0.00598  0.07110  0.51236
```

```
Coefficients:
             Estimate  Std. Error  t value  Pr(>|t|)
(Intercept)   2.22990    0.01027    217.2    <2e-16 ***
vspell2       2.83923    0.01347    210.8    <2e-16 ***
--- Signif. codes:
0 `***' 0.001 `**' 0.01 `*' 0.05 `.' 0.1 ` ' 1
Residual standard error: 0.1201 on 6970 degrees of freedom
Multiple R-Squared: 0.8644,  Adjusted R-squared: 0.8644
F-statistic: 4.444e+04 on 1 and 6970 DF, p-value:
< 2.2e-16
```

Figure 6.10 was produced by these commands.

```
> plot(vspell2,vcog2,xlab="Spelling distance",
   ylab="100 - %cognates")
> curve(exp(2.2299+2.83923*x)-5,add=T)
```

6.5 Multidimensional Scaling: A Language Similarity Space

Multidimensional scaling (MDS) is a method for visualizing dissimilarity data. The basic idea is that we can make a map using estimated distances between the points on the map by using a method of triangulation and iterative improvement between the data and the map. For example, if you know that the distance between Albany and Albuquerque is 2,040 miles, and the distance between Albany and Atlanta is 1,010 miles, and the distance between Albuquerque and Atlanta is 1,400 miles, then you can construct a map showing the relative locations of these cities. Chapter 4 of my *Acoustic and Auditory Phonetics* (2002) has a fairly long non-technical discussion of MDS, and if you want to use MDS in any serious way you should study Kruskal and Wish (1978).

The spelling distance matrix can be used to plot a "similarity" space of languages using multidimensional scaling. This approach to the analysis of Indo-European might be valuable if we wish to explore similarities among the languages without assuming the genetic relationships as depicted in a family tree. Note that unlike principal components analysis, in order to perform multidimensional scaling we

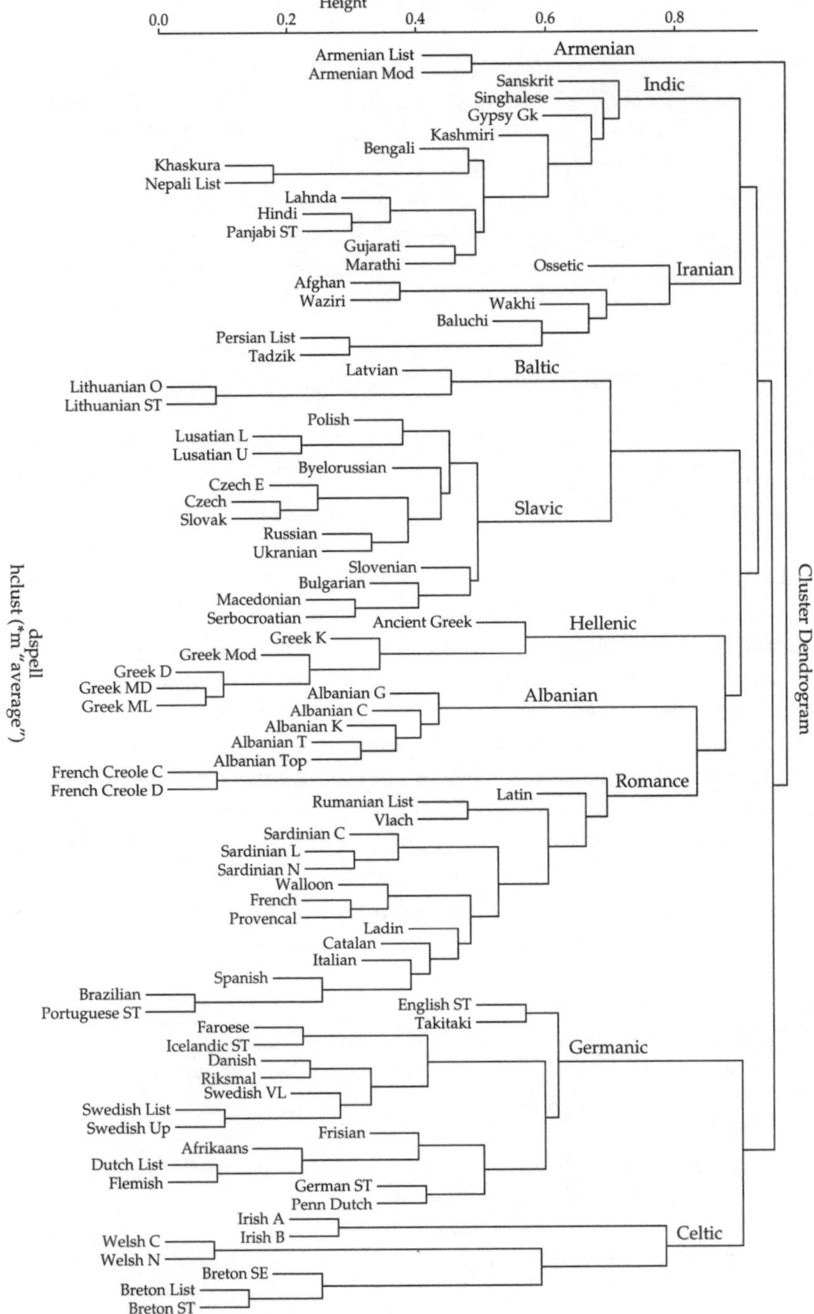

Figure 6.9 Dendrogram of clusters produced in a hierarchical clustering analysis of spelling distances.

R note. The Perl script that I used to calculate the spelling distances between languages is "get_IE_distance." There are also a couple of support scripts, to condition the data into a distance matrix. You can get these on the book web page, and read the comments in the scripts to see what I did. The R commands to produce Figure 6.9 are pretty much the same as those we used to produce Figure 6.3.

```
> m <- read.table("IE-distmatrix.txt",sep = ",")
> dspell <- as.dist(m[1:87]) # dyen's 84 languages + 3
    ancient langs.
> names(dspell) <- m$V88
> plot(hclust(dspell,"ave"))
```

Perhaps one could measure the impact of borrowing in the spelling similarity analysis by correlating genetic distance from Dyen et al.'s (1992) "percent cognates" distance measure with this simple spelling distance measure. I did this by regressing the spelling distance measure against the percent cognates distance measure. As Figure 6.10 shows, the relationship between these two measures of language similarity is nonlinear so I regressed the log of cognate distance against the spelling distance. The R^2 value gives a proportion of genetic similarity that is accounted for by spelling similarity. The value that I obtained for this R^2 value was 0.86, indicating that 86% of the variance in the cognate judgments can be predicted from the spellings of the words. The remaining 14% of variance is possibly contributed by borrowing.

R note. I converted the distance matrices that were read for the cluster analyses above into vectors using the command:

```
> vcog = c(m$V1,m$V2,.... m$V84)
```

I removed the diagonal of the matrix, where distance values were zero, and then did a regression analysis.

```
> vcog2 = vcog[vcog>0]
> vspell2 = vspell[vspell>0]
```

I had looked at the graph and knew that the relationship was nonlinear so I did the regression on the log of the cognates distance see also Heeringa & Braun, 2003 and Heeringa & Gooskens, 2003; and especially Sankoff & Kruskal, 1983/1999), and in the analysis of phonetic reduction in conversational speech (Johnson, 2004). However, in both my earlier work and in Heeringa's work, the method calculates pronunciation differences using phonetic transcriptions, so in this study there was no guarantee that spelling similarity would produce a sensible analysis of the Indo-European language family. The reason that I decided to try this is that it is often very difficult to know whether two words are cognate with each other in two languages – especially if the languages are distantly related. Additionally, it might be of some interest to compare a historical relatedness tree with a tree of language similarity which takes into account borrowing as a source of similarity. This spelling similarity method, though very crude, makes the beginnings of such a comparison possible. Perhaps there is a way to measure how much of language similarity is due to "genetic" relatedness, and how much is due to chance similarity or borrowing.

In the spelling comparison algorithm, the spellings are aligned with each other allowing for insertion, deletion, and substitution of symbols, so that identical symbols will be aligned with each other and so that vowel symbols will tend to line up with each other. Three example spelling alignments are shown in Table 6.7. In this table, the only difference between English "animal" and Italian "animale" is the deletion of the final "e" in English (or insertion of "e" in Italian, if you want to think of English as the base). Vowel substitutions added 1 to the distance. Insertions and deletions added 1.5, and substitutions involving consonants added 2 to the distance. The reported distance is the

Table 6.7 Spelling "distance" produced by the dynamic time warping algorithm. The letters align with each other in columns according to the algorithm's choice for the best possible alignment of the spellings.

English	a	n	i	m	a	l	.				
Italian	a	n	i	m	a	l	e	0.115			
English	.	a	n	i	m	a	l				
Kashmiri	j	a	n	a	w	a	r	0.499			
English	.	a	.	.	.	n	i	m	a	l	
Russian	z	i	v	o	t	n	o	.	e	.	0.856

average distance. For example, the total distance between the English and Italian words is 1.5 so the average is 1.5/(6 + 7) because there are six letters in "animal" and seven in "animale" (Heeringa, 2004, prefers to divide by the length of the longest string).

Now to come up with an overall measure of similarity between English and Italian, for example, we take the average of the 200 word similarities. This value for English and Italian is 0.755. The speech variety that scored the most similar to English is Frisian with an average distance of 0.566, though in the cluster solution below Frisian groups with Afrikaans, Dutch, and Flemish rather than with English because it is even more similar to these (particularly Dutch with a distance of only 0.391).

With a matrix of overall spelling similarities among the languages we can apply hierarchical clustering as we did with the percent cognates data. The results are shown in Figure 6.9. What is interesting about these results is that the major language families are again found, despite the very crude methodology used to compare languages. Some of the differences between a family tree based on cognation (Figure 6.3) and this one based only on spelling similarity must result from chance similarity, and perhaps also from the presence of borrowed word similarity. For instance, Albanian, a separate branch of Indo-European, shows greater affinity for the Hellenic branch (from which it has borrowed many words) in this spelling similarity analysis.

You will notice in Figure 6.9 that I also added Sanskrit, Ancient Greek, and Latin word lists to the lists that were analyzed in Dyen et al. (1992). Interestingly, in the analysis of spelling similarities, these ancient languages cluster with their historical descendants, being the last to cluster with their family near the top of the tree. Of course you wouldn't want to make too much of this because creole languages, like French Creole, and languages that have many borrowed words, like English and Ossetic, also cluster more weakly with their relatives. Nonetheless, it is very interesting that such a crude analysis of overall language similarity could produce such an informative picture of the language family.

Naturally, there is a caveat. It could be that much of the successful grouping found in Figure 6.9 arises from the borrowing of writing systems, or more recently shared conventions of romanization. This analysis needs to be done on the basis of broad phonetic transcription rather than on orthography. Despite this concern, I'll mention a couple of other steps of analysis using the spelling similarity data.

---------------- Interacting with the **retree** program ----------------

```
Tree Rearrangement, version 3.65

Settings for this run:
U        Initial tree (arbitrary, user, specify)?  User tree from file
N Format to write out trees (PHYLIP, Nexus, XML)?  PHYLIP
0                   Graphics type (IBM PC, ANSI)?  (none)
W     Width of terminal screen, of plotting area?  80, 80
L                       Number of lines on screen?  24

Are these settings correct? (type Y or the letter for one to
change)
```

The cladistic method for combining character-based trees is a pretty intuitively simple one and does yield sensible trees. However, the results are not stable depending on luck of the draw in the random orderings that get tested, and more importantly on the accuracy of particular judgments that the linguist makes in establishing the character sets used as input to the process. In fact Nakhleh, Warnow et al. (2005) conclude their methodological study with the sobering suggestion that "it seems possible that phylogenetic reconstruction methods are best suited to working out, in a maximally rigorous fashion, the consequences of linguist's judgements" (p. 22). This is a useful thing to do, but does indicate that cladistic analysis is not a magic method that will automatically deliver the phylogenetic tree of a language family.

6.4 Clustering on the Basis of Spelling Similarity

There are some problems with cladistics that limit its utility in some circumstances. In order to use the method we have to know enough about the history of each language under investigation to be able to identify words as cognates. For comparisons at a fairly shallow time depth, or with a small number of languages, this is not a problem, but for more distant undocumented relationships we can't really know whether languages are similar because of borrowing or direct descent. Nakhleh et al. (2005) indicate this in their "phylogenetic networks" approach when they add links for borrowing in a tree determined on the basis of cognate words (among other things). It may be that no methodology is immune from this concern, but I would like to consider an additional technique here, as an additional tool for historical phonetic research.

Even for comparisons of relatively shallow time depth, in working with languages for which we don't have a body of documentary evidence we can't always know whether words are cognates with each other. Especially for non-Indo-European languages it would be convenient to be able to explore the similarities among speech varieties even when historical information may not be available or reliable.

For example, Ladefoged, Glick, and Criper (1971: 34) in their study of the languages of Uganda (now Tanzania) noted some cases of historical uncertainties in the movements and interactions among peoples. They suggested that, "because of mixtures of this kind, and because we do not know enough about the past relations between the tribal groupings in Uganda, the historical method is not very useful in trying to make a detailed classification of the languages of Uganda." They introduced a technique for clustering languages on the basis of their phonetic similarities. This section presents an extension of their method.

> I told Peter Ladefoged about this "new" clustering method that I was toying with. He was gracious about it but basically told me that he had also thought of exploring language similarities on the basis of phonetic comparisons of words – when I was in junior high school! One of the homework exercises at the end of this chapter involves constructing a map of Bantu languages using data from Ladefoged et al. (1971).

To explore the utility of cluster analysis without historical reconstructions I used a dynamic time warping method to calculate the distances between words on the basis of their spellings and then entered these distances into a cluster analysis of Indo-European. I should say that I don't think that this takes the place of making cognate decisions on the basis of systematic sound changes. Instead, I am offering this method as an exploratory tool that may be valuable in the investigation of language prehistory.

The dynamic time warping method has been used to calculate the similarities of dialects in computational dialectology (Heeringa, 2004;

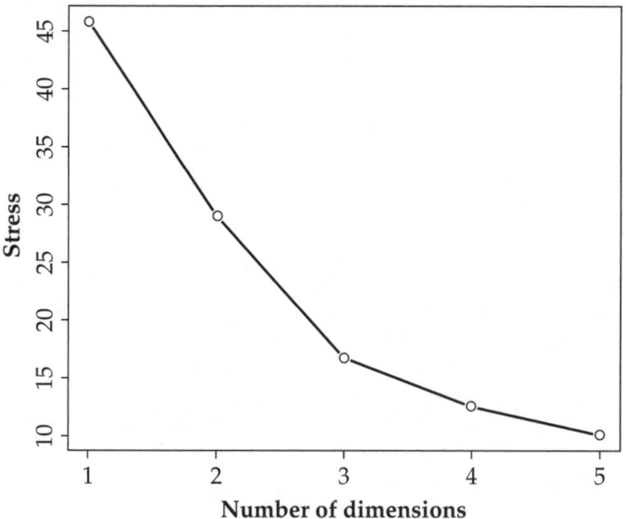

Figure 6.11 Stress of MDS solutions of 1 to 5 dimensions. Adding a fourth or fifth dimension does not substantially improve over the three-dimensional solution.

do not need to measure the languages on any variables – the only information we need is some measure of distance between languages, it could even be subjective judgments given by Indo-Europeanists if we wish!

The MDS solution for a three-dimensional similarity space is produced using Kruskal's nonmetric MDS (see Kruskal & Wish 1978) to map the language differences as measured by our spelling distance comparison.

Unlike a road map, in our map of Indo-European we don't know how many dimensions to include in the language similarity space so we try a number of maps and measure how well the map matches the data using a parameter called "stress" (Figure 6.11). This is a number on a scale from 0 (perfect fit) to 100 (the map captures nothing about the data). Generally, we are looking for a stress value less than 20 and an "elbow" in the stress by number of dimensions plot. The elbow indicates a point of diminishing returns where adding new dimensions to the similarity space does not result in much increase in correspondence between the map distances and the raw data distances.

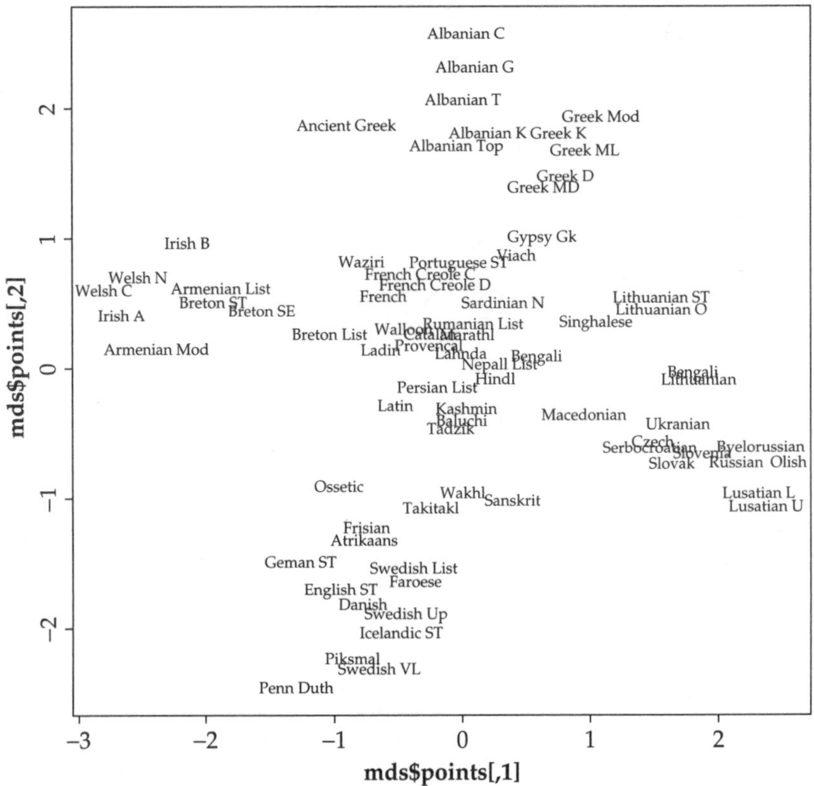

Figure 6.12 A plot of dimension one (horizontal axis) and dimension two (vertical axis) of the MDS similarity map of Indo-European speech varieties.

Figure 6.11 indicates that the best solution is probably the one with three dimensions. This three-dimensional solution is shown in detail in Figures 6.12 and 6.13, and in a slightly less detailed way in Figure 6.14. These views of Indo-European are complicated and rich, and perhaps informative about the historical and contemporary relations among the languages in ways that a cladistic view may not be capable of representing. Whether or not MDS will be of much use in historical linguistics is an open question, though the technique has been used with success in dialectology and language documentation (e.g. Ladefoged et al. 1971).

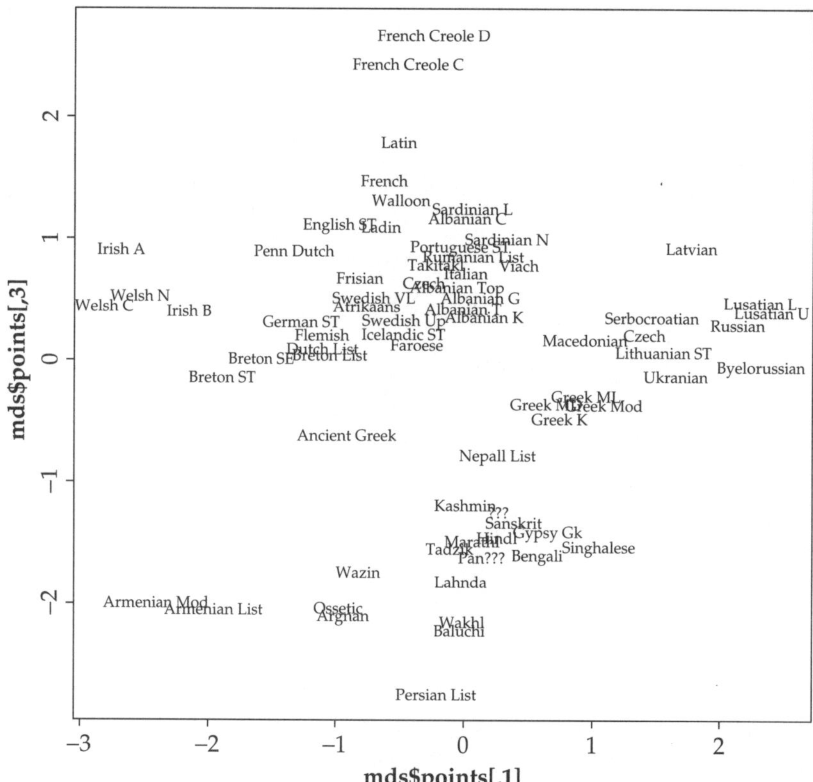

Figure 6.13 A plot of dimension one (horizontal axis) and dimension three (vertical axis) of the MDS similarity map of Indo-European speech varieties.

R note. You can use the "metric" or "classical" multidimensional scaling procedure `cmdscale()` to produce a map from city distances. For example, try out this code for a map of cities starting with the letter "A."

```
> m <-
matrix(c(0,2040,1010,2040,0,1400,1010,1400,0),
nrow=3,ncol=3,byrow=T,
dimnames=list(c("Albany","Albuquerque","Atlanta"),
c("Albany","Albuquerque","Atlanta")))
```

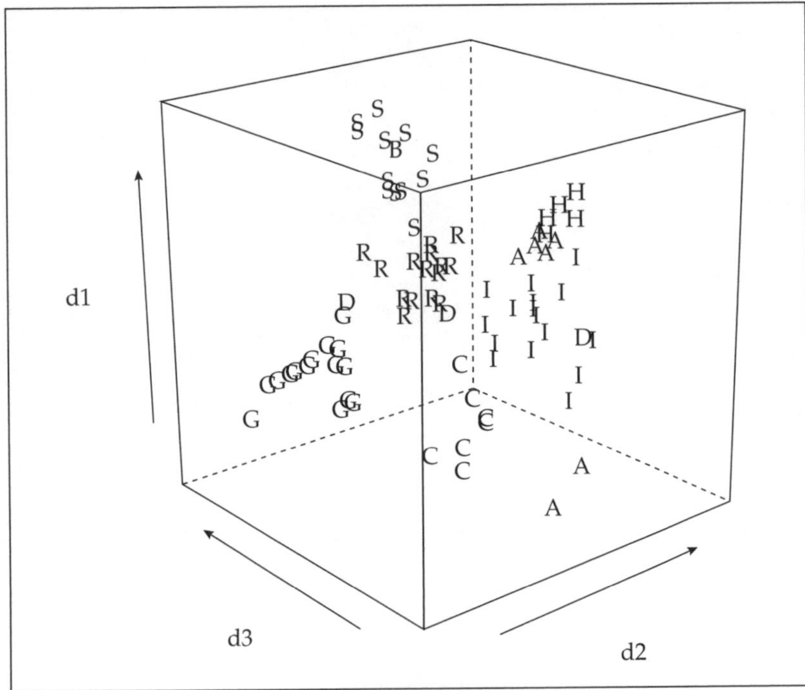

Figure 6.14 A plot of the three-dimensional similarity space of Indo-European languages, based on spelling similarity. Germanic languages are coded with "G," Hellenic with "H," Slavic with "S," Romance with "R," Baltic with "B," Celtic with "C," and the dead languages with "D." Indic and Iranian are both coded with "I," and Albanian and Armenian are both coded with "A" – Albanian is closer to Hellenic. The letters are also coded in different colors in the original.

```
> d <- as.dist(m)
> d
              Albany  Albuquerque
Albuquerque    2040
Atlanta        1010         1400
> mds <- cmdscale(d)
> plot(mds,ylim=c(500,-300),xlim=c(-1500,1200),type="n")
> text(mds,as.character(dimnames(m)[[1]]))
```

The nonmetric, rank-order multidimensional scaling procedure that I used to visualize our language similarity data is implemented by the isoMDS() command, which is in the R library MASS. Here are commands to load that library and ask for a two-dimensional solution for the dspell data set.

```
> library(MASS)
> m <- read.table("IE-distmatrix.txt",sep=",")
> d <- as.dist(m[1:87])
> names(d) <- m$V88
> mds <- isoMDS(d,k=3)
initial  value  37.282523
iter  5  value  22.490628
iter 10  value  17.671007
iter 15  value  17.073035
final    value  16.780951
converged
```

The final "stress" value measures the degree of correspondence between distances in the data and distances in the map and is given on a scale from 0 to 100 (in some implementations the stress scale is 0 to 1). As the fit improves the stress value approaches zero, and generally fits that have stress greater than 15–20 are considered unstable and not to be trusted. The the three-dimensional solution represents a 12-point improvement over the two-dimensional solution (stress = 29 versus stress = 16.8) and so is presented here.

```
> stress <- c(45.86,29.09,16.78,12.64,10.11)
> dim <- c(1,2,3,4,5)
> plot(stress,dim,type=b,xlab="Number of dimensions",
    ylab="Stress")
```

The two figures showing the MDS similarity space (Figures 6.12 and 6.13) were created with:

```
> plot(mds$points,type="n")
> text(mds$points,as.character(names(d)),cex=0.5)
> plot(mds$points[,1],mds$points[,3],type="n")
> text(mds$points[,1],mds$points[,3],as.character
    (names(d)), cex=0.5)
```

I made a data frame that I called "space" to hold the language names, and the mds$points columns from the multidimensonal scaling solution. I also added a column that identifies the language family of each language, as revealed in the cluster analysis – except that I created a group called "DEAD" that includes Latin, Ancient Greek, and Sanskit so we can more easily see where they fall in the three-dimensional similarity space.

```
> space <- read.delim("3dspace.txt")
> space
    language    group            d1          d2          d3
1     Afghan  Iranian -0.9160043711  0.28414069 -2.08811418
2  Afrikaans Germanic -0.7752611315 -1.32240609  0.44734323
3  Albanian C Albanian  0.0338698088  2.57451648  1.16025233
4  Albanian G Albanian  0.1064020998  2.30977783  0.51065756
```

To produce the three-dimensional graph in Figure 6.14, I used the "lattice" library of graphics commands (steeper learning curve than the other plotting routines in R, but fancier graphs).

```
> library(lattice)
> lset(col.whitebg())
> lset(list(superpose.symbol=list(pch
      =c("A","A","B","C","D","G","H","I","I","R","S"))))
> cloud(d1 ~ d2*d3,groups=group,data=space,cex=1.7,
    screen=list(z=40,x= -70))
```

EXERCISES

1 File "bantu_matrix.txt" contains a distance matrix for eight Bantu languages from the Tanzanian Language Survey (http://www.cbold.ddl.ish-lyon.cnrs.fr/Docs/TLS.html). I selected 33 words in the survey and judged whether the languages seemed to have the same stem for the word. The distance value in this table then is the number of times the two languages had a different stem out of 33. Construct, by hand, a hierarchical clustering tree of the languages using the single-linkage method, just as I did for the Celtic languages in section 6.2 of this chapter.
2 Using the distance matrix in file "bantu_matrix.txt" of Bantu languages in Tanzania, perform hierarchical cluster analyses using

average linkage, complete linkage, and Ward's method. How do these differ from each other and how do they differ from the single linkage tree you drew by hand for question 1. Explain any differences that you find.

3 File "LGC_phonetic.txt" contains phonetic distance data from Ladefoged et al. (1971). These data contrast Bantu languages in Tanzania according to how phonetically different they are for a set of 22 words. Phonetic differences were defined in terms of the number of phonetic features the stems of the words shared. Produce a hierarchical analysis of the data.

4 File "bantu_pars.txt" contains data for the eight Bantu languages in the Tanzanian Language Survey (see question 1) in a format that is appropriate for phylogenetic parsimony analysis by the Phylip program "pars." Follow the steps outlined in section 6.3 to produce a phylogenetic tree of these languages. How does this differ from the hierarchical clustering tree? Can you identify the language named "Gwere" with any of the languages in the Ladefoged et al. data set?

7 Syntax

In syntactic research, it is important to distinguish between judgments that bear on grammaticality and those that bear on semantic anomaly. For example, though it is syntactically well-formed, and thus grammatical, the phrase *colorless green ideas* is semantically anomalous. Table 7.1 illustrates the distinction between grammaticality judgments and semantic anomaly judgments.

However, the grammaticality/anomaly distinction is over-simple. For example, with the appropriate discourse context leading up to it, the apparently anomalous *colorless green ideas* can be judged as semantically well-formed. Similarly, when a phrase is grammatically ill-formed like *subversive ideas communist* is given an appropriate context, it isn't clear that it actually has a compositional semantic interpretation. Nonetheless, the distinction between grammaticality and anomaly is central to any discussion of syntactic theory.

I bring this up because recently researchers have been turning to naive speakers for syntactic data (Bard, Robertson, & Sorace, 1996; Schütze, 1996; Cowart, 1997; Keller, 2000, and many others). The problem is that

Table 7.1 Illustration of the difference between grammaticality and semantic anomaly.

	Grammatically well-formed	**Grammatically ill-formed**
Semantically well-formed	*subversive communist ideas*	*subversive ideas communist*
Semantically anomalous	*colorless green ideas*	*colorless ideas green*

naive speakers can't tell you that *colorless green ideas* is syntactically OK but semantically odd. They just think it isn't nearly as natural, or acceptable, as *subversive communist ideas*. So, to use data given by naive speakers we have to devote a good deal more effort to acquiring syntactic data, and still there are likely to be concerns that we don't actually know why a person judged one phrase to be relatively unacceptable while another is perfectly fine.

Why bother then? Why not just continue to use judgments given by people (linguists) who can factor out semantic anomaly and report only the grammaticality of a sentence or phrase? There are two very good reasons to bother. First, linguists' grammaticality judgments are suspect. Our experience of language is unusual because we have encountered, and even memorized, example sentences from the linguistic literature. Students who first encounter this literature often remark that the judgments are really not clear to them, and it may be that a part of acculturation in the study of syntax is the development of intuitions that are not really present in normal language processing (for a spectacular example of this, see Ferreira 2003). Now one argument is that what is happening is that the budding linguist is developing the distinction between grammaticality and anomaly, but it seems just as likely that we are learning to have stronger opinions or intuitions about grammaticality than nonlinguists. The possibility that the "data" are infected with the researcher's expectations is a fundamental concern that appears to be driving the push to get syntactic data from naive speakers (see Inton-Peterson, 1983; and Goldinger & Azumi, 2003 for evidence that expectations can color the results even in "low-level" tasks).

The second good reason to bother getting data from naive speakers has to do with sampling theory. If we want to say things about English syntax, for example, then we need to get data from a representative sample of the population of people who speak English (of some variety).

I don't think that there is much disagreement about these problems with using linguists' intuitions as the data base for syntactic theory, but there has to be a viable alternative. One of the most serious concerns about "experimental" or "empirical" alternatives has to do with whether information about grammaticality can be gleaned from naive speakers' acceptability judgments. Consider Table 7.1 again. If we collect acceptability judgments for items in all four cells of the table we can distinguish, to a certain degree, between judgments that are responsive primarily to semantic anomaly (the rows in the table) from judgments that are responsive to grammaticality. Here we are using a hypothesis testing approach, in which we hypothesize that these utterances differ in the ways indicated in the table on the basis of our linguistically sophisticated judgments.

7.1 Measuring Sentence Acceptability

In syntax research an interval scale of grammaticality is commonly used. Sentences are rated as grammatical, questionable (?, or ??), and ungrammatical (*, or **). This is essentially a five-point category rating scale, and we could give people this rating scale and average the results, where ** = 5, * = 4, ?? = 3, ? = 2, and no mark = 1. However, it has been observed in the study of sensory impressions (Stevens 1975) that raters are more consistent with an open-ended ratio scale than they are with category rating scales. So, in recent years, methods from the study of psychophysics (subjective impressions of physical properties of stimuli) have been adapted in the study of sentence acceptability.

The technique that I am talking about here – using an open-ended ratio scale for reporting impressions – is called magnitude estimation. Lodge (1981) lists three advantages of magnitude estimation over category scaling. First, category scaling has limited resolution. Though you may feel that a sentence is something like a 4.5 (a little worse than prior sentences that you rated as 5 and a little better than sentences that you rated as 4), gradient ratings are not available in category scaling. Magnitude estimation permits as much resolution as the rater wishes to employ. Second, category scaling uses an ordinal scale. So, though we may average the ratings given on a category scale, there is no guarantee that the interval between * and ** represents the same difference of impression as the difference between ? and ??. Magnitude estimation provides judgments on an interval scale for which averages and standard deviations can be more legitimately used. Third, categorical scaling limits our ability to compare results across experiments. The range of acceptability for a set of sentences has to be fit to the scale, so what counts as ?? for one set of sentences may be quite different than what counts as ?? for another set of sentences. You'll notice that I've employed a set of instructions (Appendix 7A) that imposes a similar range on the magnitude estimation scale. I did this by giving a "modulus" phrase and instructed the raters to think of this as being an example of a score of 50. I did this to reduce the variability in the raters' responses, but it put the results onto an experiment-internal scale so that the absolute values given by these raters cannot be compared to the ratings given in other experiments that use different instructions with a different modulus phrase.

In sum, magnitude estimation avoids some serious limitations of category scaling. But what exactly is magnitude estimation? The best way I know to explain it is by way of demonstration, so we'll work through an example of magnitude estimation in the next section.

7.2 A Psychogrammatical Law?

Keller (2003) proposes a psychogrammatical law relating the number of word order constraint violations and the perceived acceptability of the sentence, using magnitude estimation to estimate sentence acceptability. The relationship can be expressed as a power function:

$R = kN_v^p$ a syntactic power law

where R is the raters' estimation of sentence acceptability and N_v is the number of constraint violations in the sentence being judged, p is exponent of the power function and k is a scale factor. Note that this relationship can also be written as a simple linear equation using the log values of N_v and R:

$\log R = \log k + p \log N_v$ expressed as a linear regression equation

The exponent (p) in Keller's power law formulation for the relationship between acceptability and constraint violations was 0.36.

In the example discussed in this chapter we will be looking for a power law involving violations of an adjective order template in English adjective phrases.

Hetzron (1978) proposed a word order template for prenominal adjectives in English (Table 7.2) that putatively follows universal constraints having to do with semantic or pragmatic properties of adjectives, but apparently the *best* predictions of adjective ordering in English corpora come from considerations of language-specific and often adjective-specific conventions rather than universal principles (Malouf, 2000). Nonetheless, Hetzron's template accounts for at least some portion of the prenominal adjective order patterns found in spoken English (Wulff, 2003).

Table 7.2 The Hetzron (1978) template of prenominal adjective order.

13	epistemic qualifier	"famous"
12	evaluation*	"good," "bad," "nice"
11	static permanent property*	"wide," "tall," "big"
10	sensory contact property	"sweet," "rough", "cold"
9	speed	"fast," "slow"
8	social property	"cheap"
7	age*	"young," "new," "old"
6	shape	"round," "square"
5	color*	"blue," "red," "orange"
4	physical defect	"deaf," "chipped," "dented"
3	origin*	"Asian," "French"
2	composition*	"woolen," "silk," "steel"
1	purpose	"ironing"
0	NOUN	

* I used these in the experiment.

So we will use Hetzron's word order template to make predictions about acceptability, in search of a psychogrammatical law similar to the one Keller suggested. In Hetzron's template, position 0 is the head noun of the phrase and prenominal adjectives in a noun phrase typically come in the order shown in table 7.2 (with some of these categories being mutually exclusive). The hypothesis that I wish to test is that placing adjectives in the "wrong" order will result in a greater decrease in acceptability if the adjectives are from categories that are further apart from each other on this scale. This predicts that "woolen nice hat" (transposing adjectives from category 12 and 2) is worse than "woolen Asian hat" (categories 2 and 3). In some cases this seems intuitively to be true, in others it may not be quite right. An empirical study is called for.

I created a small grammar with the following lexicon (these are annotated lines from the Perl script that I used to generate noun phrases for the experiment):

```
[12]attitude = ("good","nice","pleasant","fun","tremendous",
  "wonderful","intelligent");
[11]size = ("big","tall","small","large","tiny","huge","wide",
  "narrow","short");
```

```
[7]age = ("old","young","new");
[5]color = ("black","white","red","blue","pink","orange");
[3]origin = ("French","Dutch","English","Asian","Irish","Turkish");
[2]material = ("steel","woolen","wooden","lead","fabric");
[0]noun = ("hat","plate","knob","wheel","frame","sock",
  "book","sign","dish","box","chair","car","ball");
```

Phrases were then generated by selecting randomly from these sets to form phrases with differing degrees of separation along the template. Random generation of phrases produces some that are semantically odd ("pleasant Asian sock") and others that are semantically fine ("old pink plate"). I used different randomly generated lists for each participant in order to provide a rough control for the effects of semantic anomaly, because the results were then averaged over semantically anomalous and non-anomalous phrases. However, a more careful control would have not left the factor of semantic anomaly to chance, instead controlling anomaly explicitly on the basis of a pretest to insure that either no anomalous phrases were used or that each participant saw a fixed number of anomalous and non-anomalous phrases.

There were four types of stimuli involving adjectives at four different degrees of difference on the Hetzron template. The group 1 pairs of adjectives come from slots that are close to each other on the template, while the group 4 pairs come from distant slots. If the template distance hypothesis is on the right track, group 4 order reversals will be less acceptable than group 1 order reversals.

The experiment (Appendix 7A) starts with a demonstration of magnitude estimation by asking participants to judge the lengths of a few lines. These "practice" judgments provide a sanity check in which we can evaluate participants' ability to use magnitude estimation to report their impressions. Previous research (Stevens 1975) has found that numerical estimates of line length have a one-to-one relationship with actual line length (that is the slope of the function relating them is 1).

Figure 7.1 shows the relationship between the actual line length on the horizontal axis and participants' numerical estimates of the lengths of the lines. The figure illustrates that participants' estimates are highly correlated ($R^2 = 0.952$) with line length and the slope of the line is about equal to one (1.13) – a one-to-one relationship between length and estimated length. In general, this result assures us that these

Table 7.3 Adjective order template distance of the four groups of phrases used in the experiment. Template "distance" is the difference between the indices in the Hetzron template of the two adjectives in the phrase.

Group 1		
attitude, size	12 – 11 = 1	
size, age	11 – 7 = 4	average distance = 2
age, color	7 – 5 = 2	
origin, color	3 – 2 = 1	
Group 2		
attitude, age	12 – 7 = 5	
size, color	11 – 5 = 6	average distance = 4.5
age, origin	7 – 3 = 4	
color, material	5 – 2 = 3	
Group 3		
attitude, color	12 – 5 = 7	
size, origin	11 – 3 = 8	average distance = 6.33
age, material	7 – 2 = 5	
Group 4		
attitude, origin	12 – 3 = 9	average distance = 9
size, material	11 – 2 = 9	

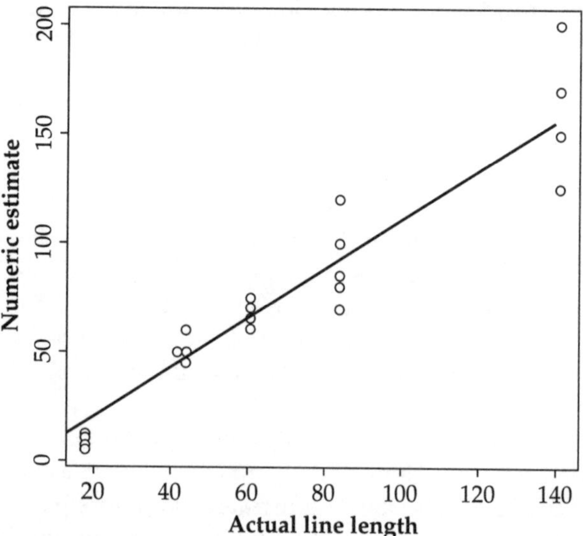

Figure 7.1 Participants' numerical estimates of line length are highly correlated with actual line length.

people can use magnitude estimation to report their subjective impressions.

R note. The actual lengths of the lines (in mm) are put in "x" and the numeric estimates are put in "y."

```
> x <- c(42,18,61,141,44,84)
```

You can enter data for more than one person into a table of rows and columns like this:

```
> y<- rbind(c(50,50,50,50,50,50,50,50,50,50,50,50),
c(10,5,10,10,12.5,10,12.5,10,10,7,10,10),
c(75,65,70,70,75,70,75,60,70,65,70,60),
c(150,150,170,200,150,150,125,150,150,150,150,150),
c(50,50,60,50,50,50,50,50,45,50,50,50),
c(100,100,120,100,100,100,100,70,85,80,100,100))
```

which produces a table where rows are for different lines and columns are for different participants:

```
> y
     [,1] [,2] [,3] [,4]  [,5] [,6]  [,7] [,8] [,9] [,10] [,11] [,12]
[1,]   50   50   50   50  50.0   50  50.0   50   50    50    50    50
[2,]   10    5   10   10  12.5   10  12.5   10   10     7    10    10
[3,]   75   65   70   70  75.0   70  75.0   60   70    65    70    60
[4,]  150  150  170  200 150.0  150 125.0  150  150   150   150   150
[5,]   50   50   60   50  50.0   50  50.0   50   45    50    50    50
[6,]  100  100  120  100 100.0  100 100.0   70   85    80   100   100
```

If you wish to examine the means estimated line length, averaging over participants, you can use a little "for" loop:

```
> mean.y = vector()
> for (i in 1:6) { mean.y[i] = mean(c(y[i,])) }
```

and this gives us a vector of the six average responses given by the participants (one mean for each row in the table of raw data):

```
> mean.y
[1] 50.0 9.75 68.75 153.75 50.42 96.25
>x
[1] 42.0 18 61 141 44 84
```

Clearly, the average subjective estimate (mean.y) is similar to the actual line length (x). The relationship can be quantified with a linear regression predicting the numeric responses from the actual line lengths. The function as.vector() is used to list the matrix y as a single vector of numbers. The function rep() repeats the x vector 12 times (one copy for each of the 12 participants).

```
> summary(lm(as.vector(y)~rep(x,12)))

Call:
lm(formula = as.vector(y) ~ rep(x, 12))

Residuals:
    Min       1Q  Median      3Q      Max
-32.583  -7.583   2.304  4.569  42.417

Coefficients:
              Estimate Std.   Error  t value  Pr(>|t|)
(Intercept)    -2.14910 2.29344  -0.937     0.352
rep(x, 12)      1.13285 0.03017  37.554    <2e-16  ***
---
Signif. codes: 0 '***' 0.001 '**' 0.01 '*' 0.05 '.' 0.1 ' ' 1

Residual standard error: 10.09 on 70 degrees of freedom
Multiple R-Squared: 0.9527,  Adjusted R-squared: 0.952
F-statistic: 1410 on 1 and 70 DF, p-value: < 2.2e-16
```

The average residual standard error of the participants' judgments is about 10 mm and the correlation between estimated line length and actual line length is high ($R^2 = 0.952$). As Figure 7.1 shows, larger errors occur for the longer line length. This may be related to Weber's law – sensitivity to differences decreases as magnitude increases – so that judgments about long lines are likely to be less accurate than judgments about short lines.

The degree of fit of the regression line can be visualized in a plot (see Figure 7.1). Try adding log="xy" to this plot command to see why psychophysical judgment data are often converted to a logarithmic scale before analysis:

```
> plot(rep(x,12),as.vector(y),xlab="actual line length",
   ylab="numeric estimate")
> curve(-2.1490 +1.13285*x,0,140,add=T)
```

Participants in this example experiment were asked to judge phrases in two ways: (1) by giving a numeric estimate of acceptability for each phrase, as they did for the lengths of the lines in the practice section; and (2) by drawing lines to represent the acceptability of each line. Bard et al. (1996) found that participants sometimes think of numeric estimates as something like academic test scores, and so limit their responses to a somewhat categorical scale (e.g. 70, 80, 90, 100), rather than using a ratio scale as intended in magnitude estimation. People have no such preconceptions about using line length to report their impressions, so we might expect more gradient, unbounded responses by measuring the lengths of lines that participants draw to indicate their impressions of phrase acceptability.

We have two measures of adjective order acceptability – line drawing and numerical estimation. These should have about a one-to-one relation with each other as they did in the numerical estimation of line length, so we will look for a slope of 1 between them as a measure of the validity of magnitude estimation as a measure of acceptability (see Bard et al. 1996). As you can see in Figure 7.2, looking at all of the raw data points in the data set, participants' judgments of phrase acceptability using line length were correlated with their numerical estimates.

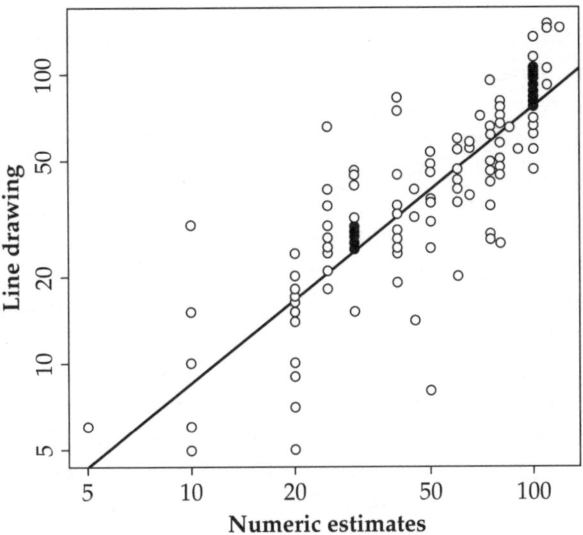

Figure 7.2 Cross-modal validation of adjective phrase acceptability judgments. log(lines) = –0.0335 + 0.96 * log(numbers), $R^2 = 0.744$.

The slope of this relationship is nearly exactly 1, but there is a certain amount of spread which seems to indicate that their impressions of the acceptability of the phrases were not as stable as were their impressions of line length.

Note also that the dots in Figure 7.2 appear in vertical stripes. This indicates that there were some "favorite" numbers given in the numerical estimates. For instance, the cluster of dots over x = 2 indicates that the numerical estimate 100 was given by many of the participants.

R note. I saved the raw line length and numeric estimate data in a text file "magest2.txt."

```
> mag <- read.delim("magest2.txt")
```

Figure 7.2 was made with the following commands.

```
> summary(lm(log(mag$lines)~log(mag$numbers)))
> plot(mag$numbers,mag$lines,log="xy",xlab="numeric
estimates",ylab="line drawing")
> abline(lm(log(mag$lines)~log(mag$numbers)))
```

Now, finally, we are ready to consider the linguistic question under discussion, namely whether acceptability is a function of the distance on the Hetzron (1978) template of preferred adjective order. We are concerned primarily with the consequences of putting the adjectives in the "wrong" order, testing the hypothesis that violations of the order predicted by the template will be more unacceptable the further the adjectives are from each other in the template.

I coded Hetzron distance as 1 if the adjectives were in the order predicted by the template, and 1 + the number of template slots that separate the adjectives when they were not in the correct order. I did this on the average distances in the four groups of experimental stimuli, so for each participant there were five categories of stimuli – correct, and then incorrect order with adjectives from group 1, 2, 3, or 4. There were 12 students in my class, who participated in this experiment (thanks guys!). Five of them were native speakers of English and 7 were non-native speakers of English.

Figure 7.3 shows the averaged results (again using the geometric mean to take the averages) separately for native speakers and nonnative

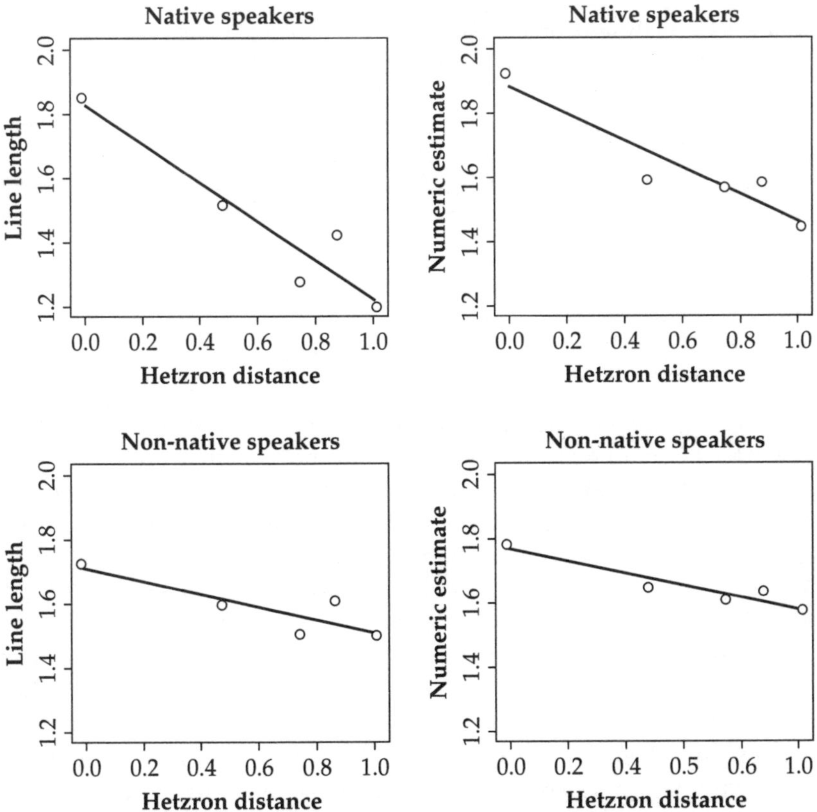

Figure 7.3 Adjective ordering acceptability, measured by line length responses (left panel) or by numerical estimates of acceptability (right panel), as a function of group number. Responses from native English speakers are in the top graphs and by nonnative speakers of English are in the bottom graphs.

speakers. Interestingly, the hypothesis is generally supported by the data. We find that acceptability goes down (on the vertical axis) as Hetzron distance goes up (on the horizontal axis). This was true for both native and nonnative speakers whether they were using numerical estimates of acceptability (the graphs on the right) or drawing lines to indicate acceptability (the graphs on the left).

Table 7.4 summarizes the line fits shown in Figure 7.3. The linear fits (in this log-log representation of the data) were generally quite good

Table 7.4 Analysis of an adjective ordering psychogrammatical law for native speakers of English and nonnative speakers of English.

		Slope	Fit
Native	lines	−0.61	0.90
	numbers	−0.42	0.89
Nonnative	lines	−0.20	0.75
	numbers	−0.19	0.91

for both groups of participants, with three of the four R^2 values near 0.9. The nonnative speakers produced functions that are about half as steep as the native speakers, indicating that their impressions of the acceptability of the phrases were generally less extreme than the impressions recorded by the native speakers. Interestingly, the slope of the line fitting the native speakers' responses was steeper for the line-drawing task than it was for the numerical estimation task. This may have been due to a tendency to limit the upper bound of their responses at 100.

In sum, this example magnitude estimation experiment illustrates the use of an empirical technique to elicit acceptability judgments. The hypothesis I tested is a somewhat naive one, but I hope that this demonstration will be provocative enough to cause someone to want to use magnitude estimation to study syntax.

R note. Figure 7.4 was drawn with these R commands. I also used `lm()` to calculate the regression coefficients used in the `curve()` commands here, and for the report of slopes and fits in Table 7.4.

```
> nl <- c(70.5, 33,19, 26.3, 15.8)
> fl <- c(52.6, 39.2, 31.8, 39.9, 31.5)
> nn <- c(83.1, 38.8, 36.7, 38.1, 27.7)
> fn <- c(59.9, 44.1, 40.8, 42.9, 37.4)
> d <- c(1,3, 5.5, 7.33,  10)
```

The Hetzron distance (d) that I entered into these graphs is 1 plus the number of slots that separate the adjectives in the template (see Table 7.3) for those phrases in which the adjectives are in the wrong order. Phrases in which the adjectives were in the correct order were given a 1 on the distance axis (d) in these figures. The log10 of d then ranges from 0 to 1.

```
> par(mfrow(c(2,2))
> plot(log10(d),log10(nl),ylim = c(1.2,2),main="Native
    speakers",xlab="Hetzron distance", ylab="line length")
> curve(1.82853 - 0.60942*x,0,1,add=T)

> plot(log10(d),log10(nn),ylim = c(1.2,2),main="Native
    speakers",xlab="Hetzron distance", ylab="numeric
    estimate")
> curve(1.88125 - 0.42488*x,0,1,add=T)

> plot(log10(d),log10(fl),ylim = c(1.2,2),main="Non-native
    speakers",xlab="Hetzron distance", ylab="line length")
> curve(1.70625 - 0.1996*x,0,1,add=T)

> plot(log10(d),log10(fn),ylim = c(1.2,2),main="Non-native
    speakers",xlab="Hetzron distance", ylab="numeric
    estimate")
> curve(1.76282 - 0.18694*x,0,1,add=T)
```

7.3 Linear Mixed Effects in the Syntactic Expression of Agents in English

In this section we will be using a data set drawn from the *Wall Street Journal* text corpus that was used in the CoNLL-2005 (Conference on Computational Natural Language Learning) shared task to develop methods for automatically determining semantic roles in sentences of English. Semantic roles such as agent, patient, instrument, etc. are important for syntactic and semantic descriptions of sentences, and automatic semantic role determination also has a practical application, because in order for a natural language processing system to function correctly (say to automatically summarize a text), it must be able to get the gist of each sentence and how the sentences interact with each other in a discourse. This kind of task crucially requires knowledge of semantic roles – who said what, or who did what to whom.

Well, that's what the CoNLL-2005 shared task was. In this section, I'm just using their database for an example of mixed-effects modeling asking a very simple (if not simplistic) question. We want to know whether the size (in number of words used to express it) of the noun phrase that corresponds to the "agent" role in a sentence is related to the size (again in number of words) of the material that comes before the clause that contains the agent expression. The idea is that expression of agent may be abbreviated in subordinate or subsequent clauses.

What we will do in this section is investigate a method for fitting linear "mixed-effects" models where we have some fixed effects and some random effects. Particularly, we will be looking at linear mixed-effects models and a logistic regression extension of this approach to modeling linguistic data. As I mentioned in the introduction to the book, this is some of the most sophisticated modeling done in linguistic research and even more than with other methods introduced in this book it is important to consult more detailed reference works as you work with these models. In particular, the book *Mixed-Effect Models in S and S-Plus* by Pinheiro and Bates (2004) is very helpful.

In the example here, we will use the *Wall Street Journal* corpus data compiled for CoNLL-2005 to build linear mixed-effects models that predict the size (in words) of the agent expression. Some examples will help to clarify how the data is coded.

With "take" in the sense of "to acquire or come to have" (this is verb sense 01 for "take" in Verbnet), argument zero (A0) is the *taker*, and argument one (A1) is the *thing taken*. So the sentence "President Carlos Menem took office July 8" is tagged as:

(A0 President Carlos Menem)(V took)(A1 office)(AM July 8).

where the tag "AM" is a generic tag for modifiers. In almost all cases A0 is used to tag the agent role.

In the longer sentence below, the clause containing "take" is embedded in a matrix clause "the ruling gives x." The phrase "pipeline companies" is coded as A0, and "advantage" as A1. In addition to this, the fact that there was earlier material in the sentence is coded using the label N0. So the argument structure frame for the verb "take" in this sentence is:

(N0)(A0)(V=take)(A1)(A2)

> According to industry lawyers, the ruling gives pipeline companies an important second chance to resolve remaining disputes and take advantage of the cost-sharing mechanism.

The question that we are concerned with in this example is whether there is any relationship between the number of words used to express the agent, A0, and the number of words earlier in the sentence, N0. There are a number of indeterminacies in the data that will add noise to our predictive models. The N0 labels do not contain information as to whether the target verb, "take" in the examples above, is the matrix verb of the sentence, or in an embedded clause. Additionally, the dependent measure that we are looking at here, the number of words used to express A0, is a very rough way of capturing the potential syntactic complexity of the agent expression (if indeed an agent is specifically mentioned at all). Nonetheless, this little exercise will help to demonstrate mixed-effects modeling.

7.3.1 Linear regression: Overall, and separately by verbs

The relationship between the number of words used to express the agent (a_0) and the number of words present in an earlier portion of the sentence (n_0) is shown in Figure 7.4. This figure illustrates that agent size is clearly not determined by the quantity of prior material in a sentence. There may be some non-trivial, reliable relationship but there are clearly other factors at work. This is normal. In a complicated system such as language many factors (including randomness and experimenter error) are at work. We'll be investigating our ability to detect patterns in such noisy data.

The data in Figure 7.4 are plotted on a log scale, and all of the analyses described here were done with log transformed data because the raw data are positively skewed (the size of a clause cannot be less than zero). The log transform removes some of the skewness and decreases the impact of some of the rare longer agent phrases (the longest of which was 53 words!).

The negative slope of the regression line in Figure 7.4 (a simple linear regression predicting a_0 from n_0) indicates that, overall, there is a relationship between the size of the agent phrase (a_0) and the size of the preceding words (n_0). As the size of the preceding material increases, the size of the agent clause decreases.

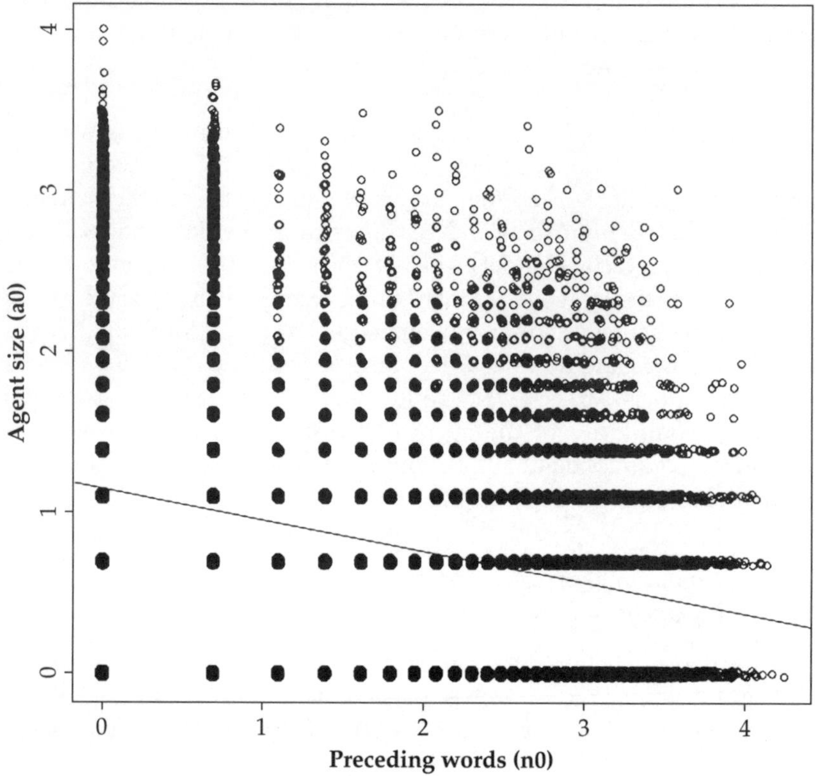

Figure 7.4 A scatter plot of the relationship between the (log) number of words prior to the target verb clause (n_0) and the (log) number of words in the agent of the clause (a_0). Symbols are "jittered" so it is more apparent that there are many instances of particular combinations of a_0 and n_0.

Although the linear regression model does find a significant relationship between a_0 and n_0 [t(30588) = –53.46, p < 0.01] (see table 7.5), the amount of variance in a_0 that is captured by this regression is only 8.5% ($R^2 = 0.085$). The large number of observations in the corpus sort of guarantees that we will find a "significant" effect, but the magnitude of the effect is small.

Additionally, the overall regression in Figure 7.4 and Table 7.5 assumes, incorrectly, that all of the verbs in the corpus have the same negative relationship between agent size and the size of the preceding material in the sentence. Furthermore, the overall regression assumes

Table 7.5 Coefficients in an overall linear regression predicting a_0 from n_0.

	Coefficients:			
	Estimate	Std. Error	t value	Pr(>|t|)
(Intercept)	1.146171	0.005827	196.68	<2e-16 ***
n0	-0.194533	0.003639	-53.46	<2e-16 ***

that each observation in the database is independent of all of the others, when we should suspect that observations from different verbs might systematically differ from each other. We have seen a situation like this in the chapter on psycholinguistics above (Ch. 4), where we dealt with data containing repeated measurements over an experimental "unit," like people or language materials, by performing separate ANOVAs for subjects as a random effect and items as a random effect. Mixed effects modeling (the topic of this section) is an alternative approach for handling data with mixed random and fixed factors, and is particularly appropriate for data with uneven numbers of observations on the random effects because it uses maximum likelihood estimation procedures (as is done in `glm()` for logistic regression) rather than least squares estimation. This is important for these agent complexity data because the number of observations per verb is not equal. "Say" occurs in the data set 8,358 times while there are only 412 occurrences of "know." (The implications of this asymmetry regarding the type of reporting in the *Wall Street Journal* is beyond the scope of this chapter.)

We will analyze these agent complexity data with mixed-effects models in which the verbs are treated as random – as if we were selecting verbs from a larger population of verbs. This is not entirely accurate because I simply selected data for all of the verbs that occur at least 400 times in the corpus, so the sample is biased so that our results characterize frequent verbs more than infrequent ones.

Figure 7.5 shows the intercept and slope values (with their confidence intervals) for 32 separate linear regressions – one for each of the verbs in the "vbarg" data set. This figure shows that the intercept values particularly, and perhaps also the slope values, are different for different verbs. Two of the verbs ("rise" and "fall") never occur with an explicit

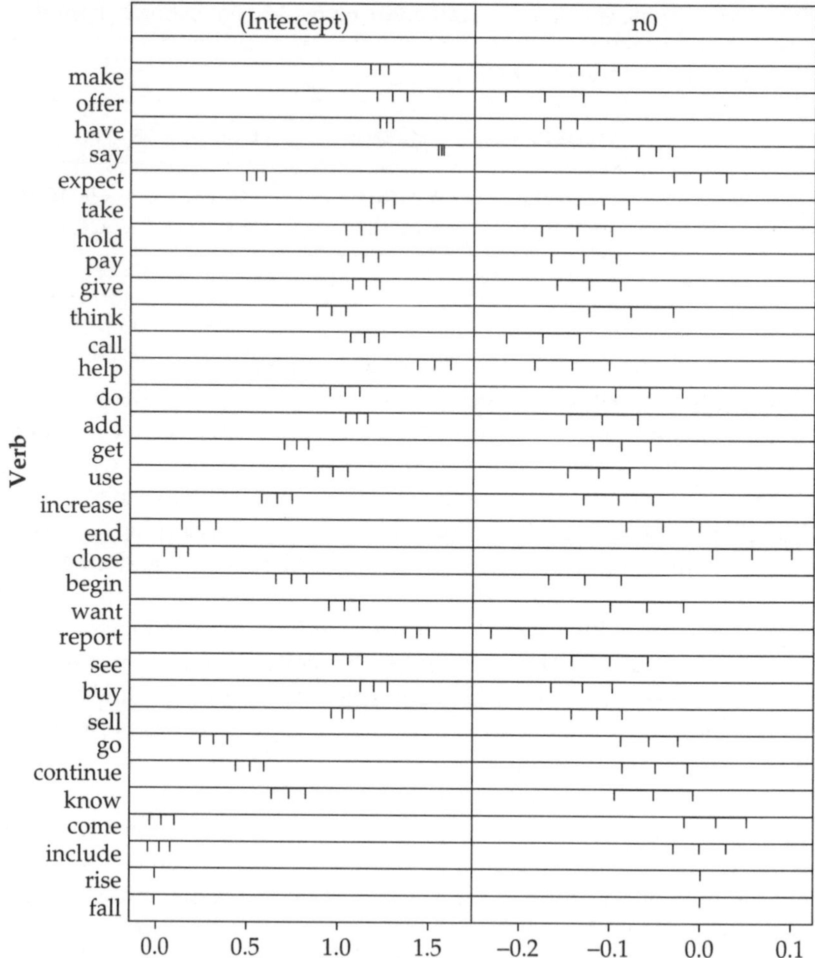

Figure 7.5 Intercept and slope (labeled "n_0") and their confidence intervals from separate linear regressions predicting a_0 from n_0 for each of 32 verbs in vbarg.txt.

agent in this corpus, so they always have a_0 of zero, while "say" tends to have a long a_0 (an average length of about five words).

Because the verbs differ from each other in how n_0 and a_0 are related to each other, we need to devise a model that takes verb differences into account in order to correctly evaluate any general (verb independent) relationship between n_0 and a_0.

R note. The agent complexity data are in the text data file "vbarg.txt." This file has columns indicating the location of the verb in the sentence (vnum) counting from 0 up, the identity of the verb, the verb sense number (see http://verbs.colorado.edu/framesets/ for a complete listing), a text field that shows the argument structure of the verb, a number indicating the location of A0 in the argument structure where –1 means that A0 immediately precedes the verb and 1 means that A0 is immediately after the verb. The next column in the dataset similarly codes the location of the patient (A1). The remaining columns have numbers indicating the number of words that are used to express A0–A3 and that occur before (N0) or after (N1) the verb clause.

```
vnum,verb,sense,args,A0loc,A1loc,A0size,A1size,A2size,A3size,
N0size,N1size
1,take,01,(N0)(A0)(V)(A1)(AM)(N1),-1,1,2,2,0,0,17,25
0,say,01,(A0)(V)(A1),-1,1,4,14,0,0,0,0
1,expect,01,(N0)(A0)(V)(A1),-1,1,1,12,0,0,5,0
0,sell,01,(A0)(AM)(V)(A1)(AM),-2,1,4,2,0,0,0,0
0,say,01,(A0)(V)(A1),-1,1,9,18,0,0,0,0
0,increase,01,(A0)(V)(A1)(A4)(A3),-1,1,3,2,0,5,0,0
```

The data set can be read into R using csv() and you can see the column headings with names(), and an overall summary of the data with summary().

```
>vbarg <- read.csv("vbarg.txt")
>names(vbarg)
[1] "vnum"   "verb"   "sense"  "args"   "A0loc"  "A1loc" "A0size"
[8] "A1size" "A2size" "A3size" "N0size" "N1size"
```

The summary results indicate that "say" is the most frequent verb in this dataset (I should mention that I only included verbs that occurred at least 400 times in the larger training set). The most common argument structure was (A0)(V)(A1), and the median values for A0loc and A1loc (–1 and 1) are as we would expect given the most frequent argument structures. A0size tends to be smaller than A1size and N0size.

I added log transformed counts for A0size and N0size with the following commands. These commands add new columns to the data frame.

```
> vbarg$a0 <- log(vbarg$A0size+1)
> vbarg$n0 <- log(vbarg$N0size+1)
```

For some of the plotting commands in the nlme library it is very convenient to convert the data frame into a grouped data object. This type of data object is exactly like the original data frame but with a header containing useful information about how to plot the data; including a formula that indicates the response and covariate variables and the grouping variable, and some labels to use on plots.

```
> library(nlme) # this line loads the nonlinear mixed effects
    library
> vbarg.gd <- groupedData(a0~n0|verb,vbarg)
```

The overall linear regression shown in Figure 7.4 was done with the familiar `lm()` command and a simple `plot()` and `abline()` command. Note the use of the `jitter()` function to displace the points slightly during drawing.

```
> summary(lm(vbarg$a0~vbarg$n0)->alla0n0)
> plot(jitter(vbarg$a0,4)~jitter(vbarg$n0,4), ylab="Agent
    size (a0)", xlab="Preceding words (n0)")
> abline(lm(vbarg$a0~vbarg$n0))
```

The graph of 32 separate linear regression fits (Figure 7.5) was produced using the very convenient function `lmList()` in the nlme library of R routines. The formula statement for this command is the same as the one we use in a standard linear regression, except that after a vertical bar, a grouping factor is listed, so that in this `lmList()` statement, the data are first sorted according to the verb and then the $a_0 \sim n_0$ regression fit is calculated for each verb. The `intervals()` command returns the estimated regression coefficients for each verb, and gives the high and low bounds of a 95% confidence interval around the estimate.

```
> library(lattice) # graphics routines
> trellis.device(color=F) # set the graphics device to black
    and white
> a0n0.lis <- lmList(a0~n0|verb,data=vbarg.gd)
> plot(intervals(a0n0.lis))  # figure 7.5
```

7.3.2 *Fitting a linear mixed-effects model: Fixed and random effects*

Linear mixed-effects modeling uses restricted maximum likelihood estimation (REML) to fit a mixed-effects model to the data. The model is specified in two parts. The first defines the fixed effects, which for this model is the formula $a_0 \sim n_0$ to specify that we are trying to predict the (log) size of agent expression from the (log) size of whatever occurred prior to the verb clause. In the first model, the one I named "a0n0.lme," the random component is identified as the grouping factor "verb" alone (`random = ~ 1 | verb`). This produces a separate intercept value for each verb, so that this model, unlike the overall regression, does not assume that average agent size is the same for each verb. We also do not let the most frequent verb dominate the estimate of the fixed effect. The difference between "say" and other verbs is captured in the random effects estimates, so that the fixed effects estimates represent the pattern of $a_0 \sim n_0$ found across verbs – controlling for verb-specific differences.

The `summary()` results of this analysis suggest that there is a strong effect of n_0 on a_0 even after we control for the the different average size of a_0 for different verbs (this is an intercept-only model in which we assume that the slope of the n_0 effect is the same for each verb). A *t*-test of the n_0 coefficient shows that this fixed coefficient (−0.10) is reliably different from zero [$t(30557) = -31.4$, $p < 0.01$].

Interestingly, it is not clear from the statistics literature how to compare the goodness of fit of a linear mixed-effects model and a simple linear model. Because of the extra parameters involved in calculating the mixed-effects model we should always have a better fit in absolute terms, and because the assumptions of the mixed-effects model are a better match to the data than are the assumptions of the simple linear model, we should go ahead and use linear mixed effects. Then to compare different mixed-effects models we use a log-likelihood ratio test that will be outlined below.

I offer here two ways to compare the goodness of fit of linear mixed-effects models and simple linear models. In one measure we take the root mean square of the residual errors as a measure of the degree to which the model fails to predict the data. These values are calculated using the R function `resid()`. An alternative measure suggested by Jose Pinhiero is to estimate the variance accounted for by each model (the R^2). This method uses the functions `fitted()` and `getResponse()`

Table 7.6 Degree of fit measured two ways for various models of the verb argument size data.

	RMS of the residuals		Estimated R^2	
	All data	**Subset ($a_0 > 0$)**	**All data**	**Subset ($a_0 > 0$)**
Linear model	0.77	0.615	0.085	0.080
Mixed-effects models				
slope only	0.734	0.606	0.170	0.107
intercept only	0.626	0.595	0.395	0.139
intercept and slope	0.624	0.594	0.403	0.143

to calculate the correlation between model predictions and input data. As Table 7.6 shows by both of these measures, the mixed-effects model that permits a random factor for the intercept for each verb is a better fit. The size of the residual goes down (from 0.77 in the linear model to 0.626 in the LME model) and the variance accounted for goes up (from 0.085 to 0.395).

I would mention also that I used a cross-validation technique to measure the robustness of these models. In order to be sure that the model parameters were not overfitted to the data I calculated each model 100 times using 85% of the data set to calculate the model and then using the remaining 15% of the cases as a test set to evaluate the fit of the model. The RMS and R^2 values that are shown in Table 7.6 are the mean values found in the cross-validation runs. The standard deviation of the 100 RMS estimates was always at about 0.007. Thus, the 95% confidence interval for the RMS in the slope-only model for "all data" was 0.72–0.748. The standard deviation of the R^2 was also extremely low at about 0.01. So, for example, the 95% confidence interval around the intercept-only "all data" model was 0.376–0.414. This encompasses the intercept and slope model, so we would conclude that adding slope coefficients to the model doesn't significantly improve the fit of the model. Cross-validation is an extremely powerful way to determine the success of a statistical model. Without it we don't really know whether a model will have acceptable performance on new data.

Table 7.6 also shows that in exploring these data I also looked at five other mixed-effects models. We turn now to these.

R note. In all of the models tested in this section the fixed effects formula is $a_0 \sim n_0$ – that is, we test the degree to which a_0 can be predicted from n_0. In the first mixed-effects model (the one I named "a0n0.lme") the random component is identified as the grouping factor "verb" using "random = ~ 1 | verb. The 1 in the formula indicates that we want to include the intercepts and not the slopes. This produces a separate intercept estimate for each verb, as if the only difference from verb to verb is the average size of the agent that the verb typically takes. I then used the `update()` function to change this model by modifying the random statement so that it includes a separate slope estimate for each verb as well as the different intercepts.

```
> a0n0.lme <- lme(a0~n0,data=vbarg.gd,random = ~ 1|verb)
> a0n0.lme2 <- update(a0n0.lme, random = ~ n0|verb)
```

The random statement to get by-verb estimates of slope with no random intercept values is:

```
> a0n0.lme5 <- update(a0n0.lme, random = ~ n0 - 1|verb)
```

The RMS of the residuals is calculated from the output of `resid()`. The lme() object has multiple levels of residuals depending on the number of grouping variables. Level 1 indicates that we want residuals taken using both fixed and random effects in the model. Level 0 would give residuals from the fixed-effects only model.

```
> sqrt(mean(resid(a0n0.lme2,level=1)^2))
> sqrt(mean(resid(a0n0.lm)^2))
```

Estimated R^2 values for `lme()` models can be obtained from the fitted values and the input values. That is, the output of `getResponse` is a vector of the same values that you will find in vbarg$a0. So this statement simply takes the (square of the) correlation between the model's predicted values for each verb in the data set, and the actual values in the data set. I have seen some complaints in online discussion groups that this estimate is incorrect, but it looks reasonable to me.

```
> cor(fitted(a0n0.lme2),getResponse(a0n0.lme2))^2
```

The cross-validation technique can be implemented with a small "for" loop which repeats the linear mixed-effect model fitting operation one hundred times. I used two arrays to store the RMS and R^2 results of each analysis. One trick in this procedure is that the `split()` command creates a new data set, here called "xx," which has a TRUE subset which is about 85% of the observations, and a FALSE subset which is about 15% of the observations. Thus the designation "xx$`TRUE`" is a dataset composed of 85% of the observations in "vbarg.gd." The `predict()` command takes the model specification in mod and applies it to the dataset in "xx$`FALSE`" giving a set of predicted a_0 argument sizes. We can then compare these predicted values with the actual values in the test set to derived RMS error or R^2 "variance accounted for" measures of how well a model calculated from the training data fits the test set of data.

```
# here is a loop to split the vbarg data set - 85% training,
15% test
# fit a nlme model to the training data,
# see how well the model predicts the argument size in the
# test data, and collect the results for averaging/plotting
RMS<-array(dim=100) # allocate space for results
Rsquared <- array(dim=100)
for (i in 1:100) {
  # step 1: Split the data into training and test sets
  split(vbarg.gd,factor(runif(30590)>0.15))->xx
  # step 2: estimate model parameters with the training set
  mod <-lme(a0 ~ n0, data=xx$`TRUE`,random = ~ 1|verb)
  # step 3: get model predictions for the test set
  predict(mod,xx$`FALSE`)->pred
  # calculate the root mean square error of the prediction
  RMS[i] <- sqrt(mean((pred-xx$`FALSE`$a0)^2))
  Rsquared[i] <- cor(pred,xx$`FALSE`$a0)^2
}
mean(RMS)
sd(RMS)
mean(Rsquared)
sd(Rsquared)
```

7.3.3 *Fitting five more mixed-effects models: Finding the best model*

We noticed in Figure 7.5 that the intercept values for verb-specific linear regressions were noticeably different, so we used a mixed-effects model that has random effects for the intercepts. It is also apparent in Figure 7.5, though, that the slope values relating n_0 to a_0 are also somewhat different from one verb to the next. Because we are especially interested in testing for a general trend for the slope across verbs it is important to control for verb-specific slope values. This is done by changing the specification of the random component of our model so that it includes an indication that we want to treat slope as a verb-specific random component (random = ~ n0 | verb).

Now we can perform a couple of tests to determine (1) whether this new "verb-specific" intercept and slope model is an improvement over the intercept only model, and (2) whether there is still a fixed effect for slope.

The first of these is a test of whether a model with random effects for slope and intercept (verb-specific estimates) fits the data better than a model with only verb-specific intercept estimates. And this is done with a likelihood ratio test. The likelihood ratio is familiar from the discussion in Chapter 5, where we saw that the likelihood ratio is asymptotically distributed as χ^2, and we used this likelihood ratio test to compare models. The same procedure is used with mixed-effects models. The likelihood ratio comparing an "intercept only" model with an "intercept and slope" model is 320, which is significantly greater than chance ($p < 0.001$). This indicates that adding a random factor for slope significantly improved the fit of the model.

The second test we perform is a test of the fixed effects coefficients. After adding a random effect for slope, it may now be that any effect of n_0 is to be found in the random slope values for the verbs, and there is then no remaining overall fixed effect for n_0 on a_0. A *t*-test, produced by the R `summary()` function, evaluating whether the n_0 slope coefficient is significantly different from zero, suggests that it is [$t(30557) = -8.32$, $p < 0.001$]. As in the simple linear regression, the slope coefficient is negative, suggesting that as the preceding material increases in size the agent phrase decreases in size.

R note. The anova() function is defined to calculate the likelihood ratio test for comparing two mixed-effects models (if they have different degrees of freedom).

```
> anova(a0n0.lme,a0n0.lme2) # intercept only vs. intercept
    and slope
          Model df      AIC      BIC    logLik   Test  L.Ratio p-value
a0n0.lme      1  4 58410.54 58443.86 -29201.27
a0n0.lme2     2  6 58094.34 58144.31 -29041.17 1 vs 2 320.2043  <.0001
```

To see a *t*-test of the fixed effects coefficients use the summary() function. This printout also suggests that the random effects for intercept and slope are negatively correlated with each other (Corr = –0.837) as shown in Figure 7.7.

```
> summary(a0n0.lme2)
Linear mixed-effects model fit by REML
Data: vbarg
     AIC      BIC    logLik
58094.34 58144.31 -29041.17

Random effects:
 Formula: ~n0 | verb
 Structure: General positive-definite, Log-Cholesky
 parametrization
             StdDev     Corr
(Intercept)  0.46999336 (Intr)
n0           0.06576902 -0.837
Residual     0.62275052

Fixed effects: a0 ~ n0
                 Value  Std.Error    DF   t-value  p-value
(Intercept)  0.8528160 0.08333595 30557 10.233470        0
n0          -0.1011621 0.01216013 30557 -8.319166        0
Correlation:
  (Intr)
n0 -0.814
Standardized Within-Group Residuals:
       Min         Q1        Med        Q3       Max
-2.5221371 -0.6895952 -0.1013437 0.4215483 5.0763747

Number of Observations: 30590
Number of Groups: 32
```

This is visualized in Figure 7.6. In this figure, the regression lines are those predicted by the linear mixed-effects model with random verb effects for both the intercept and slope of the regression. Note that the slopes are negative for most verbs. It is also apparent that these data are not especially well fit by a linear function (at least one with only a single predictor variable), but the modeling results do suggest that amongst all this noise there is a relationship between a_0 and n_0 – we do seem to have identified n_0 as a general predictor of agent size independent of any verb-specific effects.

Just for completeness, I also constructed a "slope only" model with random verb-specific effects only for the slope of the $a_0 \sim n_0$ regression, and again found that the "intercept and slope" model provides the best fit to the data.

However, another diagnostic plot (Figure 7.7) calls into question the conclusion that there is a general verb-independent relationship between a_0 and n_0. In Figure 7.7 we see that the random intercept and slope estimates in this model (the two random effects that were estimated for each verb) are clearly related to each other. When the intercept was bigger, the slope was more strongly negative. You can see how this might be an artifact of agentless sentences by looking again at the data in Figure 7.6.

If we hypothesize that agentless ($a_0 = 0$) clauses are more likely in embedded clauses (at least some of the sentences with $n_0 > 0$), as the scatter plots in Figure 7.6 might suggest, then it may be that the number of agentless sentences in which a verb appears determines both the slope and the intercept of the $a_0 \sim n_0$ regression. I tested whether the presence of agentless clauses might be the source of the finding that size of agent phrase is predicted by size of prior material by rerunning the analyses with a subset of the vbarg.txt data set from which I removed agentless sentences.

The conclusion we draw from this analysis of cases in which there was an overt agent expression is no different from the conclusion we arrived at using the whole data set. Even allowing for random verb-specific effects for both the average size of the agent phrase (the intercept) and the relationship between agent phrase size and size of prior material (the slope), there was a significant overall fixed effect of N0size on agent phrase size [coef = –0.108, t(21822) = –16, p < 0.001]. Recall that the slope coefficient from the best-fitting model of the whole data set was –0.101, almost the same as the slope value found in this analysis of a subset of data. The best-fitting

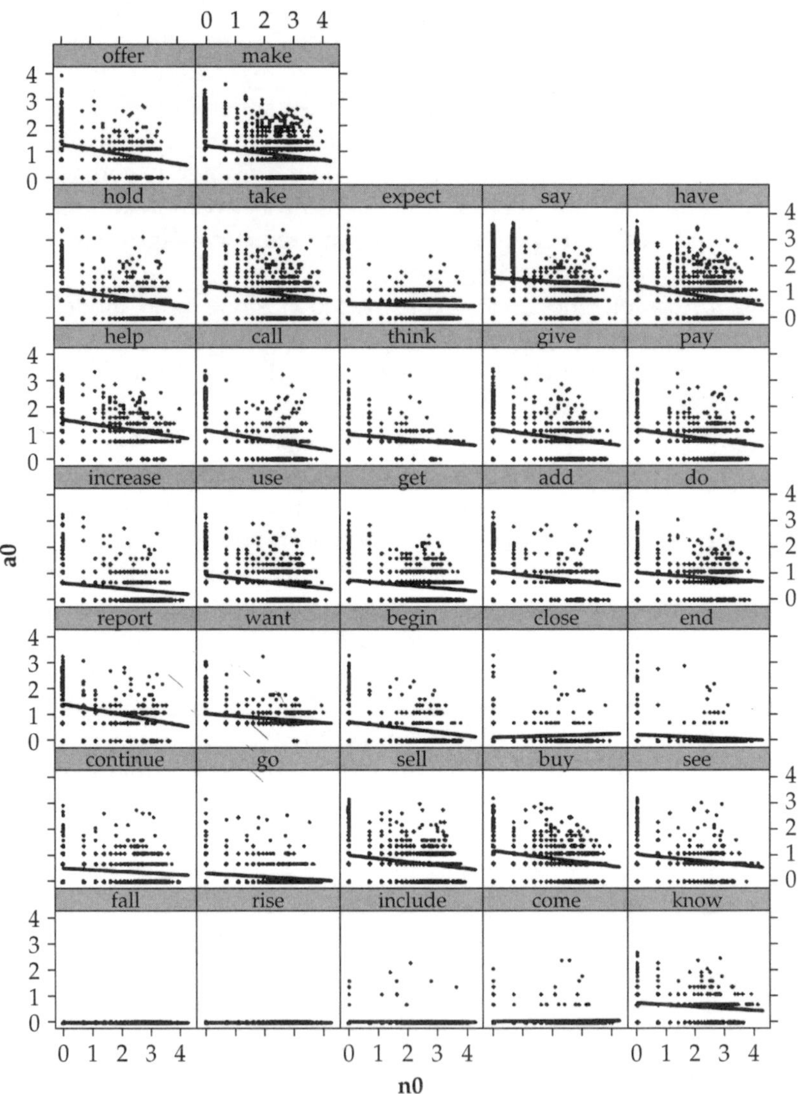

Figure 7.6 The dots in each graph show the raw data for the (log) size of the agent phrase (a_0) as a function of the (log) size of the phrase that occurs before the agent phrase (n_0). Each panel in this plot corresponds to a verb-specific plot of the data shown in Figure 7.4. This plot was generated with the R command: `plot(augPred(a0n0.lme2), col=1, cex=0.2, lwd=2)`.

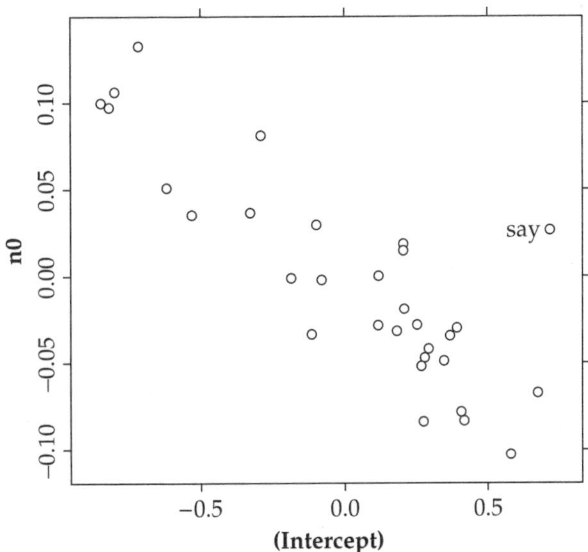

Figure 7.7 The estimates of the random effects in the mixed-effects model of the verb argument data. Each dot shows the intercept and slope parameters for one of the verbs ("say" is the only one labeled). The command to produce this graph was: `pairs(a0n0.lme2,~ranef(.), id=~verb=="say",adj=1.3)`.

lines of the two analyses are plotted against the whole data set in Figure 7.8.

R note. I used the `subset()` function to remove agentless clauses and then used `lme()` and `update()` to fit the mixed-effects model to the subset.

```
> vbarg.subset <- subset(vbarg,a0>0) # extract the subset
> vbarg.subset.gd <- groupedData(a0~n0|verb,vbarg.subset)

> a0n0.lme4 <- lme(a0~n0, data=vbarg.subset.gd, random =
    ~ 1|verb)

> a0n0.lme5 <- update(a0n0.lme4, random = ~ n0 - 1|verb)
> a0n0.lme3 <- update(a0n0.lme4, random = ~ n0|verb)
```

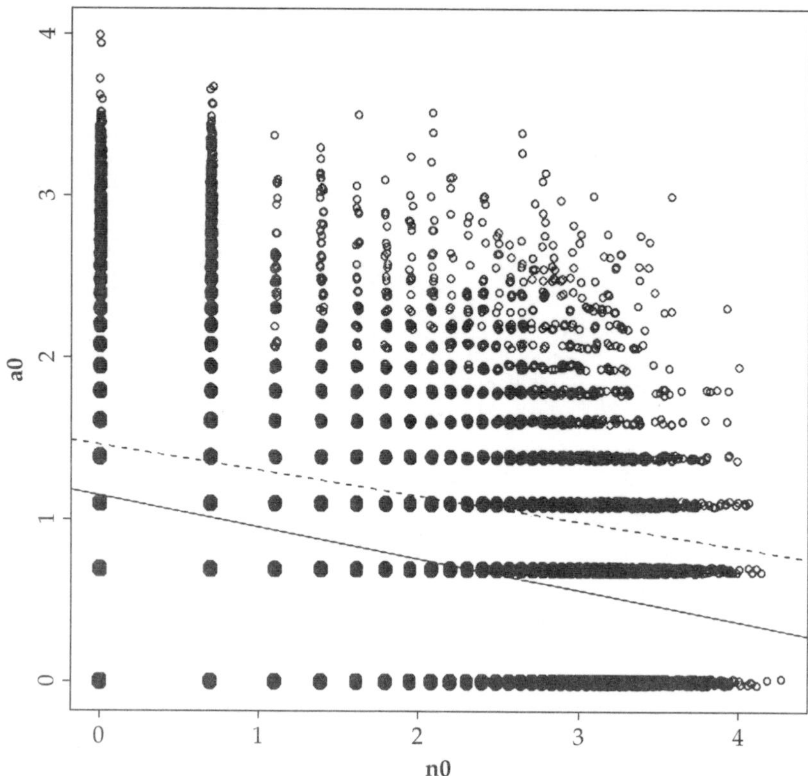

Figure 7.8 Comparison of the fixed effects regression fits for the best-fitting model that included agentless clauses (solid line) and for the best model of the subset of data that did have an overt agent expression (dashed line). The figure shows that the two models have almost identical slope values and only differ on their y-intercept.

```
> anova(a0n0.lme4,a0n0.lme3) # intercept only vs. intercept
    and slope
          Model df      AIC      BIC    logLik   Test  L.Ratio p-value
a0n0.lme4     1  4 39450.03 39481.99 -19721.01
a0n0.lme3     2  6 39412.69 39460.64 -19700.35 1 vs 2 41.33428  <.0001
```

```
> anova(a0n0.lme5,a0n0.lme3) # slope only vs. intercept and
    slope
          Model df      AIC      BIC    logLik   Test  L.Ratio p-value
a0n0.lme5     1  4 40246.02 40277.99 -20119.01
a0n0.lme3     2  6 39412.69 39460.64 -19700.35 1 vs 2 837.3299  <.0001
```

I would note here that the lme object can be passed to anova() for a test of fixed effect factors in a mixed-effects model. In these models I didn't use this because n_0 is a numeric variable and hence only a single coefficient is estimated. In this case the t-value returned by summary() suffices – and is the square-root of the *F*-value reported by anova(). But if you have a multilevel factor there will be a t-value for each dummy variable coefficient used to represent the levels of the factor, and thus anova() is a handy way to test for an overall effect of the factor.

```
> anova(a0n0.lme3)
            numDF denDF  F-value p-value
(Intercept)     1 21822 1823.516  <.0001
n0              1 21822  256.255  <.0001
```

7.4 Predicting the Dative Alternation: Logistic Modeling of Syntactic Corpora Data

Bresnan et al. (2007) published an elegant paper describing a series of logistic regression analyses of the English dative alternation. They were also kind enough to share their data with me, so this section describes how they analyzed their data. I also agree with the larger point of their paper and so I'll mention here that this analysis of the syntactic realization of data is an important demonstration of the gradient, non-modular nature of linguistic knowledge. All-or-none, deterministic rules of grammar are an inadequate formalism for capturing the richness of linguistic knowledge. This basic outlook is one of the main reasons that I wrote this book (here, finally, in the last section of the last chapter of the book I reveal my motives!). I think that for linguistics as a discipline to make any significant strides forward in our understanding of language, linguists need to be equipped with the tools of quantitative analysis.

So, let's see what the dative alternation situation is about and how Bresnan et al. used statistical analysis of corpus data to understand the facts of dative alternation.

Of the two alternative ways to say the same thing:

(1) a That movie gave the creeps to me.
    b That movie gave me the creeps.

The first is probably not as acceptable to you as the second. The question addressed by Bresnan et al. is to account for this preference. Sentences (1a) and (1b) illustrate the dative alternation in which the recipient ("me" in these sentences) can be expressed in a prepositional phrase "to me" or as a bare noun phrase. So sentence (1a) illustrates the prepositional dative structure and sentence (1b) illustrates the double object dative structure.

Although the prepositional structure (1a) is dispreferred, it doesn't take much investigation to find sentences where the prepositional dative structure is probably better. Consider for example sentences (2a) and (2b):

(2) a I pushed the box to John.
    b I pushed John the box.

Here it is likely that you will find (2a), the prepositional structure, to be preferable to (2b).

There are a number of possible factors that may influence whether the prepositional dative seems preferable to the double object dative. For example, whether the recipient ("me" or "John") is expressed as a pronoun or as a longer phrase may influence whether the prepositional dative structure or the double object construction seems more natural. So you may be happier with (3a) than (3b):

(3) a This will give the creeps to just about anyone.
    b This will give just about anyone the creeps.

Whether or not the theme has been mentioned more recently in the discourse (has greater discourse accessibility) affects realization of the dative – such that the *given* (discourse accessible) argument is more likely to occur just after the verb. For example, sentence (2a) is more likely in discourse fragment (4a) in which "box" is given in prior discourse context, while sentence (2b) is more likely in a discourse context in which John is given (4b).

(4) a I got down a box of crayons. I pushed the box to John.
  b John is one of those people who has to see for himself. I pushed John the box.

This factor in dative alternation is one of an interesting constellation of factors that seem to influence the order of verb arguments conspiring (in English at least) to "save the good stuff 'til last."

- Given information precedes new.
- Pronouns precede nonpronouns.
- Definites precede nondefinites.
- Shorter NPs precede longer NPs.

These factors can be evaluated in dative alternation.

R note. You will find the Bresnan et al. (2007) dative data in the file "BresDative.txt." This is a recoding of their original data file in which I used mnemonic labels for the codes that they applied to each example. You will note that the results discussed in this chapter are slightly different from the results given in Bresnan et al. This is because a couple of minor predictive factors that they used in their models are not available in this data set.

```
> dat <- read.table("BresDative.txt",header=T)
> names(dat)
 [1] "real"    "verb"    "class"   "vsense"  "animrec" "animth"
 [7] "defrec"  "defth"   "prorec"  "proth"   "accrec"  "accth"
[13] "ldiff"   "mod"
```

The data come from two corpora – 2,360 instances from the Switchboard corpus of conversational speech, and 905 instances from the *Wall Street Journal* corpus of text. I coded this difference with labels in the "mod" column of the data set.

```
> attach(dat)
> table(mod)
mod
switchboard  wallstreet
       2360         905
```

We will use the Switchboard and *Wall Street Journal* subsets separately so we'll pull these data into separate data frames.

```
> subset(dat,mod=="switchboard") -> SwitchDat
> subset(dat,mod=="wallstreet") -> WSJDat
```

Bresnan et al. (2007) coded 3,265 datives taken from two corpora of American English. The coding scheme marked the realization of the dative (PP = Prepositional construction, NP = double object construction) and then for each instance marked the discourse accessibility, definiteness, animacy, and pronominality of the recipient and theme. They also noted the semantic class of the verb (abstract, transfer, future transfer, prevention of possession, and communication). Finally, we also have in the data set a measure of the difference between the (log) length of the recipient and (log) length of the theme.

Obviously, the collection of such a carefully coded data set is nine-tenths of the research. The statistical analysis is the easy part (especially with a helpful chapter like this!), and no statistical analysis in the world can compensate for an unrepresentative, incomplete, or too small data set.

7.4.1 *Logistic model of dative alternation*

The variable that we wish to predict, or wish our model to account for, is the realization of the dative. This is a binary outcome variable – the person either used a preposition construction or a double object construction. In other words, the analysis problem here is exactly what we saw in the sociolinguistics chapter with variable pronunciation outcomes.

So it should come as no surprise that we can use the generalized linear model [glm()] to fit a logistic regression predicting dative outcome from discourse accessibility, semantic class, etc.

R note. The logistic model of dative alternation is fit with the `glm()` function, just as in Chapter 5.

```
> modelA <-glm(real ~ class + accrec + accth + prorec + proth
    + defrec + defth + animrec + ldiff, family=binomial,
    data=SwitchDat)
> summary(modelA)

Call:
glm(formula = real ~ class + accrec + accth + prorec + proth +
defrec + defth + animrec + ldiff, family = binomial)

Deviance Residuals:
     Min        1Q    Median        3Q       Max
-2.60321  -0.30798  -0.15854  -0.03099  3.33739

Coefficients:
                Estimate  Std. Error  z value  Pr(>|z|)
(Intercept)       0.3498      0.3554    0.984   0.32503
classc           -1.3516      0.3141   -4.303  1.68e-05 ***
classf            0.5138      0.4922    1.044   0.29651
classp           -3.4277      1.2504   -2.741   0.00612 **
classt            1.1571      0.2055    5.631  1.80e-08 ***
accrecnotgiven    1.1282      0.2681    4.208  2.57e-05 ***
accthnotgiven    -1.2576      0.2653   -4.740  2.13e-06 ***
prorecpronom     -1.4661      0.2509   -5.843  5.13e-09 ***
prothpronom       1.5993      0.2403    6.654  2.85e-11 ***
defrecindef       0.8446      0.2577    3.277   0.00105 **
defthindef       -1.1950      0.2202   -5.426  5.78e-08 ***
animrecinanim     2.6761      0.3013    8.881   < 2e-16 ***
ldiff            -0.9302      0.1115   -8.342   < 2e-16 ***
---
Signif. codes: 0 '***' 0.001 '**' 0.01 '*' 0.05 '.' 0.1 ' ' 1

(Dispersion parameter for binomial family taken to be 1)

    Null  deviance:  2440.1  on  2359  degrees of freedom
Residual  deviance:  1056.9  on  2347  degrees of freedom
AIC: 1082.9

Number of Fisher Scoring iterations: 8
```

Table 7.7 The coefficients and observed percentages of prepositional realizations of dative (%PP) are shown for several of the factors in a logistic model of dative realization in the Switchboard corpus.

	Percent prepositional dative (PP)
Accessibility of recipient (1.13)	
Given	12%
Not given	58%
Accessibility of theme (–1.26)	
Given	62 %
Not given	12%
Pronominality of recipient (–1.47)	
Pronoun	12%
Not pronoun	60%
Pronominality of theme (1.6)	
Pronoun	62%
Not pronoun	13%
Definiteness of recipient (0.85)	
Definite	17%
Not definite	64%
Definiteness of theme (–1.2)	
Definite	44%
Not definite	11%
Animacy of recipient (2.68)	
Animate	19%
Not animate	49%

Let's see how to interpret this model by discussing a few of the coefficients. These are listed under "Estimate" in the `summary()` of the model.

Discourse accessibility of the recipient (accrec) influenced realization of the dative (see Table 7.7). When the recipient was "given" in the preceding discourse the prepositional dative construction was used only 12% of the time, but when the recipient was not given the prepositional dative construction was used 58% of the time. The regression coefficient was 1.13 indicating a positive correlation between "not given" and "PP" (prepositional dative construction). One way to interpret the logistic regression coefficient is in terms of the odds ratio. In this case, the prepositional dative construction is about 3 times [exp(1.13)] more likely when the recipient is not given in prior discourse. If we keep in mind that in the prepositional dative construction ("give theme to recipient") the theme comes before the recipient, then we can see that when the recipient is given in prior discourse it is usually mentioned first in the dative construction (only 12% of the "given" recipients are mentioned in prepositional construction). This fits with the idea that good stuff – in this case new information – is saved 'til last.

The pattern of realization as a function of the discourse accessibility of the theme also follows this pattern – when the theme is given in prior discourse is it is mentioned first by using the prepositional dative construction (62%). This is because the theme in "give theme to recipient" comes first in the prepositional construction.

All of the other factors in the logistic regression model of dative alternation fit the general idea that "good stuff" (new, non-pronominal, definite, animate objects) comes later in the sentence.

7.4.2 Evaluating the fit of the model

So far here is what we have. Using logistic regression we have found that several factors are included in a predictive statistical model of dative realization, and these factors are consistent with a harmonic set of constraints on syntactic forms.

It is reasonable to ask at this point whether this statistical model is really very good at predicting the realization of dative in English, because it could be that our model does account for some nonrandom component of variance in the corpus data, but fails to correctly predict the majority of cases. This can happen when we fail to include some important factor(s) in the model. In this section we will look at three ways to evaluate the fit of the logistic model.

The first is to consider how well the model predicts the training data. The general linear model fitting procedure `glm()` finds model parameters (the regression coefficients) that produce the best possible predictions given the predictive factors included in the model. Therefore, our first test is to evaluate the goodness of this fit. The function `predict(modelA)` returns a "prediction score" for each data case in the data frame used to find the coefficients in modelA. This is the application of the linear regression formula to each data case: score = intercept + $\text{coeff}_1 \bullet \text{data}_1 + \text{coeff}_2 \bullet \text{data}_2 + \ldots + \text{coeff}_n \bullet \text{data}_n$. If this score is greater

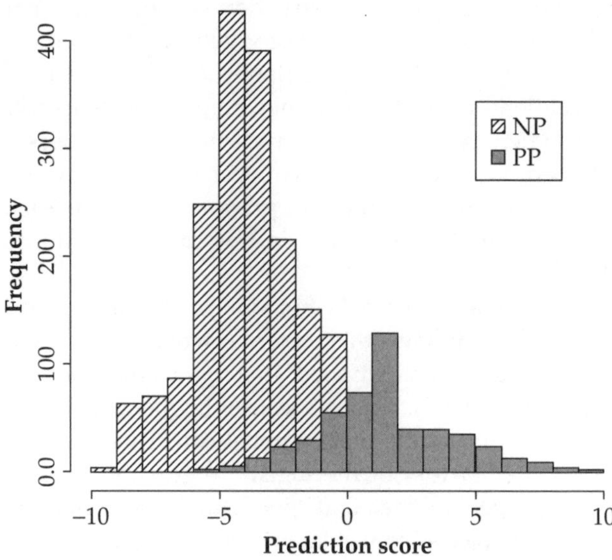

Figure 7.9 Prediction scores for the Switchboard dative data.

than zero the predicted realization is prepositional and if it is less than zero the predicted realization is double object. Figure 7.9 shows the distributions of the prediction scores for the datives from the Switchboard corpus. In this figure the gray bars below zero plot cases of prepositional dative construction which were incorrectly predicted to be double object construction, and the hatched bars above zero (hidden behind the gray bars) show cases of double object construction which were incorrectly scored as PP.

To evaluate the statistical model we tabulate the actual realizations and the predicted realizations it produces using these prediction scores. The result is that for 91% of the data cases the model gives the correct prediction. Tabulating comparisons of model predictions and actual realizations for various subsets of data will show where this model may be more or less accurate. Note that the imbalance of realization in the data set makes it possible to produce a model with no parameters at all that correctly predicts 79% of the data cases by simply predicting that dative is always realized in the double object construction (because 79% of the cases are actually realized as double objects). This is the lower bound of possible model predictions. Still, 91% correct predictions from a model that only uses a few general properties of sentences is pretty good.

A second test of the success of our statistical model of dative alternation uses the `split()` function to randomly hold back 15% of the data set as a group of test sentences. We estimate the model parameters using 85% of the sentences and then, using `predict()`, calculate dative realization scores for the test sentences. This split-glm-predict procedure is repeated 100 times to get a stable estimate of how well the statistical model can predict dative realization in sentences that were not part of the training data.

Testing a model on unseen data is an important test of a model because it is possible to "over-fit" a statistical model and have model parameters that capture information in only one or two outlier observations rather than capturing generalizations over many observations. Testing on never-before-seen data is a good way to test for over-fitting.

The dative alternation model gets an average of 91% correct in 100 random splits into 85% training and 15% test data. This is very close to the 91% correct observed for the model fit to all of the data and the good match between the two procedures indicates that the model is not over-fit. The distribution of these 100 test results is shown in Figure 7.10.

Finally, we can evaluate the validity of the statistical model of dative alternation by testing its predictions on a completely different data set. Recall that in addition to Switchboard, Bresnan et al. coded 905 datives from the *Wall Street Journal* corpus. Switchboard is a conversational speech corpus in which about 79% of datives are realized in the double object construction, while the *Wall Street Journal* corpus, as the name implies, is a corpus of written and edited text. The dative is usually also realized in the double object construction in this corpus, but at 62% the base probability of double object is quite a bit lower. If the model is capturing something real about English syntax then we would expect good predictive power despite these corpus differences.

Using the `predict()` function to calculate dative scores for the *Wall Street Journal* corpus we find a much higher number of predicted PP cases than in Switchboard, and also good prediction accuracy (83% – up from a base line of 62%).

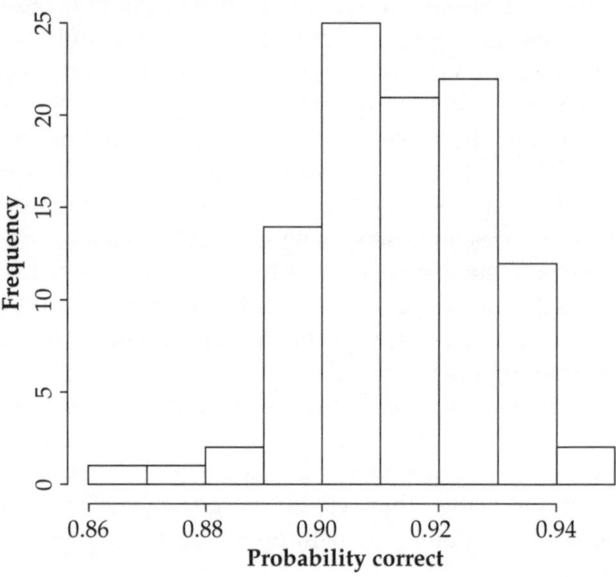

Figure 7.10 Distribution of 100 tests of the logistic model of dative alternation showing that most of the 100 random splits (into training and testing data sets) produced correct prediction of the dative alternation in over 90% of the test sentences.

R note. The commands for our three ways of evaluating the dative alternation logistic regression are shown in this note.

The first method, using `predict()`, is a vision of simplicity. Simply compare the prediction score with the actual realization code.

```
>table((predict(modelA)>0.0)==(SwitchDat$real=="PP"))
FALSE  TRUE
  201  2159
> 2159/(2159+201)
[1] 0.9148305
```

To get a little more information about the fit we can cross-tabulate the prediction score accuracy as a function of the predictor variables. For example, discourse accessibility of the recipient was a less consistently useful predictor than was the accessibility of the theme:

```
> table((predict(modelA)>0.0)==(SwitchDat$real=="PP"),
    accrec)
accrec
            given  notgiven
FALSE          98       103
TRUE         1773       386
% correct     95%       79%
```

```
> table((predict(modelA)>0.0)==(SwitchDat$real=="PP"),
    accth)
accth
            given  notgiven
FALSE          40       161
TRUE          401      1758
% correct     91%       92%
```

Bresnan et al. also showed a useful cross-tabulation (their table 1) produced with this command:

```
> table((SwitchDat$real=="PP"),predict(modelA)>0.0)
      NP   PP
NP  1788   71  96%
PP   130  371  74%
```

The following commands produce Figure 7.9.

```
> hist(subset(predict(modelA),real=="NP"), dens=c(10), angle
    =c(45), main="",xlab="prediction score",xlim=c(-10,10))
```

```
> hist(subset(predict(modelA),real=="PP"), add=T,
    breaks=c(-9,-8,-7,-6,-5,-4,-3,-2,-1,0,1,2,3,4,5,6,7,8,
    9,10),col="gray")
```

```
> legend(5,350,legend=c("NP","PP"),fill=c("black","gray"),
    density=c(10,-1), angle=c(45,-1),cex=1.5)
```

The second evaluation method discussed in this section involves the use of a "for" loop to produce 100 separate partitions of the data set into training and test components, with model fits and evaluations produced for each random split of the data set. I used runif() to produce 2,360 random numbers in the range (0,1) and then produced a factor that had 2,360 values, either true or false, coding whether the random number was above or below 0.15. This produces a split that has approximately 15% of the data cases in the TRUE subset and 85% in the FALSE subset.

```
> split(SwitchDat,factor(runif(2360)>0.15))->xx # split
    approximately 85/15

> table(xx$`TRUE`$real) # this set will be used for training
    a model
  NP   PP
1571  441

> table(xx$`FALSE`$real) # this set will be used for testing
    the model
 NP  PP
288  60

# here is a loop to split switchboard - 85% training, 15% test
#  fit a glm model to the training data,
#  see how well the model predicts the Dative realization in the
#  test data, and collect the results for averaging/plotting

pcorrect<-array(dim=100) # allocate space for results
for (i in 1:100) {
  # step 1: Split the data into training and test sets
  split(SwitchDat,factor(runif(2360)>0.15))->xx

  # step 2: estimate model parameters with the training set
  mod <-glm(real ~ class + accrec + accth + prorec + proth
      + defrec + defth + animrec + ldiff, family=binomial,
      data=xx$`TRUE`)

  # step 3: get model predictions for the test set
  predict(mod,xx$`FALSE`)->pred

  # bookkeeping 1: tabulate the responses
  table((pred>0.0)==(xx$`FALSE`$real=="PP"))->tab

  # bookkeeping 2: save the probability of a correct answer
  pcorrect[i] <- tab[2]/(tab[1]+tab[2])
}
```

After running this "for" loop (you can type it directly at the R command prompt) pcorrect contains 100 values: one record for each test set telling how accurately the test data could be predicted by the model. We can then take the average of these 100 tests and plot the distribution of the test results.

```
> mean(pcorrect)
[1] 0.9107247
> hist(pcorrect) # this produces figure 7.10
```

Here is how to use the model built on the Switchboard corpus to predict dative realization in the *Wall Street Journal* corpus. We get 83% correct on the WSJ.

```
> predict(modelA, WSJDat)
> table((WSJDat$real=="PP")==(predict(modelA,WSJDat)>0.0))
FALSE  TRUE
  151   754  83% correct

> table((WSJDat$real=="PP"),predict(modelA,WSJDat)>0.0)
      NP   PP
NP  510   47  92%
PP  104  244  70%
```

7.4.3 *Adding a random factor: Mixed-effects logistic regression*

So far we have pooled sentences regardless of the verb used in the sentence, as if the verb doesn't matter. This is an erroneous assumption. For whatever reason – the particular semantics of the verb, some fossilized conventions associated with a particular verb, or whatever – it is apparent that some verbs are biased toward the double object construction while others are biased toward the prepositional dative. More than this, it seems clear that verb bias relates to the particular sense of the verb. For example, "pay" in its transfer sense (e.g. "to pay him some money") tends to take an animate recipient and tends to appear in the double object construction, while "pay" in a more abstract sense (e.g. "to pay attention to the clock") tends to take an inanimate recipient and tends to appear in the pre-positional dative construction. We don't know which is the true predictive factor – the particular verb sense, or general predictive factors such as the animacy of the recipient, or some combination of these random (verb) and fixed (animacy) factors.

Therefore, we need to be able to evaluate the effect of animacy (and the other predictive factors that we included in the models above) while simultaneously taking into consideration the possibility that the verb senses have their own preferred constructions, the choice of which is independent of the general "predictive" factors. This requires a mixed model directly analogous to the models we explored in section 7.3 – though in this case the response variable is a binary choice (double object versus prepositional dative) and thus we need to fit a mixed-effects logistic regression model. The R function `glmmPQL()` – generalized linear mixed models fit using Penalized Quasi-Likelihood – is analogous to `lme()` in that we specify a fixed component and a random component of the model, while also providing the capability of `glm()` to allow us to fit a logistic model.

In the case of dative alternation we specify the fixed factors in our model exactly as we did with the `glm()` function, but we also add a random formula (random= ~1/vsense) which adds an intercept value for each verb sense (where the verb senses are pay.t for "pay" in the transfer sense, pay.a for "pay" in the abstract sense, etc.) to account for bias attributable to each verb sense. The main question we have is the same type of question we have in repeated measures analysis of variance – if we include a term to explicitly model particular verb sense biases do we still see any effect of discourse accessibility, pronominality, definiteness, animacy, or argument size difference? If these factors remain significant even when we add a factor for verb sense then we have support for a model that uses them as general predictive factors.

The mixed-effects logistic regression correctly predicts the dative alternation in 94% of the Switchboard sentences. This is up from 91% correct prediction for the `glm()` logistic model. Interestingly though, as figure 7.11 shows, the regression coefficients for the fixed factors that the two models share are very similar to each other, and as the summary table shows, all of these factors (with the exception of a couple of specific semantic classes) continue to have regression coefficients that are significantly different from zero.

I won't go through the procedure for splitting the Switchboard corpus into training and test sets to evaluate whether over-fitting might be a problem with this model (this could be an exercise for you to try), but we could certainly do this. We can also evaluate how well our new mixed-effects model deals with the *Wall Street Journal* corpus, and here

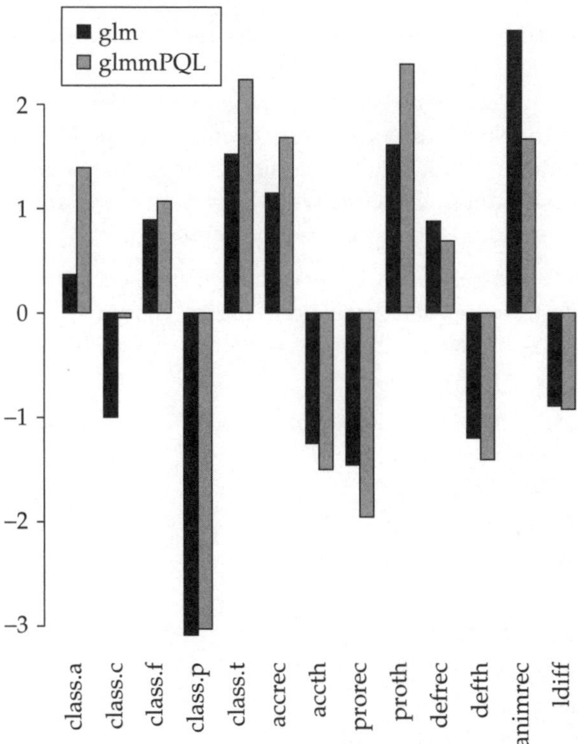

Figure 7.11 A comparison of logistic regression coefficients for a `glm()` model with the fixed effects shown on the *x*-axis of the figure, and a `glmmPQL()` mixed-effects model with the same fixed effects but also treating verb sense as a random effect.

what we find is also an increase in prediction accuracy – 86% correct with the mixed-effects model where we had found 83% correct with the simpler `glm()` model.

R note. The mixed-effects logistic model is fit with the function `glmmPQL()` which can be found in the MASS library of routines. So load MASS.

```
> library(MASS)
```

The model formula for `glmmPQL()` is just like the formulas that we have used before. Adding –1 to the list of factors removes the intercept so that we will then have coefficients for each semantic class. What is new in this model is that we can specify a random factor as with `lme()` in section 7.6. Here we specify that each verb sense is modeled with a different intercept value. We also specify the binomial link function which causes this to be a logistic regression model in the same way that `family=binomial` produces a fixed effects logistic regression model with `glm()`.

```
> modelB <-glmmPQL(real ~ -1+class+accrec+accth+prorec+
    proth+defrec+defth+animrec+ldiff, random = ~1|vsense,
    family=binomial, data=SwitchDat)

> summary(modelB)
Linear mixed-effects model fit by maximum likelihood
Data: SwitchDat
  AIC  BIC  logLik
   NA   NA      NA

Random effects:
  Formula: ~1 | vsense
          (Intercept) Residual
StdDev:      2.214329 0.774242

Variance function:
  Structure: fixed weights
  Formula: ~invwt
Fixed effects: real ~ -1 + class + accrec + accth + prorec +
proth + defrec + defth + animrec + ldiff
                    Value Std.Error   DF   t-value p-value
classa          1.3963671 0.7207442   50  1.937396  0.0584
classc          0.0283174 0.9258208   50  0.030586  0.9757
classf          1.0472398 1.1229654   50  0.932566  0.3555
classp         -3.0380798 1.9301478   50 -1.574014  0.1218
classt          2.2155467 0.7306823   50  3.032161  0.0038
accrecnotgiven  1.6576244 0.2644031 2298  6.269308  0.0000
accthnotgiven  -1.5084472 0.2500311 2298 -6.033039  0.0000
prorecpronom   -1.9662302 0.2556799 2298 -7.690202  0.0000
prothpronom     2.3641768 0.2232062 2298 10.591895  0.0000
defrecindef     0.6747985 0.2451833 2298  2.752221  0.0060
defthindef     -1.4160615 0.2116592 2298 -6.690291  0.0000
animrecinanim   1.6529828 0.3669455 2298  4.504709  0.0000
ldiff          -0.9410820 0.1059198 2298 -8.884858  0.0000
```

```
> table((SwitchDat$real=="PP"),predict(modelB)>0.0)
       FALSE  TRUE
FALSE   1804    55  97%
TRUE      78   423  84%
                    94%
```

I used three commands to set up the arrays for Figure 7.11.

```
> a <- modelA$coefficients  # get the glm() coefficients
> b <- modelB$coefficients$fixed # get the glmmPQL coefficients
> barnames = c("class.a", "class.c", "class.f", "class.p",
    "class.t", "accrec", "accth", "prorec", "proth",
    "defrec", "defth", "animrec", "ldiff")
```

Then barplot() and legend() produce the figure.

```
> barplot(matrix(c(a,b),ncol=13,byrow=T),names.arg
    =barnames,beside=T)
legend(1,2.5,fill=c(1,0),legend=c("glm","glmmPQL"))
```

Predictions for the *Wall Street Journal* corpus can be generated exactly as we did for the glm() model. However, not all instances in the WSJ corpus are available for use.

```
> table((WSJDat$real=="PP")==(predict(modelB,WSJDat)>0.0))

FALSE  TRUE
  109   669

> 669/(669+109)
[1] 0.8598972 = 86% correct
```

Only 778 out of 905 (86%) of tokens in WSJDat can be tested with the glmmPQL() model because predictions are only available for tokens with verbs that are also found in Switchboard. The other 127 tokens have verbs that were not found in Switchboard and are thus given values of NA in the results of predict().

```
> 669+109
[1] 778
> length(WSJDat$real)
[1] 905
> 778/905
[1e 0.8596685
```

To conclude this discussion of mixed-effects logistic regression, and to conclude the book, I would like to point out that the modeling strategies that we have been considering here in the context of analyzing a syntactic pattern in English can be applied to many of the quantitative analysis methods described in earlier chapters of the book. For example, in sociolinguistics, phonetics, and psycholinguistics we often take data from several subjects and we could construct more accurate statistical models by adding random factors to capture idiosyncratic differences between people in addition to the effects of the fixed factors in our models. Perhaps lme() and glmmPQL() should be more widely used in all branches of linguistics. Similarly, we have explored in this last section some very appealing methods for evaluating the success of a statistical model – splitting a large data set into training and testing portions to evaluate the robustness of a model when it faces new data and applying model predictions to a second data set that differs in some important regards from the original data are both very powerful methods for model evaluation which should be used in other disciplines of linguistics – not just syntax.

EXERCISES

1 Use the magnitude estimation technique to evaluate the claims that I made in section 7.4 about the relative acceptability of sentences 1a, 1b, 2a, 2b, 3a, 3b, 4a, 4b. Make up a number of filler sentences spanning a clear range of grammaticality and present the sentences in random order. Are your results consistent with the claims I made in the chapter?

2 Using the data set vbarg.txt (section 7.3) and lme() determine whether the relative locations of A0 and A1 (A1loc-A0loc) is related to the size of the agent (A0size).

3 With only one factor (the animacy of the recipient), we can accurately predict the dative realization in 79% of the cases in the Switchboard corpus (the R code for this test is shown below). Are you impressed by this number (why or why not)? Which of the factors in the Bresnan et al. data set gives the most accurate prediction in a one-factor model? How does this best one-factor model do with the *Wall Street Journal* corpus?

```
> mod1 <-glm(real ~ animrec, family=binomial, data=SwitchDat)
> table((fitted(mod1)>0.5)==(SwitchDat$real=="PP")) -> tab
```

```
> tab[2]/(tab[1]+tab[2])
TRUE
0.7877119
```

4 With two factors interacting with each other (the definiteness of the theme and the discourse accessibility of the theme), we can accurately predict the dative realization in 85% of the cases in the Switchboard corpus. Can you find a better combination of factors than this? What happens with a three-factor or four-factor model?

```
> mod <-glm(real ~ defth*accth, family=binomial,
data=SwitchDat)
> anova(mod,test="Chisq")

Analysis of Deviance Table

Model: binomial, link: logit

Response: real

Terms added sequentially (first to last)

            Df  Deviance  Resid. Df  Resid. Dev  P(>|Chi|)
NULL                          2359     2440.11
defth        1    302.75      2358     2137.36  8.302e-68
accth        1    186.31      2357     1951.05  2.033e-42
defth:accth  1     58.84      2356     1892.22  1.715e-14

> table((fitted(mod)>0.5)==(SwitchDat$real=="PP")) -> tab
> tab[2]/(tab[1]+tab[2])
0.8529661
```

Appendix 7A

This appendix contains example instructions for a magnitude estimation experiment. I adapted parts of this appendix from Frank Keller's Magnitude Estimation demo at http://www.webexp.info.

MAGNITUDE ESTIMATION INSTRUCTIONS.

Section 1 Judging the lengths of lines

I'm going to ask you to judge how long lines are relative to each other. This is practice for a linguistic judgment task. For instance, let's say that the line below has a length of 50.

____________________ 50

Now if you had to judge this new line you might give it a length of 18.

_________ 18

And this one might be 85.

______________________________________ 85

There is no limit to the range of numbers you may use. You may use whole numbers or decimals.

Now I'm going to give you a series of lines and your job is to estimate their lengths assuming that the length of the first line is 50. Write your best estimate of the length of each line.

Section 2 Judging the acceptability of phrases: Practice.

Now for the linguistic part of the task. I'm going to present you with 16 phrases. Each phrase is different. Some will seem perfectly OK to you, but others will not. Your task is to judge how good or bad each phrase is by drawing a line that has a length proportional to the acceptability of the phrase. Suppose, for example that the phrase "pink narrow hat" is the first item in the list. We'll rate the acceptability of "pink narrow hat" with the "50" line from the line-judging task on the previous page. If you now are confronted with a phrase that is less acceptable than this one you should draw a shorter line, so that the length of the line is proportional to the acceptability of the phrase. And if the next phrase is more acceptable you should draw a longer line, proportional to the acceptability of the phrase.

For example, if "nice Dutch sock," the second phrase in the list, is about equally acceptable as "pink narrow hat," then the line you give it should be about the same length as the one for "pink narrow hat." If you think "nice Dutch sock" is less acceptable, then the line you draw should be shorter than the one for "pink narrow hat," and if "nice Dutch sock" seems more acceptable the line you draw should be longer than the one for "pink narrow hat."

Here are some practice phrases. Draw lines next to these according to your estimate of their acceptability as phrases of English.

1 pink narrow hat ____________________
2 nice Dutch sock
3 old blue plate
4 old tiny hat
5 Irish good frame

Section 3 Judging the acceptability of phrases: Line length

You have been given a list of 16 phrases. Please estimate the acceptability of these phrases by drawing lines, indicating your impression of the acceptability of the phrase by the length of line you draw for the phrase. Once again, we'll start with a line for the phrase "pink narrow hat" as a reference for your other lines. Please look at this item and then work down the list of 16 phrases, drawing one line for each phrase.

There are no "correct" answers, so whatever seems right to you is a valid response. We are interested in your first impressions, so please don't take too much time to think about any one sentence: try to make up your mind quickly, spending less than 10 seconds on each phrase.

0 pink narrow hat ____________________
1
2
...
14
15
16

Section 4 Judging the acceptability of phrases: Numerical estimation

Now I'll ask you to look again at the list of 16 phrases. This time, please estimate the acceptability of these phrases the way we did with line length at the beginning by indicating your impression of the acceptability of the phrase with a number. We'll start with the number 50 for the phrase "pink narrow hat" as a reference for the other numbers. Please look at this item and then work down the list of 16 phrases giving one number for each phrase. Remember that if the phrase is more acceptable than "pink narrow hat" you would give it a larger number, and if it is less acceptable than "pink narrow hat" you would give it a smaller number.

You can use any range of positive numbers that you like, including decimal numbers. *There is no upper or lower limit to the numbers you can use,* except that you cannot use zero or negative numbers. *Try to use a wide range of numbers and to distinguish as many degrees of acceptability as possible.*

There are no "correct" answers, so whatever seems right to you is a valid response. We are interested in your first impressions, so please don't take too much time to think about any one sentence: try to make up your mind quickly, spending less than 10 seconds on each sentence.

0 pink narrow hat 50
1
2
. . .
14
15
16

References

Aldenderfer, M. S. and Blashfield, R. K. (1984) *Cluster Analysis*. Beverly Hills, CA: Sage Press.

Bard, E. G., Robertson, D., and Sorace, A. (1996) Magnitude estimation of linguistic acceptability. *Language* 72: 32–68.

Boersma, P. and Hayes, B. (2001) Empirical tests of the Gradual Learning Algorithm. *Linguistic Inquiry* 32: 45–86.

Bresnan, J., Cueni, A., Nikitina, T., and Baayen, R. H. (2007) Predicting the dative alternation. In G. Bouma, I. Kræmer, and J. Zwarts (eds.), *Cognitive Foundations of Interpretation*. Amsterdam: Royal Netherlands Academy of Science, pp. 69–94.

Cedergren, H. and Sankoff, D. (1974) Variable rules: Performance as a statistical reflection of competence. *Language* 50: 333–55.

Chambers, J., Cleveland, W., Kleiner, B., and Tukey, P. (1983) *Graphical Methods for Data Analysis*. Boston, MA: Duxbury Press.

Clark, H. H. (1973) The language as a fixed-effect fallacy: A critique of language statistics in psychological research. *Journal of Verbal Learning and Verbal Behavior* 12: 335–59.

Cohen, J. and Cohen, P. (1983) *Applied Multiple Regression/Correlation Analysis for the Behavioral Sciences*. Hillsdale, NJ: Lawrence Erlbaum.

Cowart, W. (1997) *Experimental Syntax: Applying Objective Methods to Sentence Judgments*. Thousand Oaks, CA: Sage Publications.

Dyen, I., Kruskal, J. B., and Black, P. (1992) An Indoeuropean classification: A lexicostatistical experiment. *Transactions of the American Philosophical Society* 82(5): 1–132.

Ferreira, F. (2003) The misinterpretation of noncanonical sentences. *Cognitive Psychology* 47: 164–203.

Goldinger, S. D. and Azuma, T. (2003) Puzzle-solving science: The quixotic quest for units in speech perception. *Journal of Phonetics* 31: 305–20.

Hays, William L. (1973) *Statistics for the Social Sciences*. New York: Holt, Rinehart and Winston.

Heeringa, W. (2004) Measuring Dialect Pronunciation Differences using Levenshtein Distance. PhD dissertation, Rijksuniversiteit Groningen.

Heeringa, W. and Braun, A. (2003) The use of the Almeida-Braun system in the measurement of Dutch dialect distances. *Computers and the Humanities* 37: 257–71.

Heeringa, W. and Gooskens, C. (2003) Norwegian dialects examined perceptually and acoustically. *Computers and the Humanities* 37: 293–315.

Hetzron, R. (1978) On the relative order of adjectives. In H. Seiler (ed.), *Language Universals*. Tübingen: Narr, pp. 165–84.

Inton-Peterson, M. J. (1983) Imagery paradigms: How vulnerable are they to experimenters' expectations? *Journal of Experimental Psychology: Human Perception and Performance* 9: 394–412.

Johnson, K. (2002) *Acoustic and Auditory Phonetics* (2nd edn.). Oxford: Blackwell. (1st edn. 1997.)

Johnson, K. (2004) Aligning phonetic transcriptions with their citation forms. *Acoustic Research Letters On-line* 5: 19–24.

Johnson, K., Flemming, E., and Wright, R. (1993) The hyperspace effect: Phonetic targets are hyperarticulated. *Language* 69: 505–28.

Johnson, K., Ladefoged, P., and Lindau, M. (1993) Individual differences in vowel production. *Journal of the Acoustical Society of America* 94: 701–14.

Johnson, K., Strand, E. A., and D'Imperio, M. (1999) Auditory-visual integration of talker gender in vowel perception. *Journal of Phonetics* 27: 359–84.

Katchingan, S. K. (1991) *Multivariate Statistical Analysis: A Comprehensive Introduction* (2nd edn.). New York: Radius Press.

Keller, F. (2000) Gradience in Grammar: Experimental and Computational Aspects of Degrees of Grammaticality. PhD dissertation, University of Edinburgh.

Keller, F. (2003) A psychophysical law for linguistic judgments. In R. Alterman and D. Kirsh (eds.), *Proceedings of the 25th Annual Conference of the Cognitive Science Society*, Boston, MA: Cognitive Science Scoeity, pp. 652–57.

Kruskal, J. B. and Wish, M. (1978) *Multidimensional Scaling*. Beverly Hills, CA: Sage Press.

Ladefoged, P., Glick, R., and Criper, C. (1971) *Language in Uganda*. Nairobi: Oxford University Press.

Lodge, M. (1981) *Magnitude Scaling: Quantitative Measurement of Opinions*. Beverly Hills, CA: Sage Publications.

Luka, B. J. and Barsalou, L. W. (2005) Structural facilitation: Mere exposure effects for grammatical acceptability as evidence for syntactic priming in comprehension. *Journal of Memory and Language* 52: 436–59.

Malouf, R. (2000) The order of prenominal adjectives in natural language generation. *Proceedings of the 38th Annual Meeting of the Association for Computational Linguistics*. Hong Kong: Asociation for Computational Linguistics, pp. 85–92.

Manning, C. D. and Schütze, H. (2000) *Foundations of Statistical Natural Language Processing*. Cambridge, MA: MIT Press.

Nakhleh, L., Ringe, D., and Warnow, T. (2005) Perfect phylogenetic networks: A new methodology for reconstructing the evolutionary history of natural languages. *Language* 81(2): 382–420.

Nakhleh, L., Warnow, T., Ringe, D., and Evans, S. N. (2005) A comparison of phylogenetic reconstruction methods on an IE dataset. *Transactions of the Philological Society* 3(2): 171–92.

NIST/SEMATECH e-Handbook of Statistical Methods, http://www.itl.nist.gov/div898/handbook/, accessed September 2004.

Pinheiro, J. and Bates, D. M. (2004) *Mixed-effects Models in S and S-PLUS*. New York: Springer.

Pitt, M. and Shoaf, L. (2002) Revisiting bias effects in word-initial phonological priming. *Journal of Experimental Psychology: Human Perception and Performance* 28: 1120–30.

Raaijmakers, J. G., Schrijnemakers, J. M. C., and Gremmen, G. (1999) How to deal with "the language-as-fixed-effect fallacy": Common misconceptions and alternative solutions. *Journal of Memory and Language* 41: 416–26.

Sakamoto, Y., Ishiguro, M., and Kitagawa, G. (1986) *Akaike Information Criterion Statistics*. Dordrecht: D. Reidel.

Salsburg, D. (2001) *The Lady Tasting Tea: How Statistics Revolutionized Science in the Twentieth Century*. New York: W. H. Freeman.

Sankoff, D. (1978) *Linguistic Variation: Models and Methods*. New York: Academic Press.

Sankoff, D. (1988) Variable rules, In U. Ammon, N. Dittmar, and K. J. Mattheier (eds.), *Sociolinguistics: An International Handbook of the Science of Language and Society*. Berlin & New York: de Gruyter, pp. 984–97.

Sankoff, D. and Kruskal, J. (eds.) (1983/1999) *Time Warps, String Edits and Macromolecules: The Theory and Practice of Sequence Comparison*. Reading, MA: Addison-Wesley. Reprinted 1999 Stanford, CA: CSLI Publications.

Schütze, C. (1996) *The Empirical Base of Linguistics: Grammaticality Judgments and Linguistic Methodology*. Chicago: University of Chicago Press.

Stevens, S. S. (1975) *Psychophysics: Introduction to its Perceptual, Neuronal, and Social Prospects*. New York: John Wiley.

Swadesh, M. (1952) Lexico-statistic dating of prehistoric ethnic contacts: With special reference to North American Indians and Eskimos. *Proceedings of the American Philosophical Society* 96: 452–63.

Wulff, S. (2003) A multifactorial corpus analysis of adjective order in English. *International Journal of Corpus Linguistics* 8: 245–82.

Index